T0087946

TALES FROM THE
CINCINNATI BEARCATS
LOCKER ROOM

A COLLECTION OF THE GREATEST
BEARCAT STORIES EVER TOLD

MICHAEL PERRY

FOREWORD BY
NICK LACHEY

SPORTS
PUBLISHING

For
my wife, my partner, my co-captain Valerie

In memory of
my brother Norty
(1947-2003)

Sports Publishing books may be purchased in bulk at special discounts for sales promotion, corporate gifts, fund-raising, or educational purposes. Special editions can also be created to specifications. For details, contact the Special Sales Department, Sports Publishing, 307 West 36th Street, 11th Floor, New York, NY 10018 or sportspubbooks@skyhorsepublishing.com.

Sports Publishing® is a registered trademark of Skyhorse Publishing, Inc.®, a Delaware corporation.

Visit our website at www.sportspubbooks.com.

10 9 8 7 6 5 4 3 2

Library of Congress Cataloging-in-Publication Data is available on file.

Cover design by Tom Lau
Cover photo credit AP

ISBN: 978-1-61321-715-3
Ebook ISBN: 978-1-61321-741-2

Printed in the United States of America

CONTENTS

Foreword..v

Acknowledgments viii

CHAPTER 1
The Hall of Famers 1

CHAPTER 2
Five Unforgettable Games....................................14

CHAPTER 3
John Wiethe Era (1946-1952) 28

CHAPTER 4
George Smith Era (1952-1960) 48

CHAPTER 5
Ed Jucker Era (1960-1965)...................................75

CHAPTER 6
Tay Baker Era (1965-1972) 88

CHAPTER 7
Gale Catlett Era (1972-1978) 102

CHAPTER 8
Ed Badger Era (1978-1983)................................118

CHAPTER 9
Tony Yates Era (1983-1989)...............................130

CHAPTER 10
Bob Huggins Era (1989-2005) 160

CHAPTER 11
Andy Kennedy Era (2005-06).............................249

CHAPTER 12
Mick Cronin Era (2006-present) 259

FOREWORD

S oon after my wife Vanessa and I found out we were going to have a son, I had the same dreams as any other father: I could not wait to share my love of sports and my favorite teams with my child. I envisioned us watching games on TV together. I got excited at the thought of going to games with my son. How could I not think about all that?

For me, University of Cincinnati basketball has definitely been a family tradition. It started with my grandfather, Robert Fopma, a longtime professor of mathematics and a vice provost who was at UC during the championship years in the 1960s. Both my parents, John and Cate, went to UC. My uncle went there. Even though I never attended school there, I was definitely raised on Cincinnati basketball. I remember going to games down at Riverfront Coliseum.

So now, my son Camden is 18 months old, and I've got him cheering, "Go Bearcats." He's even got his Bearcat face—and he growls. He's a fan already. That's so much fun.

He had a Bearcats onesie that he rocked for a while, and now he has a UC jersey he wears. He's definitely into basketball. He's all boy. He loves any type of ball and loves playing with his little toy basketball hoop at the house.

When the Bearcats are on TV he recognizes the C-Paw. He knows it's the Bearcats. He's my little good luck charm.

Being a big sports fan and having a son and being able to share moments together and pass those traditions down is something I am enjoying immensely. He'll sit with me for as long as his attention allows. We love playing basketball together as much as an 18-month-old can play.

He loves sports in general. We had his first birthday party at Great American Ball Park. It was obviously a baseball theme.

He watches the Bengals games with me, too. He's all in with Cincinnati sports.

My love of the Bearcats has never been a secret. I get to as many games as I can, and I was a vocal supporter of former coach Bob Huggins. I even sat down in a hotel room in Stockholm, Sweden, in the middle of the night the day Huggins and UC parted ways and wrote what I call my "manifesto" that I sent to The Cincinnati Enquirer. I was upset. Because I am a fan, I was disappointed in the way it went down and I was concerned about the direction of the program.

By the time the 2005-06 season started, I was cool with Andy Kennedy, who was the interim coach. I knew him from the Huggins era because he was an assistant coach on Huggs' staff. I didn't get to any games that season, but that was not intentional. In fact, I was going to be in New York and planned to attend the Big East Conference Tournament at Madison Square Garden. But then Gerry McNamara of Syracuse hit that running game-winning 3-point shot with .3 seconds left that knocked UC out of the tournament. That was so disappointing.

I also knew Mick Cronin from when he was an assistant under Huggs, and I always thought he would be a good candidate to come back to UC as head coach. As it turned out, that's exactly what happened.

It's amazing what he has accomplished since returning in 2006.

It's to Mick's credit that he has resurrected a program from the ashes—if you will. It took some time, but Cincinnati is again competitive every year and back to being a perennial top-25 team.

Mick and I do talk and know each other somewhat. We've gotten to know each other better over the course of eight years since he's been back. If we're out somewhere and we get a chance to sit down and talk, I enjoy doing that.

I think Mick's loyalty to the city and to the university is pretty evident. I think he's done a good job of repairing a program that was left in shambles after the Huggins fiasco. He deserves credit for hanging in there and putting in the hard work and getting the program back to a place where we can all be proud of it again.

He's done a great job of being competitive in the Big East and now the American Athletic Conference, competing against programs with a lot more resources to draw from than he does. I'd like to see that improve for him. Now that the program is facing another fork in the road, I hope Mick gets the support for the facilities and amenities that could help UC compete for the country's upcoming top players.

It's not a just a job for Mick; it's a passion.

He grew up loving UC and loving the program, something I definitely can relate to. He deserves a great deal of appreciation for his support for the program, the university, and the community.

I haven't been to a game with my son yet, but that day is coming soon. It's one of those moments you dream about. It's going to be special for me.

Hopefully he'll enjoy it and we'll attend many games together as he grows up. I hope we have the opportunity to see the quality players that form great UC teams. Even as I write this, I find it hard to contain my excitement and anticipation for those magical moments I will get to spend with my son. University of Cincinnati basketball is going to be a big part of that.

Can't wait.

Nick Lachey
Cincinnati native, singer, member 98 Degrees, host of television shows "Big Morning Buzz Live" on VH1 & "The Sing-Off" on NBC

ACKNOWLEDGMENTS

These are not *my* memories. These stories come straight from approximately 85 University of Cincinnati basketball players, coaches, staff members and recruits, dating back to the 1940s and spanning 10 coaching eras.

They generously gave their time on the phone and in person, a few even calling or Skyping from overseas. *They* "wrote" this history of the Bearcats basketball program. I appreciate all their patience and candor and am grateful they shared their stories with all of us.

My thanks to everyone who spoke with me for this book:

Jim Ard, Ed Badger, Tay Baker, Lou Banks, Lloyd Batts, Corie Blount, Tony Bobbitt, Ron Bonham, Carl Bouldin, Corey Brinn, John Bryant, Anthony Buford, Darnell Burton, Vic Carstarphen, Steve Collier, Cheryl Cook, Mick Cronin, Pat Cummings, Dick Dallmer, Jamaal Davis, Connie Dierking, LaZelle Durden, Damon Flint, Tarrice Gibson, Danny Gilbert, Cedric Glover, Chris Goggin, Bob Goin, Keith Gregor, Eric Hicks, Paul Hogue, Jim Holstein, Dennis Hopson, Bob Huggins, June Huggins, Myron Hughes, DerMarr Johnson, Junior Johnson, Herb Jones, Doug Kecman, Andy Kennedy, Sean Kilpatrick, Armein Kirkland, Sandy Koufax, Bill Lammert, Melvin Levett, Chuck Machock, Danny Manning, Erik Martin, Kenyon Martin, Jason Maxiell, Roger McClendon, Derrick McMillan, Alex Meacham, Steve Moeller, Terry Nelson, Ray Penno, Dan Peters, Ralph Richter, Rick Roberson, Oscar Robertson, Levertis Robinson, Steve Sanders, Doug Schloemer, Hal Schneider, Larry Shingleton, Keith Starks, Lance Stephenson, Leonard Stokes, Andre Tate, Jermaine Tate, Tom Thacker, Mike Thomas, Luther Tiggs, Tony Trabert, Jack Twyman, Deonta Vaughn, Mike Waddell, Hal Ward, Phil Wheeler, Bob Wiesenhahn, George Wilson, Cashmere Wright, Raleigh Wynn, Tony Yates, and Gary Yoder.

We are reminded of the value of this kind of anecdotal history by the losses of several UC greats since the book first was published in 2004: Cummings (1956-2012), Dierking (1936-2013), Hogue (1940-2009), Holstein (1930-2007), Twyman (1934-2012), and Wheeler (1934-2012).

Thank you to Mike Pearson, from Sports Publishing L.L.C., who originally signed me up to write *Tales from Cincinnati Bearcats Basketball in 2004*; editors Joe Bannon Jr. (2004) and Julie Ganz (2014); *former* UC video coordinator Andy Assaley; Enquirer librarians Frank Harmon (2004) and Jeff Suess (2014); long-time Enquirer beat reporter and friend Bill Koch; guest editor Sadie Browning Johnson; University of Cincinnati photographer Lisa Ventre; and Andre Foushee (2014), Ryan Koslen (2014), Brian Teter (2004), and Tom Hathaway (2004) from UC's sports information office.

It's important to recognize my brother Jack, a 1974 UC graduate, who took me to my first Bearcats basketball game in February 1974 (an 83-61 victory over George Washington in the Armory Fieldhouse), launching a 40-year association with the university.

Of course, the most special thanks of all goes to my wife, Valerie, and children, Ben, Olivia, and Dan, who made the real sacrifices (twice) for this book to happen.

Lastly, I am grateful to the many former players who joined me for book signings in 2004-05. I will never forget all the laughs with Terry Nelson, the incredible popularity of Melvin Levett, or the classiness of Jack Twyman, one of UC's all-time greats on and off the court and a true gentleman.

My favorite story, though, came from a book signing with Corie Blount and Steve Logan. A young boy with an unusual first name came through the line to get a copy of the book signed to him. A few minutes later, his mother was standing before us with the boy and a store manager explaining that they did not pay for the book or intend to buy it; the boy thought it was free. She apologized and handed it back.

Without hesitation, Blount stood, reached into his pocket, pulled out cash, handed it to the store manager, and told the mother that the book was now a gift from him and that the boy should keep it. I don't remember how many books were sold that day, but I sure remember Corie's kindness.

Michael Perry

1

THE HALL OF FAMERS

Any book about the history of the University of Cincinnati basketball team should begin with Oscar Robertson. It was his wondrous talent that put the Bearcats on the national map and helped integrate the school's basketball program.

Considered one of the greatest basketball players ever, Robertson remains the school's all-time leading scorer and rebounder despite playing just three years (freshmen were ineligible in 1956-57). His jersey No. 12 was retired after his senior season, and a nine-foot-tall bronze statue of Robertson was unveiled outside Shoemaker Center in 1994. Robertson set the standard for every player who would put on a Cincinnati uniform.

He is one of four Hall of Famers to play in the UC basketball program—but (surprise!) only two are known for their basketball ability. That would be Robertson and Jack Twyman (there's more on both in later chapters).

OSCAR ROBERTSON

"The eye-witness accounts could look exaggerated to those who never saw this phenomenon."
—Bob Collins, *The Indianapolis Star,* 1956

"I really wanted to go to IU," Oscar Robertson starts out. "I would've crawled to go to school down there."

That's enough to give any true University of Cincinnati fan pause.

Robertson was a star at Crispus Attucks High School in Indianapolis. As the state's top high school player, he was, of course, pursued by Indiana University and Purdue University, two Big Ten Conference schools.

Robertson had no real interest in Purdue. But he longed to be in a Hoosiers' uniform.

He was unable to make college visits until late in the spring of 1956, his high school senior year. Robertson was also a track star at Crispus Attucks, and after the track season, he competed in the Indiana-Kentucky All-Star basketball series, wearing No. 1 as Indiana's Mr. Basketball.

His coach, Ray Crowe, finally had a chance to take Robertson to Bloomington to meet Hoosiers coach Branch McCracken. When they arrived, they were told McCracken was busy.

So they waited. And waited. And waited.

At least a half hour passed.

Finally McCracken came out of his office. Robertson and Crowe then followed him in and had a seat.

Robertson recalls McCracken looking right at him. The first thing he said was, "I hope you're not the type of kid who wants money to go to school."

What? Robertson thought. "I didn't know what he was talking about; I didn't know you could get money to go to school," Robertson said.

Oscar Robertson's No. 12 is one of three retired University of Cincinnati men's basketball jersey numbers. The others are No. 27 (Jack Twyman) and No. 4 (Kenyon Martin). (Photo by University of Cincinnati/Sports Information)

Robertson immediately turned to Crowe and said he wanted to leave. They did just that.

"That one statement is all that he said to me. I think he was insinuating that I was going to demand money to go to IU, which really was an insult to me," Robertson said.

"From that point on, I never said one word to Branch McCracken nor had any other conversations with him or about him. For some strange reason, Branch McCracken didn't want Oscar Robertson."

George Smith did.

Smith was a former Bearcats football player (1932-35) who became the University of Cincinnati's head basketball coach in 1952.

UC had a co-op program that appealed to Robertson. He thought that getting practical experience in a job while attending school would be valuable. He said he was eventually pulled out of the program (a co-op job at Cincinnati Gas & Electric) when the NCAA determined it gave UC an unfair recruiting advantage.

But, as Robertson recalls, a major reason he thought Cincinnati would be a good place for him was his perception of its African-American community.

He and friends would occasionally travel to Cincinnati and Crosley Field when Jackie Robinson and the Brooklyn Dodgers were in town to face the Reds. Robinson, of course, was the first African-American to play in the major leagues.

"For some strange reason, I used to see all the blacks in one section in the stands. I said, 'Wow, there are a lot of African-American people there. It'd be a great place to come,'" Robertson said.

"I didn't know the university had no blacks whatsoever. I was totally shocked. I went to class, I didn't see anyone black in my class. I didn't see anyone black, period. The only blacks I saw were four guys I entered school with who played football and (another student) who was in a couple of my classes in business school."

Robertson didn't take long to confront Smith.

"Coach, there aren't any black people here," Robertson said.

"I know," Smith replied.

"Why didn't you tell me that?" Robertson asked.

The answer was obvious. Smith didn't want to give Robertson any reasons *not* to attend UC.

Robertson was only the fifth African-American UC basketball player (Chester Smith was the first in 1932). Of course, none before him attracted the same kind of attention locally and nationally.

JACK TWYMAN

Jack Twyman was cut from the Pittsburgh Central Catholic High School basketball team three consecutive years.

But as a senior in 1950-51, he not only made the Central Catholic team, he was a star. At the time, most players in the Pittsburgh area wanted to go to Duquesne University, which had gone 23-6 and advanced to the prestigious National Invitation Tournament in 1950. The Dukes were in the midst of 16 consecutive winning seasons.

Duquesne recruited four top Pennsylvania products: Twyman, Maurice Stokes (Westinghouse High School), Ed Fleming (Westinghouse High School), and Dick Ricketts (Pottstown High School), all of whom visited Duquesne during spring break of their senior years. During the trip, they scrimmaged the Dukes—*and won.*

"Everybody was excited about all of us going to Duquesne," Twyman said.

Only Stokes decided to go to St. Francis College, and Fleming chose Niagara University.

Twyman was a Duquesne guy, though. He had signed up for classes and had his fall schedule planned.

Jack Twyman wasn't just a Hall of Fame player; he was a Hall of Fame-caliber person. Cincinnati Royals teammate Maurice Stokes suffered a head injury in the final regular-season game in 1957-58. He went into a coma and was paralyzed for life. Twyman became his legal guardian and helped raise money for Stokes's medical bills. The story of their relationship was the subject of a movie, **Maurie.** *(Photo by University of Cincinnati/Sports Information)*

Near the end of July, an assistant basketball coach from Central Catholic asked a favor of Twyman. Nick Skorich played football at the University of Cincinnati in the early 1940s and was friends with former UC football player George Smith, then an assistant coach with the Bearcats basketball team.

"I know you're all set at Duquesne," Skorich said. "But would you go to Cincinnati for a tryout?"

What the heck, Twyman thought.

He took an all-night bus ride and arrived in Cincinnati at 8 a.m. on a Saturday. Head coach John Wiethe picked him up at the bus station and took him straight to the Men's Gym, where UC players Joe Luchi, Bob Frith, and Jim Holstein were waiting for him.

"Wiethe wanted to see what I had—or what I didn't have," Twyman said. "After about 10 minutes, it was obvious they were instructed to beat me up and see if I could take it. About 30 minutes into the two-on-two scrimmage, I thought, 'What the hell am I doing here? I'm all set at Duquesne. I'm going back to Pittsburgh. But before I go, I'm going to let these guys know that I've been here.'

"So I started knocking heads myself. And I guess that impressed Wiethe."

The coach took Twyman out for a big steak lunch. Players showed him around campus. Everyone urged Twyman to become a Bearcat.

"I liked the city," Twyman said. "It was close enough to get home to Pittsburgh."

I think I'm going to Cincinnati, he decided.

Just like that, a Hall of Fame career was born.

Oh, and Twyman's mother was none too happy about his change of heart. Her boy would be leaving home.

TONY TRABERT

Tony Trabert has been faced with this question a few times: Did you *really* have a tough decision to make, whether to play basketball or tennis professionally?

Trabert laughs. "Not even close," he said.

The Cincinnati native did play basketball for the Bearcats, but his accomplishments as a pro athlete came on the tennis court. Trabert was inducted into the International Tennis Hall of Fame in 1970.

"The reason I played basketball really, is because we had no indoor tennis facilities in Cincinnati," Trabert said. "And in the winter time, you couldn't play much. I wanted to stay in shape and help my hand-eye coordination.

"Was I good? I was not a very good shooter. I was a good defender and I was a good floor general."

Trabert played four years of basketball at Cincinnati's Walnut Hills High School and was team co-captain as a senior. When he went to UC in 1948, he tried out for the freshman basketball team.

To that point, Trabert had not won any national tennis titles. The national junior indoor championships were in St. Louis that December, and Trabert dropped off the basketball team in order to compete in the tennis event.

He ended up winning singles and doubles titles there, then returned to school. In the spring 1950, Cincinnati native Bill Talbert—also a future tennis Hall of Famer—called Trabert and asked him to go to Europe with him to play doubles. Trabert accepted.

Trabert rejoined the UC basketball team for the 1950-51 season. He was the sixth man until Larry Imburgia suffered a serious knee injury early in the season. Trabert then moved into the starting lineup.

"I wish I hadn't been starting because he was such a good player," Trabert said of Imburgia.

"We were just a bunch of hustling guys. No superstars. We played full-court press and fast break—which suited what I was trying to accomplish. (Coach John) Wiethe worked us hard in practice so games were easy.

"I love sports. When I was growing up, we had no money. We lived by a playground in Bond Hill. My dad said, 'I want to keep you kids occupied in sports so you don't have time to be a drugstore cowboy.' So I played tennis, baseball, and basketball and I swam. I was a catcher in Knothole baseball. Maybe at 13,

Guard Tony Trabert (33) moved into the Bearcats' starting lineup in 1950-51 after Larry Imburgia was injured. Trabert averaged seven points a game, and the team finished 18-4 after losing to St. Bonaventure 70-67 in double-overtime in the NIT. (Photo by University of Cincinnati/Sports Information)

my dad said, 'If you want to try to excel in a sport, you should give up one or another.' So I gave up baseball.

"I like team sports. I didn't have to be the guy to make the last basket, but I wanted somebody from our team to do it. And

I like the idea of the teamwork. On the other hand, I like the idea of being out there on an island by yourself, where if you do well you get credit for it and if you don't, you take the blame."

Trabert averaged 7.0 points for UC in 1950-51, then won the NCAA tennis title that spring.

In September 1951, he joined the navy. That summer, a commanding officer told Trabert not to worry about reporting to the reserves, just to keep in touch until the summer tennis season was over.

Trabert said he was able to make it to Boston to play in a tennis tournament, and his father called to tell him: "You're going to be drafted."

"Some parents wrote poison-pen letters saying, '*My* kid's in Korea, why is he playing tennis?' So they said, 'We'll just draft him,'" Trabert recalled.

He went to Bainbridge, Maryland, for boot camp, then on to Norfolk, Virginia. The next day, he went to an aircraft carrier and spent 16 months on the Coral Sea. He spent three months in North Island Coronado off the coast of San Diego. Trabert was out of the navy by June 1953.

He returned to UC and played the final eight basketball games of the 1953-54 season. He played tennis that spring, left school without a degree in June 1954 and did not return to the classroom.

"At that stage of my life, I knew tennis was going to be my career," he said.

"I did the best I could do in basketball. I had no illusions. They're all good memories for me. But I certainly had more ability as a tennis player."

He would go on to win 10 Grand Slam titles—five singles and five doubles. After Trabert captured the French Championships in 1955, the next American to win in Paris would be Michael Chang—a mere 34 years later.

Trabert's 1955 season is considered one of the greatest in men's tennis history. That year, Trabert won singles titles at Wimbledon, the French Championships, and the U.S. Championships. He also won U.S. Clay Court and U.S. Indoor championships. In all, he won 30 titles (18 singles, 12 doubles) and finished the year with a 106-7 record in singles matches, at one point winning 36 in a row.

SANDY KOUFAX

You may have heard or read that Sandy Koufax was a scholarship basketball player at the University of Cincinnati. Or, that Koufax surprised UC coaches and walked on to the Bearcats basketball team in the fall 1953. "He just showed up," assistant coach Ed Jucker was quoted as saying in Jane Leavy's book *Sandy Koufax: A Lefty's Legacy.* "I didn't know him from anything."

Neither account is exactly true, according to Koufax.

"I was *invited* to walk on," he said.

Koufax, from Brooklyn, New York, was captain of his basketball team as a senior at Lafayette High School. He said he knew two guys in New York who had played at UC—he can't recall their names—and they recommended him to Bearcats coach George Smith. They also told Koufax it would be a good place for him.

Koufax liked the idea of UC's co-op program. "Being out of school half the time sounded good to me," he said with a laugh. Koufax started as a liberal arts major and had designs on transferring into architecture.

He ended up making the UC freshman basketball team and received some form of financial aid. Koufax started and averaged 9.7 points a game.

"Sandy was a great basketball player," said Jack Twyman, who was a junior when Koufax was a freshman. "He was not very tall, but he was a great leaper. He was the first guy who could really go up over people and dunk. I was amazed at how high he could jump. He wasn't a great shooter, but just very aggressive, a very good athlete."

Born Sanford Braun, former UC basketball and baseball player Sandy Koufax (standing second from the right) went on to a Hall of Fame baseball career. In 12 years in the major leagues, Koufax went 165-87 with a 2.76 career earned-run average. He was a six-time All-Star dubbed "The Man with the Golden Arm." (Photo by University of Cincinnati/Sports Information)

"Sandy was real fluent," basketball and baseball teammate Danny Gilbert said. "He was graceful on the basketball court."

In the spring 1954, UC's baseball and tennis teams were going to take a joint trip to Florida and New Orleans. (Trabert was going to be on that trip, too, to play a match against Tulane's Ham Richardson.) Koufax had never been to New Orleans and was eager to go.

"Basically, it sounded like a great road trip," he said.

Koufax had planned to go out for the baseball team anyway, he said, but the prospects of the trip "made up my mind definitely. I kind of knew I was going to be a baseball player, I think."

Jucker, who coached UC's freshman basketball team, was in his first year as the varsity baseball coach.

"I told Jucker I wanted to play baseball," Koufax said.

Koufax attended team tryouts in Schmidlapp Gym. Gilbert and Koufax were the only freshmen basketball players to walk on to the baseball team, too. As it turns out, Koufax was a pitcher and Gilbert a catcher.

"He could really bring the ball, but he was so wild," Gilbert said. "If he could get it over the plate, nobody at the college level could really hit him. But he would have to ease up to try to get it over.

"I knew once he was able to get his control, he could be a very dominating pitcher. For a time, he was probably the hardest pitcher to hit in the history of the major leagues."

Koufax pitched just one season for the Bearcats, going 3-1 with a 2.81 ERA. He struck out 51 batters and walked 30. He never even told his family he was playing on the baseball team.

That was the only year Koufax attended the University of Cincinnati. The Brooklyn Dodgers signed Koufax, who started his major league baseball career in 1955 and went on to be arguably the greatest left-handed pitcher in history. He was elected to the Baseball Hall of Fame in 1972.

Koufax returned to the UC campus in February 2000, when the 83-year-old Jucker was honored at halftime of a UC-DePaul basketball game. "Ed was just a nice guy," Koufax said. "It was fun to play for him. He was so intense. If somebody cares that much, it's hard not to like him and not to want to play for him."

Asked if he considers himself a Bearcat, Koufax said, "I still root for them."

2

FIVE UNFORGETTABLE GAMES

LOYOLA 60, UC 58 (OT)
MARCH 23, 1963, NCAA FINAL

The University of Cincinnati had won back-to-back national championships and was going for three in a row. UC was playing in its fifth consecutive Final Four, something no school had done to that point. The Bearcats blasted seventh-ranked Oregon 80-46 in the semifinals to set up their meeting with No. 3 Loyola (Illinois), the highest-scoring team in the country, in the 1963 NCAA title game.

No. 1-ranked UC was 26-1—its only loss coming at Wichita State, 65-64, in February.

The coaches stayed up until 4 a.m. preparing for Loyola. Tony Yates, the team captain and starting guard, became sick the afternoon of the game and was taken to Methodist Hospital in Louisville for treatment. About 15 minutes before tipoff, Yates joined his teammates on the court.

Still, it didn't look like coach Ed Jucker's team was going to have to sweat it out. The Bearcats were ahead 45-30 with 14 minutes remaining.

"At that point, I was hoping we would lose respectably," Loyola All-American Jerry Harkness told *The Cincinnati Post* in 1987.

But UC players George Wilson and Tom Thacker got in foul trouble, and Loyola managed to crawl back into the game, which was played at Louisville's Freedom Hall. In the final 10 minutes, UC went into a controlled offense and tried to run time off the clock.

The strategy seemed to backfire. The Bearcats had just one field goal in the final 14 minutes of regulation. Yates got in foul trouble. So did leading scorer Ron Bonham.

Cincinnati was ahead by one point when Harkness fouled Larry Shingleton with 12 seconds left in regulation. Loyola called a timeout. Jucker had plenty to tell his players, too.

"To this day, I couldn't tell you one word he said," Shingleton said. "I was on the bench praying."

Shingleton swished the first free throw. He turned around and looked at Yates, who had a big grin on his face. UC led 54-52.

But Shingleton missed the next foul shot; the ball bounced off the rim to the right. Loyola's Vic Rouse rebounded it, threw the ball to Ron Miller, who took several steps according to players from both teams (but wasn't called for traveling) and passed the ball to Harkness, who went in for a layup that sent the game into overtime.

Loyola then won 60-58 on a rebound basket by the six-foot-six Rouse with one second left in the extra period. The Ramblers only shot 27.4 percent from the field; UC shot 49 percent.

"At halftime, we had Loyola completely under control," Bonham said. "The guy guarding me said, 'You've got one helluva team.' It just wasn't to be. You never get over that. We

The 1963 NCAA runner-up trophy came home to Cincinnati by bus without much fanfare. The trophy is now proudly displayed in the Richard E. Lindner Center, the centerpiece of the University's $105 million Varsity Village, which opened in 2006. (Photo by University of Cincinnati/Sports Information)

could've played them another 50 times and beaten them. I had 22 points and I don't think I took a shot the last 10 minutes of the game."

More than 35 years later, Shingleton was at a hardware store, signing a credit card slip at the cash register when the woman checking him out noticed the NCAA championship ring he was wearing and asked what it was for. Shingleton told her.

Then the man standing next to Shingleton in line blurted out, "Yeah, if he'd have made that damn free throw in '63, we would've won three in a row."

"Invariably, somewhere every year, somebody will say, 'Are you the guy who missed the free throw?' People often become infamous, if you will, on the basis of what they fail to do, not what they did do," Shingleton said.

"I know one thing: I didn't choke. I didn't freeze. I swished the first one. The reason I missed, the ball rolled off the wrong fingers on my left hand. I've never said (the loss) was my fault. I always said, 'Boy, I had a hell of an opportunity to be the youngest senator from the state of Ohio.' If I had made that free throw, we would've been the only team in history—at that point—to win three in a row."

That was Shingleton's last organized basketball game.

There is a picture of Shingleton missing the foul shot, with the scoreboard partially visible. Since 1964, he has sent out roughly 50 cards, often including a copy of the photo, to what he calls members of the "Woulda/Coulda/Shoulda Been a Hero Club."

Georgetown guard Fred Brown got one of Shingleton's notes of encouragement after he threw a pass right to North Carolina's James Worthy at the end of the 1982 NCAA championship basketball game. Michigan's Chris Webber got one after he called a timeout at the end of the 1993 NCAA final against North Carolina (the Wolverines were out of timeouts and were called for a technical foul). Florida State kicker Xavier Beitia got one in 2002 after missing a 43-yard field goal (wide left) as time expired in a 28-27 loss to rival Miami (Florida).

"What I always say is there's life after missed free throws, missed field goals or whatever," Shingleton said.

In 2003, he was with his mother and grandson having lunch at a Ruby Tuesday in Cincinnati. On the television, as part of Black History Month, was a replay of the 1963 NCAA final between UC and Loyola.

Shingleton couldn't help but watch. "You know," he said, "I missed that free throw again on the instant replay."

When he got home that day, he called Yates.

"All these years I've been taking the flak for losing the game," he told his former teammate. "But damn it, Thacker didn't box out!"

UC 75, BRADLEY 73 (7OT)
DECEMBER 21, 1981

No Division I game in NCAA history has lasted longer. Seven overtimes. Seventy-five minutes of playing time. Three hours, 15 minutes of high drama.

"My heart was racing the entire game," UC's Jelly Jones said afterward.

There was no shot clock, so in the overtime periods, the teams mostly held the ball. During the third overtime, neither team scored. No team got more than four points in any over-time period.

The unlikely hero would turn out to be Doug Schloemer, a senior reserve and former Mr. Basketball in Kentucky who averaged 4.8 points that season.

Schloemer had a key offensive rebound in the sixth OT, then hit a jumper to tie the game at 73 and send it to a seventh extra period.

Neither team had scored in the seventh OT. UC had the ball in the final seconds and called timeout. Point guard Junior Johnson was supposed to penetrate to the basket. If nobody picked him up, he was going to go all the way to the goal. If the defense collapsed on him, he was expected to pitch the ball out to one of the wings. Bobby Austin would be on the right side, Schloemer on the left.

Well, Johnson was swarmed and Austin was being shadowed. The ball came out to Schloemer, who was about 18 feet out, foul line extended. He caught it and launched the shot with defender Voise Winters running at him hard.

"I don't know how he missed it," Schloemer said. "He came crashing by me. It's one of those things, when you let a shot go, you know it's in. It felt good."

There was one second left. After a timeout, Bradley inbounded the ball and got off a 20-foot attempt that bounced off the rim.

"My body's tired," Bearcats forward Kevin Gaffney said after the game. "I feel like an old man. I don't know how old people feel, but if it's like this, it's a terrible feeling."

The six-foot-five Schloemer, from Holmes High School in Covington, Kentucky, finished with just six points but was three of three from the field.

"I was soaking wet," UC coach Ed Badger recalled. "I was exhausted. I was getting tired of climbing up and down on that (raised) floor (at old Bradley Arena). It was a long, long game. It was really fun when you think about it now."

"I played 68 minutes," Johnson said. "I played the last 40 with four fouls. Every pass, every dribble, every single thing was so intense. That's what you live for. I was mentally and physically drained, but you're just working off adrenaline."

The Bearcats were 7-1 after their final game before Christmas. Bradley would go on to win the 1982 National Invitation Tournament.

"I would say that was one of the highlights of an otherwise pretty mediocre career," Schloemer said with a laugh.

KENTUCKY 24, UC 11
DECEMBER 20, 1983

Shortly after Tony Yates was hired as UC's head coach in April 1983, he had a meeting with Athletic Director Mike McGee to review the upcoming schedule.

McGee told Yates he had worked out a three-game contract to play perennial power Kentucky—and the series would begin that December in what would be Yates's eighth game as a Division I head coach.

"That day I told Mike I was going to hold the ball against them," Yates said. "I don't think he took me seriously."

The Bearcats came into the game at Riverfront Coliseum with a 1-6 record, a starting center (Mark Dorris) who was just six foot six and only one player (Dorris) who would average in double figures that season.

Unbeaten Kentucky came in ranked No. 2 in the country and had a front line that consisted of future NBA players Melvin Turpin (6-11), Sam Bowie (7-1) and Kenny Walker (6-8). The Wildcats were favored by 18 points. The game was nationally televised on ESPN.

"I thought the only way we had a chance to win, was to do what we did," Yates said.

Cincinnati had worked on its "delay" game a little in practice, but there was no hint of Yates's strategy until game day. It was then, in the locker room, he told the players his plan: The Bearcats would hold the ball on every possession until they had a chance for a layup. At the time, there was no shot clock forcing teams to shoot within a certain number of seconds.

"We just kind of looked around at each other (and thought), 'You've got to be kidding?'" Luther Tiggs said. "We're going to freeze the ball on national television? This man has lost his mind."

Yates wasn't sure how his players felt about his strategy, but he knew they'd carry it out as best they could.

"And they did it to the letter," he said.

Kentucky won the opening tipoff and immediately lobbed an alley-oop pass to Bowie near the basket. He was fouled. He missed the first free throw and made the second.

The Bearcats then passed the ball 22 times on their first possession. By the seventh pass, there were boos from the crowd. Dorris hit a jumper just above the foul line for a 2-1 UC lead. Kentucky missed its next shot, and UC went into a four-corner spread, normally used to run time off the clock at the end of games.

UC took only five first-half shots and trailed 11-7 at intermission. At one point, the Bearcats held the ball for seven minutes, 22 seconds.

Kentucky ended up winning 24-11.

Yates could hear fans booing throughout the game. The crowd would start chanting: "Bor-ing." Though Wildcats coach Joe B. Hall never said anything to Yates, he did tell the media afterward that he'd never consider such a strategy.

"I would not have the guts to do that before our home fans," Hall said that night. "The real feeling I have is that our fans were somewhat exploited. Some of them bought Cincinnati season tickets to see this game."

Cincinnati scored its fewest amount of points since 1930; Kentucky totaled its fewest since 1937. Hall made it clear he would not favor resuming the series with the Bearcats after the three-game contract expired.

"We would like to continue this series," McGee was quoted as saying in *The Cincinnati Enquirer.* "But we're not going to go begging. And if that's the way it is, that's the way it is."

Yates said he got several letters from all over the country after that game, almost all in support. Some coaches wrote and told him, "You did what you had to do to win the game."

A year later, in December 1984, the Bearcats went to Lexington to play in the University of Kentucky Invitational. The day before the tournament started, there was a banquet attended by fans.

All the coaches spoke. When it was Yates's turn, he stood up and said: "Folks, I just want to prepare you for tomorrow

night and get you warmed up. So on the count of three, I want
you all to stand up and boo me right now.

"One...two...three..."

Sure enough, the crowd booed. Yates laughed.

"I just kind of tried to take the edge off," he said.

UC 66, MINNESOTA 64
NOVEMBER 25, 1989

Steve Sanders was a wide receiver from Cleveland, Ohio,
who played four years for the University of Cincinnati football
team. But that's not how he will forever be remembered on the
UC campus.

This is what made Sanders part of Bearcats basketball
history: It was his three-pointer from the corner as time ran
out that gave Cincinnati a 66-64 victory over 20th-ranked
Minnesota in the first regular-season game at Shoemaker
Center—and the first game of the Bob Huggins era.

Here is what led up to November 25, 1989 ...

Sanders's last football season was 1988. He knew he was
coming back to UC for a fifth year to try to complete requirements for his degree. In the spring 1989, Sanders was playing
intramural basketball and caught the eye of assistant basketball
coach Larry Harrison. Harrison, who was on the lookout for
players, asked *News Record* reporter Branson Wright about
Sanders and another football player, Roosevelt Mukes. "Steve
was our nemesis in intramural basketball," Wright says now.
Sanders played pickup games every off season with UC basketball players, felt he held his own, and often wondered whether
he could play Division I basketball.

The next fall, Sanders joined the basketball team for preseason conditioning, then had second thoughts.

"That was the hardest thing I ever did in my life," Sanders
said. "I talked to Coach Harrison and said, 'I don't know if I

can do this.' We just ran so much. I actually stopped for about two weeks."

When practices officially started, UC held walk-on try-outs. The six-foot-two Sanders and the five-foot-ten Mukes, who at the time was the school's all-time leading wide receiver, both showed up.

"Coming in, I didn't really expect to play a lot," Sanders said. "I thought maybe I could play five or 10 minutes a game and just enjoy the experience. But as time went on, I started feeling more and more comfortable."

Huggins was beginning to assert himself as the Bearcats coach and certainly grabbed the attention of the players.

"He was a maniac," Sanders said. "The yelling and the screaming didn't bother me. I came from a football background, and that's all football coaches do is yell and scream. But practice was so intense for three-and-a-half hours. He never let us cheat ourselves. I was in the best shape of my life playing basketball."

The Bearcats only had eight scholarship players. By the first game, Sanders was in the starting backcourt with Andre Tate.

"The whole time leading up to the Minnesota game, he never let us think that we weren't good enough to win," Sanders said of Huggins. "We had an awful lot of confidence, which he gave us. And the coaching staff did a great job with the scouting report. Everything he said that they would do during the game, they did."

Sanders, who would average 7.0 points and 2.5 rebounds for the season, had four points all game. Until the very end.

UC led by one with 30 seconds left. Lou Banks fouled Willie Burton off the ball on an inbounds pass, and Burton made two free throws.

Minnesota was ahead 64-63—its first lead in the second half. The Bearcats brought the ball up past midcourt and called their final timeout.

Cincinnati worked the ball around, but when Keith Starks tried to hit Tate cutting across the foul line, the ball was stolen by Minnesota's Kevin Lynch, who dribbled down the sideline in front of the scorer's table. Lynch picked up his dribble right in the front of the Minnesota bench and started falling out of bounds. He tried to throw the ball off Tate and missed, and it bounced all the way back toward the UC basket and went out of bounds on the baseline with eight-tenths of a second remaining.

The Golden Gophers called a timeout.

The first thing Huggins told his players was, "You guys are going to win this basketball game."

As the huddle broke, Huggins grabbed Sanders by the arm and said, "Steve, if they can't get it inside, you have to break around, because Andre's going to throw you the ball."

Tate had to inbound the ball against seven-footer Bob Martin. The play was designed for Tate to lob it toward the basket. Banks was covered when he cut inside. By the time Levertis Robinson broke free into the middle of the paint, Tate was looking toward his last option.

Sanders had broken toward the ball, faked back, then went to the corner in front of the UC bench. Tate delivered a short bounce pass. Sanders caught it and shot it from about 20 feet out over Martin, his first three-point attempt of the night and the Bearcats' only three-point field goal in the game.

Swish.

The arena erupted.

"It felt perfect," Sanders said. "It felt like I just placed the ball into the basket. It had to go in. I saw it and when it went in, I was so happy. There was so much energy flowing through my body I cannot explain. I jumped up and down and ran, and they chased me and caught me. They dived on top of me. They picked me up and then I got down and ran across the court and up into the stands. Everybody was off the court but me. I was still running around in the stands. Then I ran down back through the court again. When I finally got in the locker room, I was so hyped and excited, I just had to go lay down on the floor in the shower. ... It was truly amazing."

Later, Sanders was talking to Harrison.

"You know, you just went down in UC basketball history," the assistant coach said.

"Coach, in two weeks, no one will remember this shot," Sanders told him.

He couldn't have been more wrong.

UC 77, DUKE 75
NOVEMBER 28, 1998

There had been so many heartaches for the University of Cincinnati during Melvin Levett's career.

Miles Simon's buzzer-beating 65-foot bank shot that handed No. 13 Arizona a 79-76 victory in February 1996. Lenny Brown's last-second jumper that gave Xavier a 71-69 upset over the No. 1-ranked Bearcats in November 1996. Top-ranked Kansas coming back from 16 points down to beat UC 72-65 in Chicago just over a week later. The 1998 NCAA Tournament loss to West Virginia on Jarrod West's halfcourt heave with 0.8 seconds to play.

That is the context of the championship game of the 1998 Great Alaska Shootout.

No. 1 Duke vs. No. 15 Cincinnati. National TV. Midnight tipoff.

Fast forward to the end.

The Bearcats were ahead 74-73 when Pete Mickeal went to the foul line with 42 seconds left, but Mickeal missed both free throws. Duke missed two shots on its possession, and UC rebounded. Alvin Mitchell was quickly fouled with 13 seconds remaining. Mitchell missed his first foul shot, then made the second. UC led 75-73.

After a UC timeout, Duke guard William Avery hit a running jumper from the baseline over Kenyon Martin to tie the game with three seconds to play.

"We were always in that position, playing a big school, and somehow, someway, we always let it slip away," Levett said. "We knew this was our moment."

Melvin Levett (21) and Alvin Mitchell (14) leap in celebration of Levett's game-winning dunk against Duke in the 1998 Great Alaska Shootout. Levett was named by Slam *magazine in 2001 as one of the 50 greatest dunkers of all time. (Jim Lavrakas/* Anchorage Daily News*)*

The Bearcats called a timeout, and without hesitation Huggins drew up a play that the team had gone over in practice—though not often with success.

"Sometimes you'd think, 'What are we doing this for?' Because when we ran it in practice, it didn't go smoothly, or we didn't beat the buzzer," Levett said. "But this time it was like destiny."

Ryan Fletcher took the ball out of bounds from under Duke's basket. He sailed a long pass to Martin, standing at the top of the three-point arc near UC's basket. Martin jumped, caught the ball, immediately turned to his left, and—before he landed back on the ground—passed to Levett, who was streaking toward the basket on the right side. Levett snagged the ball on the run and went straight up.

"I didn't want to lay it up because you've seen guys in those situations blow the layup," Levett said. "I wanted to leave no doubt."

He jumped ... and dunked (hard) ... to complete one of the most memorable baskets in Bearcats history.

"Everything flowed. It was unbelievable," Levett said.

"You'd pray sometimes ... that maybe you could have that moment. I just burst into tears. I had to be calmed down during the timeout before they came out and ran their last play. I was losing it. I kind of got caught up in the moment."

What is almost forgotten is that Duke, with one second on the clock, almost tied it again. Shane Battier threw a full-court pass that got knocked back to Avery, who nailed a 14-foot bank shot—clearly after the final buzzer sounded.

"It was more than just us winning that game," Levett said. "It was for Cincinnati, for our school, and for all the teams that didn't win before."

3

JOHN WIETHE ERA (1946-1952)

We begin now in the 1940s.

Though the University of Cincinnati basketball program officially started in 1901, it was in the latter part of the '40s that the Bearcats first won 20 games, first averaged more than 50 points a game, first achieved a national ranking, first hired a full-time coach, and first had a 1,000-point scorer.

Most important, however, expectations were forever changed.

FOOD, GLORIOUS FOOD

More than 40 years before a driven and intense 35-year-old coach named Bob Huggins arrived in Clifton, the Bearcats

John Wiethe (center) led UC to a 106-47 record in six seasons. (Photo by University of Cincinnati/Sports Information)

were led by a man named John "Socko" Wiethe, who was equally known for his intensity and hatred of losing.

Wiethe, a Xavier University graduate who attended UC's College of Law, had a football background, having been an All-NFL guard for the Detroit Lions. He also played semi-pro baseball, pro basketball in Fort Wayne, and was an American Association umpire one year. Wiethe was a UC football team assistant coach before he took over the basketball team in 1946.

He had what could be considered an unusual way of expressing his dissatisfaction with losing to his players. He hit them where it counted—in their stomachs.

When UC played on the road and won, Wiethe would take his players out for steak dinner. When they lost? He'd give the student manager a five-dollar bill and tell him to go get 10 half-dollars. Then he'd give each player 50 cents to go buy a hamburger.

That went on until Athletic Director Chick Mileham went on a few road trips with the team, saw what was happening, and put an end to it.

SWITCHING SPORTS

Ray Penno started his athletic career at UC as a basketball player but ended up in another sport.

How did that happen?

Mileham saw Penno when he led Western Hills High School past Elder for the 1944 city league championship in Cincinnati. Mileham asked Penno if he wanted to play basketball at UC.

"Not really," Penno told him.

"All my friends were going into the service," he said. "It sounds corny, but I wanted to get in as soon as I could. But I was only 17."

Mileham told Penno that he could play one year with the Bearcats, then join the military. Which is what he did. He started every game of the 1944-45 season and was the team's No. 4 scorer with a 4.0 average.

UC closed its season with a 65-35 loss to Kentucky. The day after the game, Penno signed up with the U.S. Army and spent the next two years in The Philippines.

He returned to Cincinnati just in time for the end of the 1946-47 season. By then, the Bearcats had a new basketball coach: John Wiethe. Just before the final game of the season, Penno showed up on campus and introduced himself to Wiethe.

"Go down and get a uniform," the coach said.

Penno didn't want to, but he relented. He played maybe a minute in a 61-51 victory over Butler. In the locker room afterward, Wiethe introduced Penno to Ray Nolting, UC's football coach. "We'd like you to come out and play end on the football team," Nolting said.

Penno weighed over 200 pounds, about 30 more than when he first played basketball at UC. But, he had not played a down of high school football.

"I wouldn't even know how to put on the uniform," he told Nolting.

He got the hang of it quickly and played three years for the football team, including on the 1949 Glass Bowl team for coach Sid Gillman. He started five games in his football career.

"I just fell in love with football," Penno said.

A DIFFERENT KIND OF START

Dick Dallmer was the second player in University of Cincinnati history to score 1,000 points—Bill Westerfeld was the first—and when Dallmer graduated in 1950, he was the Bearcats' all-time leading scorer. He was also the first Bearcat to earn All-America honors. All of which are some pretty nice accomplishments for a guy who never played high school basketball—and, in fact, was cut from his team as a sophomore and junior.

Dallmer grew up in Hamilton, Ohio, and graduated from high school in 1942. Like many of his peers, he immediately reported to the military, joining the U.S. Army.

Dallmer was among the soldiers who landed on Normandy in France in June 1944 during World War II. Two months later, he was moved to the port city of LeHavre, France. At about 8 o'clock one night, he was walking through a path of rubble—the streets had been blown up—when he saw a large building with a hole in the roof. He noticed the lights were on and thought he heard balls bouncing.

Sure enough, some GIs were playing basketball and invited Dallmer to join in. He took off his boots and played in stocking feet. He went back the next night. And the next. After the fourth night of playing, he was approached by the master sergeant, who told Dallmer he was being transferred to head-quarters in Lille, France, in the morning.

"Why?" Dallmer asked. He was told that the command-ing general was a West Point graduate who wanted the best basketball team in the area.

Dallmer's team won the section title and played in Paris for the U.S. Army championship of Europe. He had left high school six feet tall, 160 pounds. Two years later, he was 6-3, 190 and holding his own against former college and pro players.

Dallmer was discharged in November 1945. He signed up for classes at UC, but it was too late to play basketball for the Bearcats that season. That winter, he played with Champion Paper Company of Hamilton, which won the state industrial championship. Dallmer was named MVP of the league and had tryout offers at Kentucky and Tennessee. Wiethe was given Dallmer's name, invited him to try out in the summer of '46, then offered him a scholarship.

"That's how I got started at UC," Dallmer said. "Now that's a different story."

Dallmer was an Associated Press honorable mention All-American in 1948 and '49 and was third-team All-America in 1950. He finished his career with 1,098 points.

ROCKY RELATIONSHIP

Cincinnati native Ralph Richter was an Elder guy. So nat-urally, coming out of the Catholic high school on Cincinnati's west side, he figured he'd go to Xavier University, the Jesuit college across town from UC.

After serving two years in the navy, Richter returned to Cincinnati in the fall of 1946 and went to XU to talk to coach Lew Hirt about joining the team. Hirt—"a Hamilton guy"—said Richter could come over for a tryout. But there was no scholarship offer.

Ralph Richter was Cincinnati's leading scorer in 1948-49, averaging 16.4 points a game for the 23-5 Bearcats. (Photo by University of Cincinnati/Sports Information)

"I knew I was in bad shape," Richter said. "He kind of favored the boys from Hamilton and Middletown. So I talked to my high school coach, Mr. Walter Bartlett, and he said, 'I think UC's trying to build up a team.'"

As it turns out, Wiethe had coached at Roger Bacon High School at the same time Richter played at Elder. But when

Richter approached Wiethe about playing for the Bearcats, the coach acted as if he knew nothing about Richter.

"Did you ever play?" Wiethe asked.

"I played some in the service," Richter told him. "I averaged about 25 points."

Richter said that Wiethe then turned to football coach Ray Nolting and said, "Listen to this clown over here."

That was the start of what would be a rocky relationship between UC's third 1,000-point scorer and his character of a coach.

The six-foot-four Richter led Cincinnati in scoring in 1947-48 and 1948-49. But he and Wiethe never did see eye to eye.

'HE WAS A DIFFERENT BREED'

This was an interesting postponement of a game.

The Bearcats were scheduled to play the University of Miami (Florida) in the Orange Bowl in Miami on February 6, 1947.

But it got so cold and windy—yes, *that cold* in Miami— that the basketball game was postponed until the next day and played in a Miami high school gym. The Hurricanes won 57-54 in the final seconds, and Wiethe was none too happy.

UC flew home that night and landed at the airport in Northern Kentucky. A school bus was waiting for the team.

Wiethe jumped in the bus and rode it back to campus. Alone. He gave the players bus fare, and they had to wait until six in the morning when the buses started running to leave the airport. Their bus stopped at every stop all the way into Cincinnati.

"We said many times he was nuts," Dallmer said. "He was a different breed. And he took pride in that."

TRIVIA QUESTION

Who scored the first basket ever at Cincinnati Gardens?

It was Richter, who hit a five-foot hook shot over a Butler defender on February 22, 1949. UC won 49-41.

"I just happened to be the guy who got the ball," he said. "I was very pleased about it, though."

Turns out it was Richter's only field goal of the game. He finished with six points.

NOT ON SAME PAGE

Richter never warmed to Wiethe. "Very difficult to get along with at times," Richter said of his coach. "The longer you were there, the more difficult it became."

In his fourth year in college in 1949-50, Richter was accepted to UC's medical school. He did not plan to play his senior year, but after a meeting with Wiethe, he agreed to participate in only Cincinnati's home games.

"That worked out for a while—until we finally had an away game," Richter said.

The 12th-ranked Bearcats had a Monday night game at No. 14 Western Kentucky on January 16. On Sunday, Richter received a phone call from a man who said he was a pilot; Wiethe—without telling Richter—had arranged for a private two-seat airplane to fly Richter to Bowling Green, Kentucky, from Lunken Airport at 4 p.m. the day of the game.

"I had classes until 5 o'clock," Richter said. "I didn't go because I couldn't miss that much school and I wasn't too anxious to fly to Bowling Green, Kentucky, at night in a two-seat airplane."

He sent Wiethe a telegram saying he couldn't make it. The players told Richter that Wiethe "hit the ceiling" after he got the telegram. Western Kentucky won 84-59. Afterward,

WKU coach Ed Dibble brought a basket of apples to the Bearcats in their locker room. Wiethe took one and slammed it off the wall.

"After that," Richter said, "things weren't too smooth."

Richter averaged 8.7 points coming off the bench that season. He went on to become an orthopedic surgeon in Cincinnati—and even worked for the Cincinnati Bengals in the 1970s.

HEADS UP

Dallmer remembers the tension between Richter and Wiethe. One day, the Bearcats were running a figure-8 drill to warm up at the beginning of practice. Wiethe watched from a chair.

After about 15 minutes, a panting Richter told Dallmer: "Next time I get the ball, I'm going to sail it over his head where he's sitting."

"Sure enough, Ralph did it," Dallmer said.

"Yeah, I missed him," Richter added.

WARMS YOUR HEART, DOESN'T IT?

Richter and Wiethe did have their nice moments together. Well, maybe one.

When UC beat St. Francis (New York) 91-62 on February 18, 1949, Richter scored 38 points and established a UC record for single-season scoring. After the game, Wiethe walked by and said, "Pretty hot, huh Slim?" Then he walked away.

"That was the only compliment I got in four years," Richter said.

He was Cincinnati's No. 3 all-time scorer (1,053 points) when his career ended—behind only Dallmer and Westerfeld.

UH, SURE, I'M A CENTER

Jim Holstein was not the first UC player drafted into professional basketball, but he was the first to play in the National Basketball Association, spending 1952-55 with the Minneapolis Lakers and 1955-56 with Fort Wayne.

But he had to lie to get on the court to start his collegiate career.

Holstein was a guard for a Hamilton Catholic High School team that was state runner-up his senior year. UC offered him a scholarship.

When he arrived on campus in 1949, Holstein realized veteran guards Dick Dallmer and Ralph Richter were back for their senior years. Forwards Jack Laub and Al Rubenstein also returned. However, center Bill Westerfeld had graduated.

Wiethe asked Holstein if he had ever played center. Seeing that it was the only position available, Holstein fibbed and said, "Yeah, I played inside occasionally."

In fact, he had never played inside.

The first day of practice, Wiethe put Holstein in at center. And because he had more of a scorer's mentality, almost every time he got the ball, he shot it.

After practice, Wiethe called over Holstein. "I can't use you at center because you shoot the ball all the time," the coach said.

Holstein pleaded for another chance. The next day, he started passing the ball—and he was back as the team's center.

"He saw I could play that part of the game, too," Holstein said.

Jim Holstein (left) averaged 15.7 points and 12 rebounds in 1951-52, John Wiethe's last season as UC's coach. (Photo by University of Cincinnati/Sports Information)

The centers in the Mid-American Conference at the time were around 6-5 and 6-6. Holstein was 6-3 and able to drive by most defenders.

"I'm not sure I was quick enough to stay with the smaller guys," he said. "Staying with the big guys was a snap. I loved center. I enjoyed the physical part of it. It just took time to get used to."

After his college career, Wiethe recommended Holstein to the Lakers, with whom he went back to playing guard.

EARLY CHALLENGE

The third game of Holstein's college career, he went up against Kansas's two-time consensus first-team All-American Clyde Lovellette, who was six foot nine—six inches taller than Holstein. The two guarded each other all night.

UC would win 56-54 at the Cincinnati Gardens on December 15, 1949, and for Holstein, it was a memorable outing.

"I don't recall how many points I got, but I held him to 15 points—and eight of them were free throws," he said. "I've got a picture (from the game) on my wall."

Holstein finished with 19 points. Afterward, Kansas coach Phog Allen did a fair amount of complaining about the referees.

GOING TOE TO TOE

Joe Luchi had served in the military and was older than most of his teammates. "But what a competitor," Holstein said. "He really came after you. He was about six feet tall, but he was all man."

Wiethe would sometimes play half-court games with the team during practice. One day, Wiethe hit Luchi, and Luchi went after his coach.

"All of a sudden, Joe was decked on the floor; John punched him good," Holstein said. "So we jumped on Joe and held him and said, 'Now, stop it, he's going to kill you.' They were punching each other while we were scrimmaging."

They didn't call the coach "Socko" for nothing.

WHAT ABOUT OUR REPUTATION?

UC played Long Island University at Madison Square Garden in New York on a Thursday night in February 1950. The Bearcats had a Saturday game scheduled against La Salle in Philadelphia.

When the team left New York on Friday morning, a student manager accidentally left his bag at the Bearcats' hotel.

The good news for the manager was that Wiethe had stayed in New York to scout high school players that Friday night. An assistant coach called back and asked Wiethe to retrieve the bag from the hotel.

That was also bad news for the manager.

The UC team was in the lobby of its Philadelphia hotel when Wiethe arrived Saturday afternoon. As soon as Wiethe walked in, he threw the manager's bag across the hotel's tile lobby floor and smack into a wall on the other side.

The manager stood still. Wiethe was steaming.

"Damn you," the coach said. "We had a good reputation up there, we were well behaved—and you've got two of the hotel towels in your handbag!"

"All I wanted was a souvenir," the manager said.

The whole team cracked up.

INNER CONFLICT

The night of March 3, 1950, Wiethe didn't know what to feed his players. Remember, he made sure they ate better when they won.

The Bearcats played in Cleveland against Western Reserve, which was coached by Wiethe's friend Michael "Mo" Scarry, also a former NFL player. Well, UC was having its way with Western Reserve and nearing the 100-point plateau.

Though Wiethe loved to win, he didn't want to embarrass an old pal. So as the final minute ticked away, he didn't want UC to score anymore. The players, however, had other ideas. No Cincinnati team had ever scored 100 points in a game. So in the final seconds, one of the Bearcats called timeout. The players decided to let Western Reserve score, then they'd go down and try to get past the century mark.

Which they did. Don Huffner made the last three UC baskets.

Final score: Cincinnati 101, Western Reserve 58. The Bearcats finished 10-0 in the Mid-American Conference.

No matter. Wiethe was furious. He came into the locker room and scolded his players.

"That's the only friend I have in the coaching business, and look what we did to him!" Wiethe yelled. "I don't know whether to give you steak or hamburger."

Interestingly, Scarry became the line coach of the UC football team in 1956.

CHANGE OF HEART

Bill Lammert had scholarship offers from UC and Xavier coming out of Roger Bacon High School, and he chose XU.

The summer after his senior year at Roger Bacon, Lammert was all set to become a Musketeer—even though he considered coach Lew Hirt's deliberate style of play to be rather boring.

Wiethe held open gym for local high school players in the off season at UC, and even though Lammert had committed to Xavier, Wiethe welcomed him to the UC campus for pick-up games. As the summer wore on, Lammert decided he was more comfortable with Wiethe's up-tempo style. Two weeks before classes were to begin at Xavier, Lammert called Hirt to tell him he had changed his mind and was becoming a Bearcat. "He really reamed me out," Lammert said.

He remembers calling from the southernmost phone booth in UC's student union. And despite making numerous calls from the building during his college career, Lammert never returned to that same booth.

Here's the kicker: Hirt never would have coached Lammert. He retired before the start of the 1951-52 season and was replaced by assistant Ned Wulk, whose teams played a completely different style.

"I guess if I had known Ned Wulk was going to be the coach, I probably would never have made the decision I made," Lammert said.

Lammert went on to score 1,119 points in his UC career and was the No. 3 scorer in school history at the time of his graduation.

JUST A SHOOTAROUND, EH?

Lammert was a freshman during Wiethe's final season. Lammert had just missed six games with an ankle injury but was scheduled to return to action January 15, 1952, at Ohio University. The Bearcats bused to Athens, Ohio, and arrived around 10 p.m. Wiethe took the players to the gym "just to get the rubber out" of their legs after the bus ride.

Lammert, whose ankle was still weak, asked whether he should get taped. "No," Wiethe told him. "We're just shooting around."

By midnight, the Bearcats were going all out and full-court pressing. Lammert turned his ankle again and missed six more games.

"That's just kind of the way he was," Lammert said. "There we were, full-court pressing at midnight the night before a game when we were just supposed to be shooting around."

CONSPIRACY THEORY

UC played at Western Kentucky on January 30, 1952, and lost 79-63. For some reason, the up-tempo Bearcats could not get out and run and had trouble keeping up with the Hilltoppers, who won their 72nd straight game at home. Another thing the players wouldn't forget was a power outage at halftime.

The players were talking on the bus ride back to Cincinnati about the nets. They noticed that Western Kentucky was shooting into a basket with very tight strings, and the Bearcats would have to wait for the ball to come through every time WKU scored giving the Hilltoppers a chance to get back and set up their defense. The UC players also realized that the strings were very loose on their basket. The ball would go right through the net, allowing the Hilltoppers to take the ball out of bounds quickly and get a fastbreak going. This was strange because, of course, the teams changed baskets at halftime.

Larry Imburgia finally made the connection: When the power went out, the nets were switched.

"It was orchestrated, of course," Jack Twyman said. "In retrospect, you realized that you'd been had."

THANKS, COACH

In 1951-52, freshmen were eligible to compete on the varsity teams, and UC freshmen Twyman and Lammert played with the upperclassmen.

This was Wiethe's last year as UC's coach. But it was a season Twyman won't forget.

On February 21, Cincinnati played St. John's in New York. It was Twyman's first trip to Madison Square Garden.

St. John's was winning 38-30 at halftime. Twyman walked into the locker room and started to take a seat. Wiethe was already ranting and raving. "This is how you dive for a loose ball," he shouted. And he dove straight at Twyman, knocking him right through a tear-away door and into the lobby.

"People are getting popcorn, and there I am laying flat on my back," Twyman said. "And Weithe's saying, 'Now *that's* how you go after a loose ball.'

"He was very intense. I feel very fortunate to have played for him. He certainly taught you to be competitive and to never give up. I learned a lot from John. I also learned a lot from George (Smith, UC's head coach from 1952-60). He was like my father away from home."

IMPRESSIVE

Imburgia, who averaged 24.2 points a game in 1950-51, had contracted polio as a child. However, he had some team-mates who didn't even know it.

"His left arm was almost useless, but he could flat-out play the game with that right hand," Holstein said. "He had a great big hand. He could handle the ball and shoot it and jump real well.

"He put the left hand up to guide the ball but his right hand did almost everything. He never said anything (about the polio). You didn't even think about it when we were playing with him. We just went out and played. We'd look at him and think: How the hell can he play? But he did a great job."

INTENSE OFF THE COURT, TOO

Wiethe was big on conditioning. The Bearcats ran few drills under him; they mostly scrimmaged for hours.

The coach liked to stay in shape, too. He was roughly six foot two, 230 pounds. Big but agile.

To lose weight in the off season, he'd put on a rubber suit and play golf at Avon Field on Reading Road in Cincinnati. Wiethe would carry a 1-iron, a wedge and a putter and run the course to try to sweat off some pounds. He'd try to play 18 holes in one hour.

One night, he hit off the first tee and his ball landed right in the fairway behind a man who was playing ahead of Wiethe. But he didn't care. Wiethe's attitude was: Get out of my way.

The man playing ahead of him knocked his shot up on the green. Wiethe hit his ball onto the green close to the man, who then knocked Wiethe's ball back at him. Wiethe grabbed his ball and approached the man, asking why he hit the ball his way. The man explained that he was upset Wiethe was hitting his shots so close to him.

Wiethe picked up the man's bag of clubs and threw it off the base of the green. The guy came after Wiethe, who then picked up the man and threw him down toward his bag.

The man sued Wiethe for $10,000.

The next summer, Dallmer saw Wiethe and asked, "Whatever happened to that lawsuit?"

"Awww," Wiethe said, "I gave the fellow a C-note and that was the end of that."

"That's just the kind of character he was," Dallmer said of Wiethe.

Dick Dallmer was a four-year starter at forward. During his career, the Bearcats went a combined 77-27. He was a team captain as a junior and senior. (Photo by University of Cincinnati/Sports Information)

ZONING OUT

And so the story goes ... it was 1948 or '49, and the Bearcats were playing some of their games at Music Hall downtown. Wiethe was driving a carload of players to a game one evening. As he was driving, he was deep in thought about that night's matchup and discussing strategies with the players in the car.

He stopped at a red light on Central Parkway, and he continued talking to the players as the light turned green, then red again. The driver in the car behind Wiethe started honking his horn.

Wiethe slowly got out of his car, walked back to the other car, opened the door, grabbed the man's keys, and threw them. Then he walked back to his car, got in, and continued driving to the game.

MAKINGS OF SUCCESS

For all the antics, Wiethe was driven to get UC among the upper echelon of college basketball programs. He would play anyone anywhere and was the first to coach a Cincinnati team at Madison Square Garden in New York City. Under Wiethe, the Bearcats would also schedule games at Chicago Stadium and the Orange Bowl in Miami.

Wiethe, a lawyer who would eventually become head of the Hamilton County Democratic Party in Cincinnati, coached the first UC team to win 20 games in a season and the first to score 100 points. He left after UC finished 11-16 in 1951-52—his only losing season.

"We were the beginning of things," Dallmer said. "We really got the program started."

4

GEORGE SMITH ERA
(1952-1960)

FATHER FIGURE

George Smith, captain of the Bearcats' football team in 1934 and a former assistant football coach, took over for John Wiethe as UC's head basketball coach in 1952. The players lost a hothead and gained a father figure.

Players loved Smith. Parents loved Smith.

Here's an example of why:

Smith's relationship with future Hall of Famer Jack Twyman was forever cemented during a period in the 1953-54 season when Twyman was feeling a little discouraged.

Smith sensed something was wrong, and he went to Twyman's hotel room when UC was in Oklahoma City to play in the All-College Tournament in December 1953. The two spent an hour or two talking while looking out the window at oil wells on the horizon.

George Smith's 154 career victories as head coach of the Bearcats rank him third only to Bob Huggins and Mick Cronin on Cincinnati's list of winningest coaches. After stepping down as head coach in 1960, Smith served as UC's Athletic Director for the next 13 years. (Photo by University of Cincinnati/Sports Information)

"He sat down on my bed and we talked about life and what I wanted and how we were going to do it together," Twyman said. "Actually, that was a turning point in my career at UC.

"I always appreciated that. He and Helen (Smith's wife) didn't have any children. I kind of thought of them as my parents away from home. We had a great relationship. I really considered him my mentor, so to speak."

KEEPING GOOD COMPANY

On February 26, 1954, the unranked Bearcats were playing host to No. 1-ranked Duquesne (21-0) at the Cincinnati Gardens (remember, Twyman, a Pittsburgh native, was supposed to play for the Dukes). UC won 66-52.

Twyman's mother was in town for the game. After it was over, Smith took Twyman, his mother, his girlfriend, Bill Lammert and his mother out to dinner at a restaurant on Reading Road. Joining them was Mike Boich, an official who worked the game. He lived in Cleveland and was a friend of Wiethe's.

Well, the bus carrying the Duquesne team, which was playing in Dayton next, stopped at the same restaurant to pick up food for the trip north.

"The whole team came into Schuller's and here's Jack Twyman and George Smith and Bill Lammert and their families eating with the referee," Twyman said. "It was so funny. They were kidding us about it."

ARMORY OPENER

Twyman's career high was 49 points, in a 101-92 victory over Western Kentucky his senior year.

But one of his most memorable performances was in the very first game played at the Armory Fieldhouse. Cincinnati opened its $2 million on-campus arena December 18, 1954, against the defending Big Ten champion Indiana Hoosiers, who had won the 1953 NCAA title. A sellout crowd of 7,000 was on hand.

Don Schlundt, IU's six-foot-10, three-time All-American who left as the school's career scoring leader, drew the assignment of defending the 6-6 Twyman.

"I remember Schlundt being very big," Twyman said. "I went outside and he wouldn't come out, so I was able to shoot over him. When he did come out, he wasn't quick enough to guard me."

Twyman finished with 35 points on 15-of-24 shooting. Schlundt, who came in averaging 26.3 points a game, had just 17 against UC. The Bearcats won 97-65.

"Twyman never looked better in his life," *The Cincinnati Enquirer* reported.

His career rebounding high came a month later when Twyman grabbed 30 boards against Miami University in an 86-80 victory in Oxford.

WILLING TO WORK

Twyman finished his college career with 1,598 points and 1,242 rebounds and was the University of Cincinnati's all-time leader in both categories until a guy named Oscar Robertson came along.

He was selected by the Rochester Royals with the 10th pick in the 1955 NBA draft and played professionally from

In 11 years in the NBA, Jack Twyman averaged 19.2 points and 6.6 rebounds and was an All-Star six times. (Photo by University of Cincinnati/Sports Information)

1955-66. Twyman was enshrined to the Basketball Hall of Fame in 1983.

After getting cut from his high school team as a junior, Twyman had two choices: Give it up, or turn it up. He told his coach, "You're not going to be able to cut me next year."

Twyman turned himself into a player by working harder than others. He said he became a pretty good shooter "because I was willing to spend the time and take the initiative to practice.

"I would take a couple thousand jump shots after practice," he said. "I wanted very badly to be a pro and was willing to forgo everything else in order to get there. I had my own key to the gym (at UC). Whenever I wanted, I could go in and turn on the lights. At 10, 11 at night, I was practicing my shooting.

"I'm proud of what we accomplished. I feel we moved the program to another level. I'm very proud of my association with the University of Cincinnati. Starting with Wiethe, it gave me a lot of ideals that served me well through business and a pro (basketball) career."

JACK BE NIMBLE

The translation of a conversation can even be lost when it involves two future Hall of Famers in their respective sports.

Tony Trabert played tennis for the United States in Davis Cup competition in Australia in December 1953, then returned to Cincinnati to play the last eight games of the 1953-54 basketball season.

He was rooming on the road with Twyman, the starting center, and was talking about his experiences Down Under.

Trabert told Twyman: "You know, we had kangaroos for ball boys. They hopped out on the court. The main thing they did is when you're practicing your serve, they'd fill their pouches with tennis balls and they stood there and you could serve and take the balls out of their pouch."

Twyman bought the whole story.

"He had me going for at least a couple of weeks," Twyman said. "I was just a kid coming out of Pittsburgh. Now I've heard the story *ad nauseum*. Every time we're in a public venue he brings that story up. But I've got to admit, it's true."

ONCE A BEARCAT . . .

Chuck Machock really wanted to attend the U.S. Military Academy. Twice he took tests to get an appointment to West Point; the closest he came was first alternate.

By July 1955, after his senior year at Elyria (Ohio) Catholic High School, Machock accepted a full scholarship offer from UC.

His father was an NCAA football official for 20 years and a basketball official for 18 years. Machock knew of Cincinnati's dominance in the Mid-American Conference from 1946-51 and was aware of the kind of talent in the program. He considered it a challenge to try to play at UC.

As a freshman, there was no choice. After two scholarship players dropped off the team, there were only five players remaining.

In his sophomore season, there were so many players that Machock rarely got in games, and when he did, it was in the final seconds.

Coach George Smith knew Machock wanted to eventually coach basketball. So at the start of his junior year (1957-58), Smith had an honest exchange with Machock, telling him that he likely wasn't going to play much—if at all.

Machock said: "He kind of took me under his wing and said, 'You want to be a coach? I'll work out a situation where you can be our manager and help coach the freshmen with Coach Jucker.'"

That worked out just fine for Machock. Ed Jucker would spend the first hour each day with the freshman team, then go help Smith with the "varsity." When he was a senior, Machock helped former Bearcat Jim Holstein, who became the new freshman team coach. During the 1958-59 season, Machock sat on the bench with the varsity as part of the coaching staff.

THE HUGGINS CONNECTION

Indeed, Machock went into coaching, starting at St. Henry High School in Erlanger, Kentucky. From there he went to Elyria (Ohio) Catholic High School, Lorain County Community College, Akron as an assistant, Steubenville College and then to West Virginia University in 1972-73. There, he recruited a high school player out of Northeast Ohio named Bob Huggins. Machock had worked at Bob's father Charlie's camp as a guest coach when Huggins was just starting high school.

Machock left the Mountaineers to join Holstein's staff at Ball State. From there, Machock went to Ohio State and worked for Eldon Miller in 1976. When there was an opening on the staff, Machock suggested Miller hire Huggins, who was a graduate assistant at West Virginia. Huggins and Machock coached two years together with the Buckeyes.

In 1983, when Machock became head coach at Central Florida, he hired Huggins as his No. 1 assistant.

Machock left coaching to work in securities and ran his own office out of Lancaster, Ohio. He would occasionally meet up with Huggins to go scout high school players.

When Huggins got hired as UC's coach in 1989, he called Machock. "You want to get back into coaching?" Huggins asked. "Transfer down to Cincinnati and I'll wait for you to get off work at four to start practice. You can be a part-time coach."

Machock's wife, Dottie, is from Cincinnati. Her mother and brother lived there.

Offer accepted.

Machock was a volunteer assistant coach at UC with Huggins—more than 30 years after he helped coach the Bearcats freshman team—for three years before the NCAA changed the rules for men's basketball staffs. Machock could no longer be a part-time coach, so in 1992 he became the radio analyst and continued to be a frequent visitor to practice. He is one of Huggins's greatest supporters and confidants.

"I watched him grow up and play basketball," Machock said. "He was a phenomenal basketball player. No one shot it with any more consistent rhythm than Bob Huggins. I saw him score 40 or more in three straight games. He was the No. 4 scorer in Ohio high school history when he graduated (with 2,438 career points, he ranked ninth in 2004).

"I knew he was going to be a damn good college coach. Nobody has a better work ethic than Bob Huggins, to prepare a team for a game and to prepare a team for a season. He is relentless. He is super, super intelligent. That's what got him to where he is today."

REBOUNDING MACHINE

For all the great rebounders in the history of UC basketball, nobody ever had a game like six-foot-nine junior Connie Dierking did against Loyola (Louisiana) on February 16, 1957.

UC won 82-77 at the Armory Fieldhouse, but what was memorable about that day was that Dierking pulled down 33 rebounds, a single-game school record still standing in 2004. (He also scored 34 points that night.)

"Things just happened to be falling my way that day, I guess," Dierking said. "I knew I had a lot. But I had no idea how many I had. You don't need a lot of ability to rebound; what you need is a lot of heart. If you go after the ball, you're going to get it."

It was no fluke, either.

The next season, during his senior year, Dierking grabbed 31 rebounds—second-most in UC history—during a 70-point Bearcat victory over North Texas State. When he was a sophomore, Dierking had 30 rebounds against George Washington.

The only other player in UC history to get 30 rebounds in one game: Twyman, who had 30 on March 2, 1955 against Miami University.

REPORT TO ROOM 116, PLEASE

Dierking was born in Brooklyn and went to high school in Valley Stream, N.Y. Jucker, a UC assistant coach, had spent some time coaching at Rensselaer Polytech Institute in New York, and, well, he knew somebody who knew somebody who knew about Dierking. Jucker told Bearcats head coach George Smith about the kid.

One day during his senior year in 1955, the front office called Dierking's classroom and asked that he be sent to room 116.

"If anybody was sent to room 116, that meant you were in big trouble," Dierking recalled. "I said, 'Oh, what did I do?' I didn't remember doing anything.

"George Smith was on the phone. He asked, 'How would you like to come and visit the University of Cincinnati?' I never even went to Times Square. I said I've got to go home and talk to my parents about it."

Dierking came for a recruiting visit and never left town. He has lived in Cincinnati for roughly 50 years.

"Primarily I wanted to get away from home," he said. "My father was a.tough cookie, and I just wanted to get away. As it turned out, it was a good move."

RAINDROPS KEEP FALLIN'
ON MY HEAD

Phil Wheeler remembers going to pick up Dierking, who was taking his recruiting visit, at the airport while driving his convertible with the top down. Problem was, the weather was not fit for an open-air ride.

"We drove down the old Dixie Highway," Wheeler said. "It was a very sunny day, but there was a cloud over us and it rained on us all the way into Cincinnati. We expected it to stop because it was sunny everywhere. That was his entrance to Cincinnati. He never let me forget that."

"WE HAD A LITTLE PROBLEM WITH THE TROPHY"

In December 1955, the Bearcats went to Richmond, Virginia, and defeated Virginia, Seton Hall and the host school to win the Richmond Holiday Tourney championship. The final was played on December 30. Wheeler, UC's team captain, got the OK from Coach Smith to take the tournament trophy to a New Year's Eve party back in Cincinnati at the home of a UC booster.

Well, the team was celebrating. As the clock neared midnight, players were pouring some "beverages" into the trophy, passing it around and taking drinks from it. All of a sudden, someone snapped off one of the small basketball figurines on the trophy. Then off came another. And another.

"We had about eight little basketball players that weren't on the trophy anymore," Wheeler said. "It was demolished."

The next day, he took it to Smith in a box. The trophy "was in a million pieces" and reeked of alcohol. The really bad news? *The Cincinnati Post* had called Smith and wanted to take a picture of the trophy.

"Uh, George, we had a little problem with the trophy," Wheeler told his coach. "We put it on the mantle at the party and it fell off."

"George accepted that and not another word was said," Wheeler said. "Of course, he knew exactly what had happened."

The trophy was later repaired and was eventually on display in Shoemaker Center.

UPON FURTHER REVIEW

On February 2, 1956, Wheeler scored a career-high 37 points against St. John's at Madison Square Garden. He was being guarded all night by center Mike Parenti, who finished with 29 points. The Redmen were favored to win by three, but UC prevailed 93-78.

Wheeler, a senior, was feeling pretty good about that night—until five years later. In 1961, 37 players from 22 colleges were arrested in gambling scandals that had ties to the mob. In testimony against gamblers, Parenti was mentioned as one of the players involved in fixing games.

"Let's put it this way," Wheeler said laughing. "I *thought* I had a helluva game, but now I'm not so sure. How much he let me score, I don't know."

"THE BIG O"

It was the fall 1956, and freshmen were ineligible to compete on the "varsity." But soon, word got out about Oscar Robertson, the UC newcomer from Indianapolis. About 6,000 fans showed up to watch the freshmen scrimmage the varsity at the Armory Fieldhouse. The freshmen lost, but Robertson finished with 37 points, 17 rebounds and eight assists. There were times during the 1956-57 season that UC drew more fans at home for its freshmen games than for the varsity games.

The first game of his sophomore season, Robertson had 28 points, 15 rebounds and 14 assists in a 105-49 victory over Indiana State. It has been reported that Dick Baker, UC's play-by-play announcer on WSAI radio, that night dubbed Robertson "The Big O."

From 1957-60, the Bearcats would go 79-9 with Robertson in the starting lineup. He was a three-time All-American and three-time National Player of the Year. He averaged 33.8 points and scored a school-record 2,973 points.

More than 40 years after he left UC, the Basketball Hall of Famer said he remembers few details about the games in which he played. He said he doesn't recall much about the six games in which he scored at least 50 points, including his school-record 62-point effort against North Texas State in 1959-60. "I remember I didn't think I was shooting that well," Robertson said.

Not shooting well? He went 23 of 29 from the field and made a 50-foot shot at the buzzer just before halftime. And remember, there was no three-point shot.

Points weren't what mattered to him, though. It was the total game: Scoring, rebounding, passing, defense. And, of course, winning.

He remains UC's all-time leading rebounder, too, and is fifth in assists.

"He was so knowledgeable about the game of basketball," Machock said. "And he was always under control, no matter what he did."

HOW DID HE DO THAT?

John Bryant, a Withrow High School graduate, was discharged from the U.S. Army in June 1957. That summer, UC offered him a partial scholarship to play basketball.

While serving in the military, Bryant had heard about this freshman at Cincinnati named Oscar Robertson. But the two didn't meet until the fall 1957 when the Bearcats freshmen, including Bryant, went to scrimmage the varsity in the Armory Fieldhouse.

"I want you to guard Oscar," freshman coach Ed Jucker told Bryant.

Considered by many to be the most complete basketball player of all time, Oscar Robertson (12) established 19 Bearcat and 14 NCAA records during his collegiate career. After college, Robertson co-captained the 1960 U.S. Olympic basketball team that won a gold medal in Rome. (Photo by University of Cincinnati/Sports Information)

"The scrimmage started and I thought I was doing a pretty good job really, as far as playing good position basketball and not letting him get easy shots," Bryant said. "All of a sudden, Oscar went to the baseline and looked to me like he was almost out of bounds underneath the basket. He turned around and threw in a left-handed hook shot. I shook my head, of course."

At the next timeout, Bryant went over to his coach and said, "Juck, I'm playing very good defense and I've got him taking bad shots."

Jucker laughed. "With him there aren't any bad shots," he said.

Bryant and Robertson would become good friends.

SUDDEN IMPACT

Once eligible to play as a sophomore, Robertson made an immediate impact not just at UC, but in the basketball world.

The Bearcats took an 8-2 record into their game against Seton Hall at Madison Square Garden on January 9, 1958. That night, the 19-year-old Robertson—who came in averaging 29.7 ppg—put on a show, scoring 56 points. (Seton Hall finished with 54 in a 64-point loss.) That was a record outing at the 30-year-old arena for any basketball player at any level.

Robertson finished 22 of 32 from the field and 12 of 12 from the foul line. He had 30 points at halftime.

"Honey Russell was their coach; he never forgave George Smith for that," Connie Dierking said. "I just remember how unbelievable Oscar was and how lucky I was to be a part of that whole thing.

"When you play with a guy that good, you end up sometimes just watching him."

Robertson remembers there were few fans in the stands (attendance was 4,615) and that the Seton Hall coach was shouting to his players, "Get *Robinson.*" He sat out the final 2:46, left to a standing ovation and recalls being surrounded by the media in the locker room after the game.

During postgame interviews, he looked over at Machock, a former player who had just became a student manager a few weeks earlier. They were rooming together on the trip, and Machock was about packed up. "Hey, just remember, we're walking back together," Robertson yelled.

The team bus went back to the hotel without them. Robertson and Machock walked to the hotel together in a light snowfall.

"It's just the two of us," Machock said, "and he's talking about the game. We went back to our room, laid down, turned the light off and went to sleep. Now you tell me how many kids today, after scoring 56 points, would walk back three or four blocks without the rest of his team with his buddy, not even turn the TV on, and go to bed?"

During that season, Robertson would score 50 points against St. Louis, 50 against Wichita State and 56 in the NCAA Tournament against Arkansas. He averaged 35.1 points and 15.2 rebounds and was the first sophomore to ever lead the country in scoring. Robertson led the Bearcats to their first ever NCAA Tournament bid in 1958 and was named National Player of the Year.

LIFE SURE CAN TEST YOU

Robertson's on-court accomplishments are even more impressive given what he endured off the court. A law student wrote letters to the student newspaper, questioning the admittance of a black basketball player and indicating UC, then a private university, was lowering its academic standards.

Other examples:

HOUSTON, TEXAS
DECEMBER 1957

Cincinnati was staying at the Shamrock Hilton Hotel in Houston. Robertson was rooming with Machock.

Coach Smith came to their room late at night and told Robertson he had to leave.

"I thought he meant we—the whole team—had to leave," Robertson said.

"Where are we going?" Robertson asked.

"No, just you," Smith said. "They don't want *you* staying here."

"Me?" Robertson responded. "What the hell did I do?"

The hotel officials did not want an African-American staying in their establishment. He was taken to Texas Southern University and stayed on campus there.

"Don't get me wrong," Robertson said. "I wasn't naïve. But it took me by surprise. You know, you get on a university campus and your team rises to the top of college basketball and you're told a lot of things about doing all these things together."

He lay awake in bed that night and thought about how Smith preached unity and how the team was always supposed to stick together. Yet, there he was, alone. And, he said, none of his teammates ever addressed the situation the next day. He said he never felt the same about his standing on the team or attending UC functions as a player.

Robertson considered not playing the next day. Before the game, he said, he did not take any warm-up shots. He said fans were booing and throwing hot dogs and coins at him.

Before a crowd of 2,000, Robertson scored 25 points in a 70-53 victory.

"Makes you grow up fast," Robertson said. "It had nothing to do with my play. I think as an athlete, you've got to get rid of your personal problems and concentrate on playing basketball. That's the way life was."

Before leaving to play at Houston and North Texas the next season, Robertson told teammate John Bryant, the team's only other African-American player, to bring some extra money.

"Why?" Bryant asked.

"If we don't stay together as a team this year, you and I are coming back (to Cincinnati) whether we have to take a train or a bus or whatever," Robertson said. "We're going to stay together as a team or that's it."

Ever the ferocious rebounder, Oscar Robertson (12) still stands atop the UC record book for career rebounds (1,338) and rebounding average (15.2 per game). (Photo by University of Cincinnati/Sports Information)

They did. The Bearcats were housed in a dormitory on the University of Houston campus. Blacks still were not permitted in the hotels.

RALEIGH, NORTH CAROLINA
DECEMBER 1958

Before the Bearcats headed south to play in the 1958 Dixie Classic, Robertson received letters in Cincinnati from the Ku Klux Klan saying that if he showed up to play in the tournament, he'd be killed.

"If you're from the south, you get used to that," said Robertson, who was born in Tennessee. "It didn't bother me at all."

What did bother him was that UC—along with Michigan State—was not allowed to stay at a Raleigh hotel because it had African-American players on its team. The Bearcats and Spartans, who also had black players, ended up at a fraternity house outside of Raleigh.

When UC entered the arena for its first game, one man seated behind the UC bench wearing an army uniform, stood up and shouted at Robertson: "You black son of a bitch. Whoever said you were an All-American? You couldn't make Little Sisters of the Poor."

Cincinnati beat Wake Forest, then lost to North Carolina State and North Carolina. Robertson was verbally abused throughout the tournament. Each night, a sellout crowd of 12,400 attended.

In the first game, Robertson got into a brief scuffle with Demon Deacons junior David Budd, who was white, after they both dove for a loose ball. The officials called a foul on each player. The crowd was incited and stayed that way for the entire tournament.

Against North Carolina, Robertson finished with 29 points—21 in the second half—and 11 rebounds. As he walked to the locker room after the final buzzer, an eight-year-old white boy asked Robertson for his autograph.

"Hell no," Robertson responded as he continued on.

Teammate John Bryant told the kid to give him the program he wanted signed, then took it to Robertson in the locker room.

"No, I'm not signing that," Robertson said. "Did you hear what those son of a bitches are saying?"

"Yeah," Bryant said, "but this kid, in spite of everything they're saying, wants your autograph."

Robertson signed the program, and Bryant took it out to the child.

Soon after that, Coach Smith came charging into the locker room with tears streaming down his face. He was sweating and disheveled. Smith walked over to Robertson, hugged him and said, "I don't give a damn what these SOBs say, you're still the best damn basketball player in these United States."

"That helped a tremendous amount," Bryant said. "(Privately), Oscar was saying, 'Let's get the hell out of here. I'm leaving the university.'"

DENTON, TEXAS
JANUARY 1959

When in town to play North Texas State less than two weeks after the Dixie Classic, UC did stay at a local hotel. But the restaurant did not serve African-Americans. So, the owners closed the second floor so the Bearcats could eat there, separated from the other customers.

It was on that road trip, as the team approached its hotel, that a 12-year-old white boy with a thick Southern accent approached Bryant.

"Aren't ya'all from the University of Cincinnati?" he asked. "I heard what they did to Oscar over there in Raleigh. That was about the sorriest thing I ever heard of."

The child said he had talked to his minister and invited the players to come worship at his church.

That wasn't possible because UC had to practice, but Bryant did get the kid tickets to the game.

North Texas State is where someone put a black cat in the Bearcats locker room because of Robertson.

ST. LOUIS, MISSOURI
FEBRUARY 1960

In a restaurant around the corner from the team hotel in St. Louis, customers were dumping out their plates of food and leaving because the Bearcats arrived and Robertson and Bryant were being served. An elderly white woman approached them and asked, "Are you Oscar Robertson? I'm from Dickson County in Tennessee. We're awfully proud of you." That's where Robertson was born; he moved to Indiana when he was four years old.

"There were always little things that sort of offset some of the negative things," Bryant said.

When Robertson's statue was unveiled outside of Shoemaker Center in 1994, former teammate and close friend Bryant was one of the speakers. He talked about how Robertson knew he was a pioneer in helping break the color barrier in the UC basketball program and how he hoped to open doors at the university and in Cincinnati.

"As much as I marveled at the basketball talents of Oscar, I respected the man more," Bryant said.

Bryant falls in a similar category. He became the first African-American basketball coach (at Withrow) in the Cincinnati Public Schools and in 1968 became an assistant coach for the Bearcats—the first African-American on UC's basketball staff. His hiring was announced the same night Martin Luther King was assassinated in Memphis, Tennessee.

ROBERTSON IN A NUTSHELL

There was a Saturday morning pick-up game that Bryant remembers. First team to 15 baskets—you had to win by two baskets—would win. The losing players had to buy the winners 15-cent bottles of beer.

The game was tied at 16 when one of Robertson's teammates took a blind overhead shot that missed badly. Robertson stopped the game and asked, "What kind of shot was that?"

"It's only a game, Oscar," the player replied.

"Game nothing. I've got money riding on this."

"Oscar, if we lose, I'll pay your 15 cents."

"You miss the point. If I get up at 9 a.m. on a Saturday morning to play basketball, I'm playing to win and I'm playing to improve."

Bryant calls Robertson "the most precise, meticulous, basketball player you ever saw."

One day before practice, Robertson called over the six-foot-four, quick Bryant and asked him to guard him on a specific shot he was working on.

Then Robertson asked Bob Wiesenhahn, who was bigger and stronger but not as quick, to do the same.

Ditto for Paul Hogue, who was even bigger and stronger.

"He was trying the same thing on each one of us to see how each one of us would react to it," Bryant said. "He wanted to know in game situations how different people would tend to react to him."

EYE ON THE FUTURE

One day early in Robertson's junior year, after a hard practice, he and Bryant went to the student union cafeteria for dinner. Earlier that day, Robertson had been presented with a large framed black and white picture commemorating the 56 points he scored against Seton Hall at Madison Square Garden in January 1958.

One of the cafeteria servers at the student union was named Priscilla. She was a small, middle-aged African-American woman who saw the picture given to Robertson. She asked him to give it to her. Robertson told her it was special to him and that he would be glad to get her a copy of the picture from the university and sign it for her.

Priscilla was adamant. She wanted that specific picture.

"I don't know why you are being so high and mighty," she said. "In two more years, you will be washing dishes just like me."

"Priscilla," Robertson replied. "Two years from now, I'll be hiring and firing people like you."

SHOOT IT, QUICK

If there was a low moment in Robertson's UC playing career, it might be during an 83-80 overtime loss to Kansas State in the Midwest Regional of the 1958 NCAA Tournament in Lawrence, Kansas.

UC trailed 74-73 and had the ball with five seconds remaining in regulation. Naturally, the inbounds pass went to Robertson, who was fouled by Bob Boozer with one second to play. Robertson nailed the first foul shot to tie the game. He was on the line getting ready for his second shot and telling his teammates not to foul. Teammate Ron Dykes started yelling, "They're counting. Shoot the ball." Robertson had 10 seconds to shoot the ball, and the official counting was at eight.

Robertson shot it quickly and missed. The game went into overtime. Robertson fouled out with four minutes left. Robertson would blame his inexperience.

"Now I would've thrown the ball to the ref and faked tying my shoe," he said.

Feeling the officials had wronged him, Robertson took his frustration out on UC's consolation game opponent, Arkansas, scoring 56 points in a 97-62 victory.

BIG MAN ON CAMPUS

In 1994, the University of Cincinnati unveiled a bronzed statue of Robertson outside of Shoemaker Center, which became the basketball team's home in 1989.

Though he was honored and humbled at the ceremony, truth be told, Robertson was not wild about the idea when it was first presented to him.

His long-time attorney J.W. Brown was ill, and his son told Robertson that his father wanted to pay for the statue. Robertson first met Brown, a UC booster, on his recruiting visit in 1955.

"If he wants it, then I'll do it," Robertson said.

He spent a day with the artist outside of Salt Lake City, Utah, getting measured and having pictures taken.

When the statue was finally dedicated, Robertson said, it was "an emotional night for me."

"It brought up a lot of memories," he said. "It's funny. I had written a speech, but I never used it. When you have so many experiences, things just start coming to your mind.

"Fate decides things for you. (UC) wasn't my first choice, but it worked out great for me."

THE ENFORCER

There was a football coach at Austin High School in Knoxville, Tennessee, who had relatives in Cincinnati who were always telling him about this basketball player at the local university named Oscar Robertson.

"Of course, nobody believed that anybody could be that good," Paul Hogue said. "But it kind of piqued our curiosity."

Hogue just had to include UC as one of his college visits in December 1957, and as soon as he saw Robertson play, "that

This nine-foot bronze statue of Oscar Robertson sits outside of Fifth Third Arena near the entrance to the Richard E. Lindner Center, home of UC athletics. (Photo by University of Cincinnati/Sports Information)

pretty much made up my mind" where he wanted to attend college. Robertson was even better than advertised.

The six-foot-eight Hogue wasn't just big and aggressive on the court, but he had kind of an intimidating look because of his sports glasses that had a big rubber bridge across the nosepiece.

He starting wearing those glasses his sophomore year after having played in regular glasses since high school. He tried to go without glasses, but that didn't work because he couldn't see well and reacted slowly. He tried contact lenses but was never comfortable with them.

And he had to protect himself. He was always getting hit in the face with elbows. In high school, he even had his glasses split off his face a couple of times.

Hogue bristles a little at the notion he was UC's intimidating presence.

"I never bothered anybody," the MVP of the 1962 national championship game said. "I played physical; I would never tell anybody that I was a finesse ballplayer. I worked hard at rebounding and playing defense, and if you had to bump people around, you did that, too. And if you fooled with somebody on our team, you might have to come by me."

Said former teammate Carl Bouldin: "He was menacing to other teams. He had glasses that had tape all over them. It looked intimidating. You could see them while they were warming up, looking over their shoulders. I know Hogue was intimidating to other teams."

NEW RULES, ROOMIE

When Hogue was a freshman and sophomore, he was assigned to room with Robertson, who was in his final two years at UC. They were the only African-American players on the team who lived on campus.

"Oscar wouldn't let it be intimidating," Hogue said. "Oscar was never the kind of guy, until you got on the court, that would make you uncomfortable."

It was typical for upperclassmen to take the bottom bunk. But Robertson took one look at Hogue and decided he didn't want that big body coming down on him. So the "Big O" opted for the top.

5

ED JUCKER ERA
(1960-1965)

NEW COACH, NEW APPROACH

The 1960-61 season saw some significant changes in the University of Cincinnati program. Oscar Robertson, the best player in college basketball for three consecutive years, had graduated and gone on to the NBA as the No. 1 overall draft choice. Coach George Smith resigned as coach, became Athletic Director and was succeeded by assistant Ed Jucker.

Under Smith and with Robertson, the Bearcats had been a running, up-tempo team. But UC had lost two straight years in the NCAA Tournament to California, which was more deliberate in its offensive approach.

When Jucker took over, he slowed down the Bearcats and tried to put in place a system more like California's.

The players struggled early. After a 3-0 start, UC dropped three of its next five. Following a December 23 defeat at

The Bearcats, led by new coach Ed Jucker, celebrate their 1961 NCAA championship. They defeated Ohio State 70-65 in overtime in the title game. (Photo by University of Cincinnati/Sports Information)

Bradley, the Bearcats were 5-3—a season after which they lost only two games total.

After a 57-40 loss at St. Louis on December 16, Cincinnati had an emotional team meeting at its hotel. Jucker pleaded with the players to stick with him. "I know this is going to work," he told them. "We've just got to do it better." His voice cracked as he spoke.

The players told their coach they were with him all the way.

"After that, guys did seem to come together better," team captain Carl Bouldin said. "That was a factor in bringing us together."

After the Bradley defeat, the Bearcats would win 22 games in a row, including the national championship game over Ohio State.

FRIENDSHIP BUILT TO LAST

Bouldin and Bob Wiesenhahn, co-captains of UC's 1961 national championship team, began their friendship before they arrived in Clifton.

Bouldin went to Norwood High School. Wiesenhahn was from McNicholas. They met at a high school all-star game, went out for a malt afterward and remained friends, rooming together for four years at UC.

Wiesenhahn was a bigger guy, around 6-4, 220 pounds. Bouldin was 6-2, 175, and could barely eat after three hours of practice. Wiesenhahn did not have such a problem. One night, he told his roomie that he would have to learn to eat faster because he was making everybody wait for him to finish dinner.

So Wiesenhahn gave a lesson in quick consumption in the student union.

"He talked about peaches and he talked about peas," Bouldin said. "He said, 'You've got to smash some of the food with your tongue and get down closer to the plate and shovel it in there.' That was my lesson on how to eat faster. He just wanted me to hurry up."

DOUBLE DIPPING

One of the reasons Bouldin attended UC is because he could play basketball and baseball there. In fact, here's a good trivia question: Who played on an NCAA basketball championship team and pitched in the major leagues in the same year?

Yep, it was Bouldin.

After UC's 1961 title run, Bouldin went unselected in the basketball and baseball drafts. The Cincinnati Royals, Chicago Bulls and Detroit Pistons offered tryouts. But he thought he had a better chance to play professional baseball. That summer, he got a call from the Washington Senators, who expressed some interest. Bouldin said he was scheduled for a tryout with the Cleveland Indians. Washington upped its offer and gave Bouldin $20,000 to sign a contract.

He went to Rookie League, then to Pensacola. In September, the Senators called up Bouldin to the big leagues when rosters were expanded. He pitched in two games, starting one of them.

In 1963, he played in the Winter League in Caracas, Venezuela, on the same team as Pete Rose and against Matty, Felipe and Jesus Alou. In 1964, Bouldin went to Puerto Rico and had a locker right next to Roberto Clemente, who was there for two weeks to try to get in shape.

While in Puerto Rico, Bouldin injured his rotator cuff, ending his baseball career. In four years in the major leagues, Bouldin went 3-8 with 36 strikeouts and 30 walks.

WHATEVER IT TAKES

Tony Yates was born September 15, 1937. His birthday is relevant because shortly after he turned four years old, all his neighborhood playmates in Lawrenceburg, Indiana, where he was born, started kindergarten. They were a year older. Yates

In his three years as a player, Tony Yates averaged 7.4 points (1960-61), 8.2 points (1961-62) and 7.6 points (1962-63). In '63, he was selected third-team All-America by The Associated Press. (Photo by University of Cincinnati/Sports Information)

would follow them to school, then his mother would have to drag him home crying. This went on every day for a week until Yates's mom decided to enroll her son in the school. The family had no birth certificate, because the office of the doctor who delivered Yates caught on fire and his records were burned.

Mrs. Yates told school officials her son would turn five on December 15. The school accepted him with his "new" birthday.

Because he started school early, he was only 16 when he graduated from Lockland Wayne High School, a small, all-black school in Lockland, in 1954.

He had partial scholarship offers to UC and Xavier, but Yates turned them down. He was captain of a local high school all-star game his senior year and all his teammates were getting full scholarship offers to schools like XU, UC, Dayton, and Miami.

"I felt sad about that," Yates said.

He opted to wait a year—when he worked odd jobs and played on a barnstorming basketball team with older players—and then joined the U.S. Air Force.

Basic training was in Geneva, N.Y. After three months, he was assigned to Ellsworth Air Force Base in South Dakota.

"GRAMPS"

Yates was in the air force until 1959. While in the military, he played basketball, baseball, fast-pitch softball, handball, and racquetball. He knew when he got out, he wanted a full scholarship to play basketball in college.

The University of Cincinnati, however, was still only offering a partial scholarship. Yates had better offers from a few smaller schools, but he wanted to live in Cincinnati, his hometown. He was 22 years old and had gotten married in 1958 while still in the air force. And, of course, the Bearcats had Oscar Robertson, whose mere presence made UC more attractive to Yates. "Who wouldn't want to be associated with him?" Yates said.

In 1959-60, Yates played on UC's freshman team. He was older than his teammates. He was stronger mentally and physically and had a high confidence level and understanding of the game. "It was a definite advantage," he said.

He was an immediate leader.

His first season on the varsity, 1960-61, Yates was a starting guard alongside Bouldin, a senior. The players called him "Gramps," and he was Jucker's coach on the floor. If Yates felt a teammate was not playing hard or wasn't performing well, he'd dribble the ball past the bench and tell Jucker to get the guy out of the game. Didn't matter if it was a friend or fellow starter. And Jucker would listen.

"When we'd have a timeout, they'd want to get back in the game and come to me and say, 'I'll play harder,'" Yates said.

GETTING PSYCHED UP

It was the day of the 1961 national championship game. No. 1 Ohio State vs. No. 2 Cincinnati. The first time in NCAA history two teams from the same state met in the title game.

The Bearcat players were getting taped and dressing in the hotel across the street from the arena in Kansas City. A radio was turned on, and the team was listening to an Ohio State broadcaster breaking down the game's matchups. It was pretty much even, they decided, except for one position: That was UC's Wiesenhahn against OSU's John Havlicek.

"They thought he was going to whip me," Wiesenhahn said.

Now understand, Wiesenhahn was the kind of player who preferred to play on the road and loved to get booed. It made him play harder. He was, well, an emotional guy.

Getting knocked on the radio? "That's all I needed," he said. "I was a psycho. I got fired up real easy."

"Weise's face just got red because (the announcer) called him a hatchet man," Bouldin remembers. "He said, 'I'm going to kill him.'"

Wiesenhahn outscored Havlicek 17-4 and outrebounded him 9-4. The Bearcats won their first NCAA title, 70-65 in overtime. Wiesenhahn mostly tried to keep Havlicek, who finished one-of-five shooting from the field, from touching the ball.

"That was the greatest feeling that you could have," Wiesenhahn said. "That was very satisfying."

OVERCOMING SUPERSTITION

The Bearcats won their first national championship despite having to wear their white uniforms.

According to *The Cincinnati Enquirer*, there was a coin flip the morning of the NCAA final won by Ohio State coach Fred Taylor, who opted for the Buckeyes to be the "visiting team." UC was forced to wear white, even though the team considered their black uniforms "lucky."

SORRY, COACH HALAS

Wiesenhahn played one year of pro basketball with the Cincinnati Royals, then he played in the American Basketball Association/American Basketball League, which folded midway through the season. When he returned to Cincinnati, he got a strange phone call one day.

It was legendary Chicago Bears coach George Halas. Halas wanted to offer Wiesenhahn a tryout at tight end even though Wiesenhahn never played football at UC.

There was no guarantee of money or that he'd make the team. Wiesenhahn had a wife and two children at the time.

"If I would've been single, I would've tried it," Wiesenhahn said, "but you can't do that when you have a family to support."

The Bears went on to win the 1963 NFL Championship with a 14-10 victory over the New York Giants.

GOOD-BYE PURDUE, HELLO UC

Ron Bonham was getting pressure to stay in state. A star at Muncie (Indiana) Central High School, his team won 29 straight games before losing to East Chicago Washington in the Indiana high school state finals.

Naturally, Purdue and Indiana pursued him hard. Bonham picked Purdue, but was not thrilled with the choice. He went to West Lafayette, stayed a few days, then went back home and told his family he wanted to attend the University of Cincinnati.

"UC is where my heart was all along," he said.

In 1960-61, he played on UC's freshman team, which played an up-tempo style of basketball, just as Bonham's high school team did. That season, however, the "varsity" was slowing down their play under first-year coach Jucker, and they went on to win the NCAA title.

When his sophomore season started, Bonham was coming off the bench.

"I have to admit, I played very little defense when I was in high school," he said. "We pressed the whole time. I didn't know how I was going to fit in at UC. I had to get acclimated to playing defense, and that took a while. That helped me later on."

Bonham was soon a starter and was second on the team in scoring (14.3 ppg). In the 1962 national championship game against Ohio State, Bonham was matched against John Havlicek of the Buckeyes. Bonham scored just 10 points in the final, but UC won 71-59. Havlicek scored 11 points on five-of-14 shooting.

"We had scouted each other so much, I'd come off a pick and Havlicek would be waiting on me," Bonham said. "Jucker's strategy for me was to be a decoy. I just ran around and kept Havlicek right on me, and that helped them in starting the fast break."

As a junior, Bonham averaged 21 points, was UC's top scorer and a consensus first-team All-American after leading the Bearcats to the 1963 NCAA final, where they lost to Loyola (Illinois) in overtime.

He averaged 24.4 points and was second-team All-America as a senior, when the Bearcats went 17-9. Bonham left as UC's No. 2 scorer behind Robertson. Today, he still is eighth.

NO "I" IN TEAM

George Wilson was one of those guys who set a standard for role-playing when he was a Bearcat. Wilson was a high school All-American coming out of John Marshall High School in Chicago. He was a big-time scorer who continued that trend on UC's freshman team.

But when it came time to join the varsity as a sophomore, the Bearcats were not in need of a scorer. They had Paul Hogue, Tom Thacker, and Bonham. Coach Jucker told Wilson that he needed him to rebound and play defense. And so it was that Wilson became the defender always assigned to stop UC's toughest opponent.

Wilson accepted the role and took it seriously, reading about his opponent and watching film so he knew what to do in games. All of this is why he calls a two-point, one-rebound performance the best of his sophomore year and one of the best in his career.

Cincinnati was facing Creighton in its first NCAA Tournament game in 1962, and Wilson was going to be matched up with Paul Silas, who led the country in rebounding and was among the nation's top scorers.

Silas finished with just eight points and five rebounds, and UC won 66-46.

"Everybody had to do their part, and that was my role," Wilson said. "Everybody gets a ring when you win a champion-

George Wilson shared UC team MVP honors with Ron Bonham in 1963-64, then went on to play in the NBA from 1964-71 with six different teams. When Wilson left UC, he was the school's career leader with 121 blocked shots. (Photo by University of Cincinnati/Sports Information)

ship. When I speak to kids, they always ask, 'How many points did you score?' I didn't worry about scoring. I set picks. I did what I had to do."

GOOD TIMING

Tom Thacker had not hit a shot all night. He was zero of six from the field. And with the score tied in the final seconds of the 1962 NCAA semifinals against UCLA, the plan was for Thacker to give up the ball to Bonham, who would take the potential game-winning shot. Thacker dribbled to the right side, but Bonham was covered. "He couldn't get free," Thacker said. "I think everybody in the world knew Ron was going to get the ball."

Time was running out. Thacker knew he had to get off a shot quickly. So, he fired away from about 12 feet out with three seconds left.

"As soon as I let it go, I felt good," Thacker said. "It hit all net."

The Bearcats won 72-70. They would go on to the title game and defeat Ohio State 71-59 for their second consecutive national championship.

When it came to winning championships, nobody was better than Tom Thacker.

After winning two titles at UC, he won a North American Basketball League title with the 1967 Muskegon (Michigan) Panthers, an NBA title with the 1968 Boston Celtics and an ABA title with the 1971 Indiana Pacers.

Thacker, from William Grant High School in Covington, Kentucky, would also become the first African-American head coach at the University of Cincinnati, leading the women's basketball program from 1974-77.

WHAT'S IN THAT DRINK?

Thacker claims to be a naïve country kid from Covington, Kentucky. And to support that, he offers this story from one of UC's trips to New York.

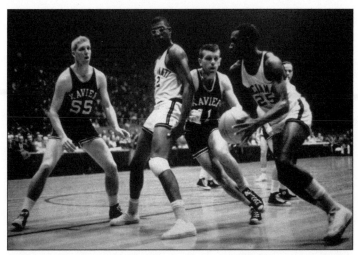

Two of the stalwarts from the Jucker championship era still rank high on the Bearcats' all-time lists. Paul Hogue (left in white, 1,391 points) and Tom Thacker (right, 1,152 points) are members of the school's 1,000 Point Club. Hogue is still the Bearcats' No. 3 all-time leading rebounder with 1,088. (Photo by University of Cincinnati/Sports Information)

An alum took the team to Club 21 for dinner. There were fans, players, coaches. And when it came time to order beverages, Thacker asked for a Tom Collins, a lemon-lime drink that was his favorite soda pop.

"I thought he was going to bring me a Tom Collins soft drink," Thacker said. "He brought me the glass, and I took a big sip because I was thirsty."

"WOW!" yelled Thacker. It was a Tom Collins mixed drink with gin.

"I couldn't really talk," Thacker said. "There was alcohol in there! That stuff burned the heck out of me. Everybody was laughing at me. That was the first time I had alcohol in my life. It went straight to my head. I thought I was spitting fire out of my mouth."

6

TAY BAKER ERA (1965-1972)

CLIMBING THE LADDER TO THE TOP

When Tay Baker became the Bearcats' head coach in 1965, it was roughly 20 years after he began his playing career at the University of Cincinnati.

The 1945 Hamilton High School graduate played three games as a freshman at UC before beginning an 18-month stint in the U.S. Army, where he was stationed at Fort Bliss in El Paso, Texas, then Fort Benning in Georgia.

He had originally come to UC when Ray Farnham was the coach. When Baker returned in 1947, John Wiethe had taken over the program. Baker played for three years and was one of the top reserves on Cincinnati's first 20-win teams (23-5, 1949; 20-6, 1950).

Tay Baker was UC's coach for seven seasons. As a player, he averaged 3.8 points off the bench in 1948-49 and 4.2 points as a reserve in 1949-50. Both those seasons, the Bearcats won the Mid-American Conference. (Photo by University of Cincinnati/Sports Information)

After graduating from UC, Baker coached at Lebanon, Miamisburg and Wyoming High Schools. In 1959, Cincinnati decided to add a third coach to its staff. George Smith was the head coach. Ed Jucker was the assistant and head baseball coach. Baker came aboard as a varsity assistant, the freshman coach, track and cross country coach and a physical education teacher. For all that, he said, he earned about $6,300 a year.

During Baker's first four years on the Bearcats staff, the team went a combined 110-9, advanced to three Final Fours and won two NCAA titles. When Jucker was named head coach in 1960, Baker became the top assistant.

When Jucker left in '65, it was only natural that Baker would succeed him.

SIGN OF THE TIMES

Baker coached UC during what he calls "a different time" in U.S. history. There were protests and riots on college campuses all over the country. The Vietnam War. Martin Luther King's assassination. Robert Kennedy's assassination. Kent State. Long hair. Drugs.

"It was a harder job," Baker said. "There was a revolution going on. It kind of detracted from athletics and from basketball.

"There was a line prior to that. There was the coach and there were the players, and whatever the coach said, the players responded to it. In the late '60s, students would question the authority of a coach. Students wanted their opinions to be heard. They wanted to be counted. There was a psychological change in coaching. Players weren't challenging me; they were challenging the system, the methods of education and participation, and the whole realm of the college experience. The drug scene became an issue. Discipline became an issue."

Not to mention the fact that other basketball teams in the country started catching up to Cincinnati, which was a national powerhouse in the late 1950s and early '60s. The Bearcats were still a top-10 team during parts of 1965-66, Baker's first season as head coach. And they were in the top 20 during parts of 1968-69 and 1969-70.

But in Baker's final two seasons, UC went a combined 31-21. His team won 10 of its last 12 games in 1972, but

Baker felt a growing dissatisfaction with his performance, so he announced February 16, the night UC was playing Xavier at the Cincinnati Gardens, that he was resigning at the end of the season.

He was criticized by some for being too nice.

"Some people thought I shouldn't be there," he said. "I probably could have stayed. I think the best thing to do was to get out of there and let somebody else have the opportunity to have it.

"If I had it all to do again, I'd probably do a few things differently. But I really feel like I had success as a player on good teams at UC. I feel like I was part of basketball history there. And I feel like the years I was there coaching we were respectable."

MEMORIES IMPROVE WITH TIME

Before Jim Ard was inducted into UC's Athletic Hall of Fame in 1996, he was informed that he had to make a speech. Say some good things about your time at the university, he was told.

That was a challenge for Ard, who scored 1,256 career points, was an honorable mention All-American in 1970, and went on to win an NBA championship with the Boston Celtics in 1976.

He had kind of forgotten he played on a UC team that went 21-6 and earned a National Invitation Tournament berth his senior year.

Like his coach, what he remembered mostly was the era.

"There were an awful lot of distractions," Ard said. "I arrived in '66 and left in '70; you can't believe what went on during that time. Nobody was happy.

"There were a lot of things changing in this country. All I can tell you was it was not conducive to concentrating on ball."

After Ard led Thornton High School to an Illinois high school state championship as a senior, he said he had more than 100 scholarship offers. But he had already narrowed his choices to Cincinnati and Wisconsin.

Freshmen were ineligible in 1966-67. In Ard's three seasons on the "varsity," UC went 56-23. He averaged 13.9 points, 16 points and 19.2 points, and he was fifth on UC's career scoring chart when he finished (he is now 26th). As a senior, he also averaged 15.2 rebounds.

Ard said he channeled his anger at the world around him onto the court. He shared top billing with teammate Rick Roberson, who was UC's No. 6 all-time scorer when his career ended.

All Ard could think about was finishing his eligibility and moving on, away from UC, away from Cincinnati, away from the college environment, away from the 1960s.

"When I look back on it now, it was just growth," Ard said. "But it took me almost 20 years to realize it wasn't UC, it wasn't Cincinnati, and it wasn't Tay Baker. Those were turbulent times. I think any coach at that time was under a big disadvantage. I have to give him credit—the older I get, the smarter he becomes. He had a whole lot of stuff he had to deal with. I have to give him a lot of respect now."

BAKING WITH MOM

Ard was home for Christmas in 1966, his freshman year at the University of Cincinnati. One day, assistant coach Lee Rose called Ard's home in Harvey, Illinois, to check in with one of his players.

Aline Ard, Jim's mother, answered the phone.

"May I talk to Jim, please?"

"He can't come to the phone right now."

"This is Lee Rose, the freshman coach at Cincinnati. Jim's doing very well down here. Can I talk to him, please?"

"No, he's making cookies with me."

James Ard, Jim's father, all but fell out of his chair. "You can't say that!" he shouted.

It was a tradition. For roughly 10 years, Jim Ard had helped his mom bake Christmas cookies. He just didn't want the UC coaches and his teammates to know about it.

"Did I catch a bunch of crap on that one," Jim said laughing. "My father even gave my mother a hard time. Lee was very nice about it. He said, 'You've got to be a good guy if you're home making Christmas cookies with your mother.'"

THE CRUTCH

Raleigh Wynn came to UC from the same Knoxville, Tennessee, high school (Austin) as former Bearcat great Paul Hogue. He was recruited by several colleges in Tennessee and could have played football at Indiana University.

But he settled on Cincinnati. And he's part of Bearcat folklore all because of one game.

It gets brought up before most Crosstown Shootouts. There have been a lot of heated moments when Xavier and Cincinnati played, but March 3, 1967 is one of those that gets singled out.

That was the night Xavier's Joe Pangrazio threw a crutch at Wynn. "Oh yeah," Wynn said, "I had a big fight in that game."

To say the 54th meeting between the teams was heated would be stating the obvious. That's the way it always is when the Bearcats and Musketeers square off.

UC came in to its final game 16-9. Xavier had lost six of its past seven and was 13-12. It was Xavier's only game of the season at the Cincinnati Gardens; it was UC's second.

The game went into overtime. The play was physical. Wynn was bringing the ball upcourt against Pangrazio.

"I was dribbling the ball and he was hitting me in the back with his fist," Wynn said. "I said, 'Take it easy.' He hit me in the back again. I dropped the ball and turned around and slugged him. That's the way it was. I hit him, and bam. He ran up in the stands and got a crutch, and the place just went wild."

According to a 1988 *Cincinnati Post* article, while chasing after a loose ball, Pangrazio felt Wynn deliberately threw him into the crowd. Pangrazio picked up a crutch belonging to a fan and went after Wynn.

"I was ready to fight at the time," Wynn said. "I didn't run or anything. Somebody grabbed him."

When a policeman stopped Pangrazio, he threw the crutch at Wynn. Both players were ejected from the game.

"After a basketball game was over, I never, ever held a grudge," Wynn said. "If I would see him today, we'd be friends. I wasn't mad about that. We were just playing a tough game. Several guys would get into it in that game.

"It's funny now. I laugh about it. The place just went wild."

IT'S "THE JUICE"

During Ard's junior season, the Bearcats headed to the West Coast for games against Southern Cal, California, and Stanford. Ard averaged 16.7 points and 13 rebounds over the three games, but that isn't what he most recalls about the road trip.

The Bearcats were on the USC campus and headed for a workout when one of the players yelled, "Hey, that's O.J. Simpson." Simpson was the Trojans' star running back who went on to, well, you know the rest of the story.

If first looks mean anything, Ard wasn't overly impressed.

"Everybody had heard of the guy," Ard said. "But he was so little, I thought, 'He's never going to make it.'"

Oops. Simpson won the 1968 Heisman Trophy, was the National Football League's MVP in 1975, and is one of the greatest running backs ever. He was inducted into the Pro Football Hall of Fame in 1985.

SCARY MOMENT

Another interesting fact about the West Coast trip was that UC's game at Stanford was called by mutual agreement with 38 seconds left. According to *Cincinnati Enquirer* reports, Bearcats sophomore Don Hess fell under the UC basket and hit his head on the floor. He started to swallow his tongue, suffered a severe cut on the inside of his mouth and went into convulsions on the court. Two people in the stands—one man and one woman—who witnessed the incident collapsed. Hess, from Trenton, N.J., was taken to Stanford Hospital. He received 12 stitches in his mouth and lip and was released the next morning complaining only of a headache. Sixth-ranked UC won the game 60-49.

TIMING IS EVERYTHING

Ard did not think much of his chances to have a pro basketball career—until early in his senior season, that is.

Cincinnati was playing host to Iowa and "Downtown" Freddie Brown at the Armory Fieldhouse. Ard scored a career-high 41 points in a 114-105 Bearcats victory and found out later a Seattle SuperSonics scout was at the game.

It was soon after that Ron Grinker, a Cincinnati attorney, told Ard, "I think you're a first-round draft choice."

"I don't believe you," Ard said. "There's no way I can play with Elgin Baylor and John Havlicek."

Grinker was one of the pioneers in representing NBA players and was well respected throughout the league. Turns out, he was absolutely right.

Seattle drafted Ard in the first round of the 1970 NBA draft.

ELVIS HAS LEFT THE BUILDING

Rick Roberson grew up in Memphis, Tennessee, roughly five miles from where Elvis Presley lived, but on "the other side of the tracks." Roberson said he had a chance to become the first African-American basketball player at Memphis State, but he thought the University of Cincinnati had more to offer him on and off the court.

A self-described "boy from the country," Roberson came to UC in 1967, played freshman ball, then led the Bearcats in scoring three consecutive seasons. He held the career blocked-shots record for about 30 years, until Kenyon Martin came along and shattered it.

"I didn't read very much about myself," Roberson said. "I didn't like to read criticism, so I opted to read magazines. My younger brother knows more about what I did in basketball than I do. I don't come with a lot of stories. I played hard; I worked hard.

"Those were the best days of my life. I loved what I was doing and I loved where I was. It was all good to me."

Roberson is one of only five players in UC history to collect a triple-double, joining Oscar Robertson, Martin, Kenny Satterfield, and Eric Hicks. After Roberson tallied 16 points, 10 rebounds and 10 blocks against Bradley on January 17, 1967, it would be 30 years and one month before another Bearcat had a triple-double. That came when Martin had 24 points, 23 rebounds and 10 blocks against DePaul in February 1997.

In 1969, Roberson was a first-round draft pick of the Los Angeles Lakers, and he played professionally from 1969-76. None of which was all that surprising.

In his Mitchell High School yearbook, Roberson said he is quoted as saying he wanted to be an NBA player.

"Rick's main purpose was that he was going to the pros," former teammate Raleigh Wynn said. "That's all he ever talked about. That was his main objective. Rick was always fun loving, always laughing. He always had something funny going on."

"I played and I played," Roberson said. "I just wanted to be drafted. I knew I could make it if I was drafted."

THOSE DARNED BUGS

Lloyd Batts was a high school star from Phoenix, Illinois, a south suburb of Chicago, who said he received more than 250 college scholarship offers, including one from the University of Cincinnati. Baker and assistant coach John Bryant were recruiting him for the Bearcats in 1970. Batts attended the same high school as Ard.

Understand, this wasn't just any player. Check the UC record books carefully, and you'll see that Batts has the second-highest career scoring average in school history behind only Oscar Robertson.

Batts could score. He played inside and could shoot long jumpers. Driving to the basket was his forte. He played small forward for two years, then was a guard his senior year.

Freshmen were ineligible to play in 1970-71 when Batts arrived in Clifton, so he only played three years for UC. If he had played four, he might very well have ended up the No. 2 all-time scorer.

Lloyd Batts (31) led the Bearcats in scoring three straight seasons and twice was the team's most valuable player. Batts (20.1 ppg) and Oscar Robertson (33.8 ppg) are the only members of the school's 1,000 Point Club to average more than 20 points a game. (Photo by University of Cincinnati/Sports Information)

On his recruiting visit, Batts met Robertson. That had a big impact on him and would've made choosing a college easy—if not for the darned bugs. You see, Batts came to Cincinnati at the same time as the 17-year cicadas.

"I decided when I left the campus I was not coming back," Batts said. "They were freaking me out. I'm not too fond of bugs, period, especially flying bugs. And they were flying all around me. I had never seen anything like that in my entire life. I wouldn't care if they had offered me a million dollars, I wasn't coming."

Before Batts boarded his airplane back to Chicago, Bryant asked about his visit. "I don't think this is the place for me," Batts said.

"Why?" Bryant asked.

Batts explained. He liked UC, thought it would be a great place to go to school, but he didn't think he could handle the bugs.

Then it was Bryant's turn to explain. He said they'd be gone before he showed up the next fall, and he'd be out of school by the time they came back.

That was all it took. Batts committed. Oscar beat out the bugs, after all.

GOING TO THE "OTHER SIDE"

Tay Baker remained at the University of Cincinnati as a physical education teacher for one year after resigning as basketball coach in 1972.

Then, a funny thing happened.

The head coaching position opened at Xavier University, the rival school across town. Baker's name ended up in the mix, and he received a call from XU Athletic Director Jim McCafferty, who wanted to talk to him.

"I had no inclination to go there at all," Baker said. "It was a tough decision to make. I don't care who you are, if you're from UC and you go to Xavier, some people are not going to like it. Or vice versa. I still wanted to coach, but I didn't want to leave town. My kids were all in school. My wife went to UC and was from Cincinnati.

"It was a tug of war in my mind. I thought, 'God, you're from UC and you're talking about going to Xavier.' There was even one guy on their selection committee who flat out told me, 'I want you to know you're not a unanimous choice for this position.'"

Xavier's program had hit rock bottom under coach Dick Campbell in 1972-73, going 3-23—that remains the worst season in XU history.

Baker decided to take the job. His former UC players were supportive, he said. Still, overall he received a "mixed reaction."

"Some people said, 'You're nuts,' and some said, 'Well, it's an opportunity,'" Baker said. "I really loved UC and wanted to pay attention to what they were doing and hoped they were winning. Well, the people at Xavier, they want them to lose every game. It was strange. It worked out for me. The people there were great to me. Mr. McCafferty was great to me."

Fans were another story. It is no wonder Baker's the only man to be head basketball coach at UC and Xavier.

"I'd be driving down (Interstate) 75 in a blue station wagon with Xavier on it and a guy would go by and give me the finger," Baker said. "You expect that with UC and Xavier. There's nothing wrong with that, really. They don't like each other and they want to beat each other, and that's the way it should be."

Baker's teams went 70-89 in six seasons at XU. He had two winning seasons (14-12, 14-13). But he had an impact on the Musketeers that went beyond wins and losses.

Baker said he was the one who encouraged and prodded McCafferty to get Xavier in a conference. The Musketeers were an independent until 1979-80.

"The schedule was a mess," Baker said. "You'd play Marquette and Notre Dame and then Wheeling."

McCafferty took Baker seriously and worked with Loyola, Butler, Evansville, Oral Roberts and Oklahoma City to form what would become the Midwestern City Conference. Baker would never get to coach in the MCC. Just like at the end of his UC tenure, he felt a faction of Xavier people wanted him out, so he resigned as head coach in 1979 and gave way to Bob Staak.

"At Xavier, I really felt good that after I left, the conference was formed and all of a sudden Xavier basketball started an upswing," Baker said. "I felt like I was a part of that development. I feel like the foundation was laid there for part of the success of the program they have even today."

It must be noted that as UC's coach, Baker went 5-2 against the Musketeers. When he was coaching Xavier, he went 0-6 against the Bearcats.

There is no question where his allegiances are.

"Even though in wins and losses it wasn't too successful a career at Xavier, the people there were very fair to me and there was some progress made," Baker said.

"But I graduated from UC and they're always at the bottom of my heart."

7

GALE CATLETT ERA (1972-1978)

CLEAN START

The University of Cincinnati community was a bit surprised when 31-year-old Gale Catlett was announced as the Bearcats' new basketball coach in April 1972. The University of Kentucky assistant under Adolph Rupp entered the picture late in UC's six-week search for Tay Baker's replacement.

The search committee had whittled the candidates down to North Carolina assistant John Lotz and Capital University coach Vince Chickerella.

When Catlett had originally expressed interest in the job, Athletic Director George Smith told him that he was too late, according to *The Cincinnati Enquirer.*

But there was obviously a change of heart. Catlett got an interview after all. "We were impressed with his credentials," Smith said after Catlett was hired.

That '70s show: Gale Catlett brought a certain flair to the UC basketball program with his, uh, flamboyant wardrobe. (Photo by University of Cincinnati/Sports Information)

Like all new coaches, Catlett showed up with his own set of rules; he also brought a reputation as a disciplinarian. One of the things he insisted at his very first team meeting was that the players shave off all facial hair and that hair be kept "neat and groomed."

That didn't sit well with a lot of the Bearcats, including Lloyd Batts, Cincinnati's top scorer who had not shaved in his life and had a slight goatee.

Batts told himself: *I've never shaved before, and I'm not about to shave for him.*

Catlett found out some of the players were considering boycotting and not shaving, so he called them in individually. "Shave or pack your bags," was his message. "You'll no longer be a part of UC basketball."

"Nobody left," Batts said. "Everybody did what he said.

"I always called him the yes-man. Any time he wanted something done, people would always say yes to him. He just had a way of getting his way."

Batts didn't appreciate what Catlett was trying to accomplish in terms of discipline and expectations until years later when he became a junior college head coach in his hometown.

Batts said he wrote Catlett a letter and thanked him for all that he tried to instill in his players.

"I think I understood what he was trying to do and the point he was trying to get across to his players," Batts said. And he wanted to tell Catlett that.

SHORT DEBUT

Catlett wasn't around long to see his first game as UC's coach. The Bearcats beat Cleveland State handily, 113-85, but Catlett was long gone by the final buzzer.

With just under seven minutes left in the first half, a referee blew his whistle while right in front of the Cincinnati bench. "You're getting paid to call all the violations, not only the fouls," Catlett yelled.

Robert James, the official, slapped Catlett with a technical foul.

Catlett got off the bench. "That's two," James said. Catlett told *The Cincinnati Enquirer* that he then said "a naughty word" and received a third technical, which was an automatic ejection. As he was leaving the court, Catlett passed James, who worked in the Big Ten Conference, and told him: "I'm writing [Big Ten commissioner] Wayne Duke immediately, and I'm telling him you'll never work another game for me."

"That's one more, four," James said.

Catlett spent the rest of the game in a photographer's booth high up in the Armory Fieldhouse. He communicated with his assistants by walkie-talkie, according to *The Enquirer*.

UC ran away with the game, which prompted Catlett to say afterward with a smile: "… Maybe I'll coach from up there all season."

HOPE AND A PRAYER

The picture is still in his home. The one game Batts won't forget is against Louisville at the Armory Fieldhouse when he hit the winning basket during his junior year (February 5, 1973).

The game was tied at 79 in the final minute and Louisville was in possession, but the Cardinals turned the ball over with 21 seconds remaining. UC called a timeout.

Lionel Harris took the inbounds pass and started dribbling. The clock was counting down. Fans started screaming.

An impatient Batts ran toward Harris, grabbed the ball and shot from about 30 feet out. The buzzer sounded. The ball went in.

"When a guy is going the wrong way, is off balance and just throws the ball up and it goes in, there's nothing you can do about it," Louisville coach Denny Crum said afterward.

I HATE SNAKES

Batts was one of several UC players who refused to visit teammate Derrick Dickey in his dorm room. They liked Dickey, who everyone agrees had one of the most infectious smiles. But one of Dickey's roommates was a boa constrictor.

He would taunt his teammates with tales of feeding the snake lots of mice. Once, Batts said, the boa got out of its cage and wrapped itself around one of Dickey's sons.

"Nobody knew that he had it except the team," Batts said. "After that, they made him get it out of there. After college, he took it with him to the pros."

That's why Batts called Dickey "The Snake."

"He called it his baby," Batts said. "I'm glad he wasn't helping recruit me," Batts said laughing. "I wouldn't have come for sure. I never stepped foot inside of Derrick's house."

TRY OUT THIS CAR

Hal Ward grew up in Loveland, Ohio, but had no intention of attending the University of Cincinnati, even though Ken Cunningham, an assistant to UC coach Tay Baker, originally recruited him.

Ward, from Loveland High School, was headed for Tennessee-Chattanooga, where on his recruiting visit he was introduced at halftime of a game and treated like royalty. He said he was going to be a "package deal" with Ted Allen, a football player from Loveland.

When Catlett became UC's head coach in 1972, Ward was his first recruit. Catlett called the family and scheduled a home visit in an area that was rural at the time. "A hick town," Ward said.

"We lived in lower-middle class crackerjack box homes— about 15 feet apart," Ward said. "I remember we were waiting for Gale Catlett to come, and he drove up in a white Cadillac. Now, nobody drove a Cadillac in that area.

"One of his assistant coaches was with him. Then he jumped out. Of course, Gale Catlett was a flashy dresser. He had a maroon-and-white-checked suit on with white buck shoes. I thought, 'This is a used car salesman.' So he came in and I'll tell you what, he had a gift of gab."

Catlett hit it off with Ward's mother. And he hit home with his message to Hal.

"You may not play one minute if you come to UC," Catlett told Ward. "But if you come and bust your back and work hard, those are the kind of guys we're looking for."

Ward thought, "That's a pretty good challenge."

"I guess I liked challenges at that time," Ward said.

At the last minute, he told the coaches at Tennessee-Chattanooga he wasn't coming and he signed with UC.

HOW TO PLAY?

Ward was surrounded by UC teammates who were scoring machines in high school, guys like Lloyd Batts and Jesse Jemison, and later Robert Miller, Steve Collier, Mike Jones and Pat Cummings.

Early in his career, Ward figured out there was only one way he was going to get any playing time: "I was going to have to play defense," he said.

As a sophomore, he started at forward. He was a key reserve his last two seasons, when the Bearcats went a combined 48-12. He said he was three times voted best defensive player on the team.

"Nobody wanted to play defense," Ward said. "Gale loved defense. I thought, 'These other guys can shoot. If I want to play, I'm going to have to do something else.' That's how I got to play."

NICE FINISH

In Batts's final home game, he treated UC fans to a special parting performance.

The Bearcats were playing No. 8 Marquette at the Armory Fieldhouse and trailed 43-36 at halftime. Then Batts went to work. He ended up with 33 points and 10 rebounds. Marquette coach Al McGuire was yelling at his players, "Can anyone stop Batts?"

Marquette would go on to the NCAA title game, where it lost to North Carolina State. Batts thinks it was the victory over Marquette that helped him get drafted by the Kentucky Colonels.

THE ALL-AMERICANS

They arrived on campus in 1974, dubbed "The All-Americans." There was Steve Collier, Indiana's co-Mr. Basketball. Pat Cummings, a prep All-American from Johnstown, Pennsylvania. Mike Jones, one of the best West Virginia had to offer. Robert Miller, an all-star in Kentucky. It is a group, recruited by Catlett, which ended UC's eight-year absence from the NCAA Tournament and would be the last Cincinnati team to go to the NCAA for another 15 years.

Collier was from Hanover, Indiana, and attended Southwestern High School. Being an Indiana All-Star, Collier was, of course, expected to go to Indiana or Purdue or stay in state at another school. He visited Indiana "almost out of courtesy," knowing he was not a Bob Knight-type of player. He also was recruited by the likes of Michigan, Wake Forest, Louisville, Kentucky and North Carolina.

Catlett worked hard to land Collier. He spoke at Collier's high school basketball team's banquet. He arranged meetings at Riverfront Stadium with Reds stars Pete Rose and—on another visit to town—Johnny Bench. "Every time I came to Cincinnati to visit, they did different things with me," Collier said. "It was fun."

Collier liked the city and saw a chance to play. He was part of a stellar freshman class that would have a chance to grow together.

Collier, Miller and Cummings started from Day One. *The Cincinnati Enquirer* referred to the Bearcats as the "Kiddie Korps." Jones eventually worked his way into the starting line-up. All four started all the time by the time they were sophomores.

23 YEARS LATER . . .

This is what Bill Lammert said about teammate Jack Twyman, who starred at UC from 1952-55: "Jack Twyman knew what he wanted to do. He was the first on the floor and the last one off. He worked harder than anyone else. He wasn't that talented. He was rather awkward, quite frankly. Nobody had any clue he would turn out the way he did."

This is what Collier said about teammate Cummings, who starred at UC from 1975-79: "He was the hardest worker I had ever seen on the court. He was always in the gym, always working on his game. You wouldn't say he was real athletic, but he would outwork you and he had a good head on him. You could see why he went to the pros and why he played for so long. He just had that mental toughness."

Twyman was six foot six and was UC's all-time leading scorer when his career ended. He played professionally from 1955-66.

Cummings was six foot nine and was UC's No. 2 all-time scorer when his career ended. He played professionally from 1979-89.

"We'd have an early morning practice and Pat would already be there shooting," Collier said. "We'd get home from a road game and we'd drop off our stuff, and then he'd go up to the Armory and shoot around. He just wanted to develop his shot."

"I had keys to every gym on campus that had a hoop in it," Cummings said.

Cummings said that he knew when he was in ninth or tenth grade that he wanted to be a pro basketball player. At Greater Johnstown (Pennsylvania) High School, that was his stated goal. By tenth grade, he was lifting weights regularly, starting with a tailpipe filled with BBs. During his college career, he lifted three times a week throughout the season.

Remember, this was in the 1970s, before strength and conditioning programs existed.

TOO GOOD OF A TIME

Catlett believed in taking his players to interesting, exciting cities and giving them a chance to see some sites. On Catlett's watch, the Bearcats went to Hawaii, Malibu, New Orleans, and New York City.

"He always wanted us to get out and experience the city," Collier said. "He always said if we didn't get out and enjoy it, we might as well take a bus up to Youngstown and play Youngstown. He'd set things up for us to see. He was a firm believer in that. I always thought it was great."

When UC played in New York City, Catlett took the team to the 21 Club. After the Bearcats won the 1976 Sugar Bowl Classic in New Orleans, Catlett kept them in New Orleans through January 1 so they could celebrate New Year's Eve on Bourbon Street.

"We really had a good time," Collier said.

In May 1975, UC went to Australia and played 17 games. The players traveled in vans through the country and stayed with Australian families for a day or two at a time.

"I remember waking up in the middle of the night looking for the bathroom, and it's out there by the cows—it was an outhouse," Cummings said. "One time I stayed with a sailor, and he wanted to take me out drinking all the time."

Then there was the basketball.

"We were 16-0 and the last game was in Melbourne," Collier said. "The country was getting upset with us, so they loaded up their National Team. We won and went 17-0. The trip was quite an experience."

There was a time Catlett's philosophy backfired.

Unbeaten Cincinnati was favored to win the eight-team 1975 Rainbow Classic in Hawaii. Catlett let his players spend time on the beach and enjoy Honolulu. When it was time for the first game, against Arizona, the sixth-ranked Bearcats were pulled out of the ocean and off the beach, then they went out and lost 71-64 to the unranked Wildcats. They lost their second game to Holy Cross 66-65, before winning their finale 83-55 over Yale.

UC finished seventh in the tournament.

"A plastic atmosphere … too many distractions," Catlett told *The Cincinnati Enquirer*. "The atmosphere just wasn't for basketball. Everybody was there primarily to have a good time."

"(Catlett) was upset, but that was early (in the season), and he stuck with what he believed in," Collier said. The Bearcats only lost four more times that season.

RIGHT PLACE, RIGHT TIME

No. 18 UC was playing host to San Francisco at the Cincinnati Gardens on February 28, 1976. A strong freshman class that included Bill Cartwright led the Dons.

Pat Cummings (42) played 12 seasons in the NBA with five different teams, averaging 9.6 points and 5.6 rebounds over his career. (Photo by University of Cincinnati/Sports Information)

The game, which the Bearcats led 62-49, ended up going into overtime. UC trailed 88-87 with 44 seconds left and came down the court for a potential game-winning shot.

UC wanted to get the ball inside. But a pass got deflected and the ball was up for grabs. In a crowd of players, Cummings reached down and picked the ball up off the floor. He sent up an 18-foot shot that gave Cincinnati the victory.

"God was with me," Cummings said that night. "I just turned and threw it."

He finished with 20 points and six rebounds. Cartwright, who would become Cummings's teammate with the New York Knicks, totaled 14 points and 16 rebounds.

LUCK OF THE IRISH

UC, ranked 15th in the country, had a golden opportunity to knock No. 7 Notre Dame out of the 1976 NCAA Tournament during a Midwest Regional game in Lawrence, Kansas. The Bearcats led the whole game and were ahead 78-77 in the final seconds. They were taking the ball out of bounds under the Irish basket with eight seconds remaining.

"We had two timeouts left," said Ward, who was inbounding the ball. "Gale said, 'If you can't get the ball in, call timeout.' I couldn't get it in and I called timeout."

Before Ward knew it, official Don Wedge blew his whistle and called him for five seconds. A turnover. The Fighting Irish would have one more chance.

"Nobody knows this—you can see it on the film—the referee puts the whistle in his mouth and he drops the whistle," Ward said. "So he's bending down to pick up the whistle. While he's bending down, I call timeout in plenty of time. He doesn't see me call timeout, he blows his whistle and points Notre Dame ball. We're all thinking, what's going on?"

Notre Dame inbounded the ball to Bill Paterno, who missed a jump shot. Toby Knight, a six-foot-eight forward, tipped in a game-winning basket for Notre Dame with two seconds left.

"He came from the foul line," UC's Gary Yoder said. "We couldn't get a body on him."

"Somebody up there loves us," Notre Dame coach Digger Phelps said afterward.

UC would have played Kentucky next in the tournament, and the players thought they matched up well with the Wildcats.

"That was a killer," Collier said. "We had the team that year. We had a good mixture of upperclassmen. We were playing well. We were clicking well. We had gone through the whole season improving. I don't think we were ever as good as we were that year. That sticks in our mind. That was the time, and it did not happen.

"Hal Ward says to this day people ask him about that. He said that still haunts him. It's not his fault. You can't blame one guy."

That was the final game of Ward's career.

"It was disappointing," Ward said. "I do know one thing: If we would've won that game, we would've gone to the Final Four. We should've been there."

I GOT THE MESSAGE

UC played sixth-ranked Marquette—which would go on to win the national championship—on February 6, 1977 at Riverfront Coliseum in a nationally televised game. The Bearcats were No. 12 in the country.

For the game-opening jump ball, Yoder was positioned next to Marquette star Butch Lee. When the referee tossed the ball in the air, Lee "gave me the biggest elbow in the middle of the sternum," Yoder said. "As all hands go up for the jump ball, he hit me. I bent over and could hardly breathe. That was sending a message. Butch is from New York. I'm some country hick."

Yoder had the last laugh. The Bearcats won 63-62.

Yoder was a junior-college All-American from Southern Idaho. He played high school ball in Topeka, Indiana, just outside of South Bend. It was a small country school with about 300 students, he said.

Yoder, who at six foot four played center in high school, started his college career at Mississippi before transferring to Southern Idaho.

He was the top scoring reserve for the Bearcats during the 1975-76 season and started in the backcourt with Collier as a senior in 1976-77 when he was named Metro Conference Player of the Year.

ALL GOOD THINGS MUST COME TO AN END

UC took a 59-game home winning streak into its matchup with 18th-ranked Florida State on December 27, 1977 at Riverfront Coliseum. The Bearcats were playing without starting point guard Eddie Lee, who had been suspended for one game for being late to a Christmas Day practice.

And this game wasn't going to end without a lot of drama.

Ten points were scored in the final 69 seconds.

A layup by Florida State's Mickey Dillard with eight seconds remaining tied it at 75. UC had to go the length of the court to prevent overtime. Junior Bobby Sherlock, playing in place of Lee, took the inbounds pass, and dribbled twice. Then he sent a pass from the top of the key on the Florida State side of the court to Collier, who was on the right sideline, about 30 feet from the basket.

Collier fired up a shot that went in. The Bearcats won 77-75 for their 60th consecutive victory at home—that tied them with UNLV for longest streak in the nation.

There was controversy, though.

Florida State insisted the ball did not leave Collier's hands in time.

"In my opinion, there was no question the shot was late," Florida State coach Hugh Durham said afterward.

"The ball was definitely in the air," Collier said.

Replays were not available at the time.

The Bearcats' next home game was 11 days later against No. 10 Louisville, which promptly ended the UC home winning streak.

PARTING OF WAYS

Catlett coached three consecutive UC teams to 20-win seasons, but in 1977-78 the Bearcats went 17-10. Some UC fans were growing unhappy with Catlett, especially after a first-round loss to Georgia Tech in the Metro Conference tournament.

He had been at UC six seasons when the job opened at West Virginia, his alma mater; he was a college teammate of Jerry West's.

Catlett left Cincinnati to take over as coach at West Virginia and he coached the Mountaineers for 24 years before resigning after the 2002 season. Who would get first crack at that job but UC coach Bob Huggins, another West Virginia alum who ended up turning down the position. (More on that in chapter 10.)

Back to Catlett.

He left the UC campus and did not return until 22 years later, when Collier was inducted into UC's Athletic Hall of Fame and asked Catlett to be his presenter.

"I've been to his house in West Virginia," Collier said. "He has all the pictures of our time (at UC). I'm sure he enjoyed our team. We had good kids. We didn't cause him any problems. He had young kids at the time and they hung out with us."

Catlett was a major reason Cummings chose Cincinnati over Memphis, Oregon, Pittsburgh, and Florida. While Cummings thought Catlett was a very good coach, there was more to it than that.

"The thing that impresses me to this day is he's been a friend, not only to me, but to my family," Cummings said. "When he went to West Virginia (in 1978), my family would go down there several times a year. And he treated them like they were family. They're still close friends.

"He's from West Virginia. My parents are from Pennsylvania. Maybe he saw something in me or my family that were a lot like his roots. They just hit it off."

8

ED BADGER ERA (1978-1983)

FROM THE NBA TO DIVISION I

In 1978, Ed Badger was nearing the end of his second year as head coach of the Chicago Bulls, who would finish 40-42. He had one year remaining on his contract with the NBA club.

After Gale Catlett left UC for West Virginia, Cincinnati attorney Ron Grinker called Badger and encouraged him to apply for the position. Grinker represented Bulls players John Mengelt and Derrick Dickey, a former Bearcat.

Badger wasn't really interested but decided to go through the interview process as a favor to Grinker. He met with a group of school officials, including UC Athletic Director Bill Jenike, at a downtown hotel.

By the end of the day, the job was pretty much Badger's if he wanted it.

Before taking over the Bearcats, Ed Badger coached the Chicago Bulls for two seasons. His 1976-77 Bulls team went 44-38 and advanced to the NBA playoffs. (Photo by University of Cincinnati/Sports Information)

Badger not only wanted to talk to his wife, he was to discuss a contract extension with the Bulls ownership. That conversation did not go well. Meanwhile, he said, UC had called to officially offer him the job. The Bulls had no problem releasing Badger from the final year of his contract.

The Bearcats had their new coach.

He promised to bring a fast-paced, pro style of play to Cincinnati.

"I didn't know what kind of a career move it was," Badger said.

STRATEGY SESSION

Soon after he accepted the UC job, Badger was in Doug Schloemer's house in Covington, Kentucky. The Holmes High School standout, named Kentucky's Mr. Basketball, had narrowed his college choices to Cincinnati and Charlotte, which had advanced to the 1977 Final Four with Cedric "Cornbread" Maxwell.

At his high school banquet soon after Badger's visit, a UC booster was pressuring Schloemer into a decision. So he went ahead and announced that he would attend UC.

In the sixth game of his career, the Bearcats were playing host to No. 6 North Carolina at Riverfront Coliseum. UC led by two points with 3:35 remaining. But North Carolina was ahead in the final minute.

Badger called a timeout.

Schloemer, a reserve who did not play much, was thinking, "Wow, this is pretty cool."

"I wanted to get up in the huddle and hear what (Badger) had to say," Schloemer said. "Probably some big-time strategy. He pointed at all five starters and said, 'Shitty, shitty, shitty, shitty, shitty. … You're making me look bad. Now get out there and win this game.' That was the extent of the huddle."

UC lost 62-59.

TOUGH START

Badger inherited a heckuva schedule from Catlett. In 1978-79, the Bearcats played in Long Beach, California, Boston, Atlanta, New York City, and Chicago. Perennial power North Carolina came to Riverfront Coliseum. UC played Earvin "Magic" Johnson's Michigan State team at the Pontiac Silverdome in front of 31,683 fans; at the time, it was the second-largest crowd to see a college basketball game. "I thought I was back in the NBA," Badger said. (By the way, Magic had just nine points and five turnovers in the fifth-ranked Spartans' 63-52 victory.)

While in St. Louis to play the Billikens on January 2, Badger received a phone call in his hotel room at 3:30 a.m. He was summoned to the lobby, where he found some of his players in handcuffs.

They were accused of breaking into the hotel gift shop and stealing more than $2,000 worth of merchandise. "It started out as a joke, but then it wasn't a joke anymore," a player anonymously told *The Cincinnati Enquirer*. Lionel Harvey and Keith Hemans were permanently suspended from the team.

A few days later, Cincinnati had a game at Virginia Tech. The Hokies were undefeated and playing host to a prominent recruit, Ralph Sampson, who watched the game from midcourt.

Well, UC won 72-68 and Badger was in a celebrating mood. He ran to the locker room and was jumping up and down.

Student manager Neil Bendesky was icing down some pop and Gatorade in a pail that he placed just inside the locker room door. When Badger came jumping in, he landed right in the pail. His shoes, socks and pants were soaked. "Everything was wet," he said.

SORRY, GALE

Perhaps the most rewarding victory of that season, however, came January 24, 1979, at West Virginia. The Mountaineers were coached by Catlett and came into the game with a 10-4 record. In December, nine months after he left UC for West Virginia, the Bearcats were placed on two years probation by the NCAA for violations that occurred during Catlett's tenure.

The Bearcats beat the Mountaineers 79-65. Catlett barely spoke to Badger, wishing him luck before the game and saying, "Good job" afterward. Catlett refused to speak to reporters after the game, leaving the arena after his postgame radio show.

ROCKY ROAD

Pat Cummings was part of a much-heralded freshman class that arrived in 1974, but he didn't get to end his career with the group.

He broke his left ankle at South Florida 18 games into his freshman season and had to watch as the Bearcats went 23-6, losing to Louisville in the 1975 NCAA Tournament.

During preseason of his junior year, 1976-77, Cummings broke the fifth metatarsal bone in his right foot. It would "pop again" while he was walking through campus. He had pins surgically inserted in his foot, sat out the season and spent months on crutches.

Cummings averaged 18 points and 7.6 rebounds as a redshirt junior. Because he had been in college four years, he was eligible for the 1978 NBA draft. The Milwaukee Bucks selected him in the third round. Rather than turn pro, Cummings opted to return to UC for the 1978-79 season, the Bearcats' first under Badger. Milwaukee retained his rights. It was the same move made that year by Indiana State's Larry Bird, who was drafted by the Boston Celtics but returned for a final year of college ball.

"I didn't even watch the draft," Cummings said. "I was in the gym shooting. I found out about it a few hours later.

"Would it happen today, I would turn pro. But it was a different climate back then. The money's different. I was probably a little naïve and really enjoyed college life. I wanted to graduate, which I did. I'm glad I stayed another year. I never regretted it. Evidently it worked out."

It didn't hurt that Badger came right from the NBA to the Bearcats and brought a pro-style offense that ran through the forward position. Badger had been an assistant for the Chicago Bulls when Dick Motta was head coach; Motta would later coach Cummings in Dallas.

Badger also had the ears of NBA personnel who were interested in Cummings, who averaged 37.5 minutes a game as a senior. The Bearcats started two freshmen, a sophomore, a junior and Cummings.

"It was going to be a tough year no matter what, with all the seniors leaving," Cummings said. "It was a transitional period. I enjoyed playing for Ed."

"He wanted to be an NBA player," Badger said. "He was pretty receptive to me. He was a little wild at times, but he was coachable. You could get on him. He was a good 6-9 kid who could shoot outside."

HITCHING TO A HIGH SCHOOL

One of Badger's favorite recruiting stories involves Doug Kecman from West Mifflin, Pennsylvania.

Two aunts raised Kecman; his mother died of cancer when he was 12, and his father was killed in a steel mill accident when he was 16.

The first time Badger went to see Kecman play, he flew in a private airplane to Allegheny County Airport. It had started to snow, and Badger did not bring a jacket. He went into the terminal and asked how to get a taxi. "We haven't had a cab here in 10 years," he was told.

Badger said he had to walk about three quarters of a mile to get to a highway.

"Here I am coaching a major college team," Badger said. "I can't get a cab. It's snowing. I don't have a coat. And I'm hitchhiking.

"All of a sudden, some kid comes along and picks me up."

Badger asked the boy whether he knew where West Mifflin High School was. Turned out the kid went there.

"It's only a few miles away," he said

"I'll give you 10 bucks to take me," Badger told him.

After the student dropped off Badger, he said, "You want a ride back afterward?"

Sure, said Badger. He watched the game sitting between Kecman's aunts, then got his ride back to the airport. Kecman eventually signed with UC.

BAD OMEN

It maybe shouldn't come as a big surprise that Myron Hughes ended up having an injury-plagued UC career given the way it started.

Hughes, who led Colbert County High School to an Alabama state championship as a senior, chose Cincinnati over Tennessee. He liked the talent Badger was bringing in, and he liked UC's business college and the kinds of companies that were in Cincinnati. His goal was to be an Academic All-American, and UC gave him the best chance to do that, he felt.

While warming up for his very first game, the 1981-82 season opener against Bellarmine at Riverfront Coliseum, Hughes accidentally ran into teammate Mike Williams and broke the ring finger on his shooting hand.

Hughes played anyway, mostly using his left hand. He nailed his first shot and finished with eight points. After the game, X-rays revealed that his finger was dislocated and broken in three places. He had surgery and missed the next eight games.

THEY DID WHAT?

Hughes traveled to Peoria, Illinois, for the December 21 Bradley game, but he was so frustrated about not being able to play, the coaching staff let him fly home to Alabama for a long Christmas break.

Hughes left the morning of the game and was traveling all day. He had no idea what happened. When he arrived home, his family told him UC and Bradley had played an NCAA-record seven overtimes before the Bearcats prevailed 75-73.

MUCH MALIGNED

From 1979-83, the Bearcats went a combined 55-57 under Badger and never played in the postseason. Nobody heard more from frustrated fans than Junior Johnson.

The six-foot blond guard from Lexington, Kentucky, who spoke with a "Kentucky accent," was a first-team all-state player as a senior when he led Lexington Lafayette to a high school state championship. He scored 1,665 career points and handed out 750 career assists. He set single-game school records for points (42) and assists (15).

"Junior is a star of the future," Badger proclaimed.

Over his four-year UC career, Johnson would never average more than 6.4 points in a season, and that came his sophomore year.

"Everybody in the school thought they were a better player than he was," teammate Derrick McMillan said. "He was a guy who was never well respected by fans and other teams but … Junior knew how to run a team. His intelligence on the floor was very eerie."

Johnson experienced more than his share of booing from fans. It was the students who were hardest on him.

"I wasn't supposed to shoot, and then when we didn't score, you had the coaches saying that we're not getting enough scoring out of our guard position," Johnson said. "My responsibility was not to score points. It was to break pressure defense and get us into our offense."

"He had a lot of pressure on him," McMillan said. "Maybe it was self-inflicted pressure because he had such high expectations."

In one stretch during his junior season, UC lost seven straight games, including to Xavier (53-51) on January 27, 1982. In that game, Johnson had no points, two assists and five turnovers in 13 minutes. Fans at Riverfront Coliseum targeted Johnson. What they didn't know was that for months, he had been driving back home to Lexington after practice four or five times a week.

His grandfather was terminally ill with cancer—and, in fact, died before the season ended. Johnson's mother had been diagnosed with "a bad form of diabetes," and he didn't know how that would affect her. Johnson was close to his family and had a hard time balancing basketball, school and his personal concerns.

"Obviously, I wasn't at the peak of my game," he said. "That's probably when I caught the most flak. We started losing, and I just wasn't playing well. If the point guard's not playing well, it's not good for the team. We had a bunch of injuries, too. Nonetheless, I was trying to do a lot as far as supporting my mom.

"I could understand people being irritated and mad, but it was hard to be stepped on when you're going through the toughest time of your entire young adult life. That was the first time anyone close to me was really, really sick."

Johnson was benched after the Xavier game. He hesitated to go public with his family problems. A month later, when he entered a home game against Florida State, he was booed again. He ended up making two free throws that secured an 84-83 victory.

"I didn't want to make any excuses," he said. "I wasn't mad. It hurt my feelings. There's a difference."

That said, Johnson said he left UC with great memories and remained involved with the program. He lived in Cincinnati and Lexington until 1996 and owned six Picture Show Video stores, three in each city. His Cincinnati store managers often hired UC players to work in the off season.

"I had nothing but good times," Johnson said. "I went to the right school. Every one of my memories is positive. Not winning more was frustrating, but we had a number of factors that contributed to that. I got a great education. I graduated on time. I met a lot of great people. I love Cincinnati. If I hadn't, I wouldn't have come around so much after I got out of school."

IF ONLY . . .

During Badger's last season at UC (1982-83), he worked hard to recruit a player out of Toledo Bowsher High School named Dennis Hopson. Badger said he saw Hopson play about 18 times and had a great relationship with his family. Hopson said that on a visit to UC to see a game, he committed.

"I was going to come there," Hopson said. "I loved Coach. Coach Badger was the man. I wanted to play against Louisville and those types of teams. I was ready to go."

Hopson went on to play at Ohio State, where he became the Buckeyes' all-time leading scorer with 2,096 points. He was the Big Ten Conference most valuable player in 1987 and was the No. 3 overall pick in the 1987 NBA draft by the New Jersey Nets.

"Actually, the reason I came to Ohio State was because of Coach Machock," Hopson said. "Great gift of gab, man. He was a great recruiter. I never even paid attention to Ohio State until (Badger was fired). Then I started searching around."

That would be UC alum Chuck Machock, who was an assistant coach on Bob Huggins's staff when the Bearcats went to the Final Four in 1992.

IF ONLY . . . PART II

Hopson wasn't the only star player who may have come to UC if Badger had remained coach.

A year behind Hopson was Danny Manning, who also crossed the Bearcats off his list after Badger's firing.

"He loved Cincinnati," Derrick McMillan said. "He loved the school."

True, says Manning, who confirms that UC was "absolutely a possibility" had Badger stayed. "They were on my list until he was no longer there," he said. "They were definitely in my top four (joining North Carolina, North Carolina State and Kansas, where he ended up)."

Ron Grinker, the same Cincinnati attorney who encouraged Badger to take the UC job, represented Manning's father, Ed, who played in the NBA and ABA from 1967-76. Ed Manning was with the Bulls when Badger was an assistant coach.

Every summer, Grinker would gather the players he represented in Cincinnati. For several years, Danny Manning would tag along and spend time in Cincinnati. He got to know the city and attended five basketball camps at UC. He became fond of Cincinnati staples like Graeter's ice cream and Montgomery Inn ribs, which to this day he orders online and has shipped to him. He also liked Skyline Chili.

"We understood that on a scale of one to 10, it was a nine he was coming to UC," McMillan said.

"From everything that we knew, Danny was coming," Hughes echoed.

In 1986, Grinker told *The Cincinnati Enquirer* the same thing.

Well, you probably know the rest. Manning became the all-time leading scorer and rebounder at Kansas, was named the consensus national player of the year in 1988, led the Jayhawks to an NCAA title, and was the No. 1 overall pick in the 1988 NBA draft.

CLEARING OUT

Badger said he never did get along with Mike McGee, hired as UC's Athletic Director in May 1980.

By end of the 1982-83 season, Badger's fifth, the coach knew his days were numbered. The day after the Bearcats lost to Tulane in their first Metro Conference tournament game at Riverfront Coliseum, Badger went to the UC campus and cleaned out his office. It was a Sunday afternoon.

When Badger came into the office Monday morning, he said, his secretary was crying.

"Coach, we've been robbed," she said. "Somebody robbed your office."

Badger thought it was funny. Then he went to meet with McGee, who told Badger what he expected to hear—that he was making a coaching change. Their meeting lasted all of three minutes.

Three months later, the Cleveland Cavaliers hired Badger as their top assistant coach.

"Cincinnati was a good move for my family," Badger said. "My wife liked it. Our two sons are still there. Cincinnati was my second favorite place (behind Charlotte)."

9

TONY YATES ERA
(1983-1989)

ONCE A BEARCAT . . .

Tony Yates was a Bearcat during three consecutive decades. He played in the 1960s. He was an assistant coach for Tay Baker, then Gale Catlett, in the '70s. And he returned to his alma mater as head coach in 1983.

Yates had been an assistant coach at the University of Illinois for nine years—one under Gene Bartow and eight under Lou Henson.

In the back of his mind, he always hoped to one day coach the Bearcats. He said he interviewed for the job in 1972 when Baker resigned, but Athletic Director George Smith went with Catlett. Yates tried again when Catlett left in 1978, but Athletic Director Bill Jenike chose Ed Badger.

Toward the end of the 1982-83 season, with growing disenchantment with Badger, some UC alums contacted Yates to see if he was still interested in the job at UC.

Tony Yates's tenure as head coach of Cincinnati did not bring the championship success of his playing days. Nevertheless, Yates brought many memorable moments to Bearcats fans, including the infamous slow-down game against Kentucky in 1983, the Bearcats' first postseason appearance (NIT, 1985) in more than eight years, the snapping of UC's 17-game losing streak to Louisville, and the recruitment of three 1,000-point scorers: Roger McClendon, Louis Banks, and Levertis Robinson. (Photo by University of Cincinnati/Sports Information)

There was no question about it.

Badger was out of work soon after the season ended. UC Athletic Director Mike McGee flew to Champaign, Illinois, to interview Yates at his home.

The other primary candidates were Lou Campanelli from James Madison and Ron Greene from Murray State. It came down to Yates and Greene after Campanelli withdrew from consideration.

Yates came to campus for a formal interview with the selection committee, which included Oscar Robertson.

On April 1, McGee called Yates at his home in Champaign and offered him the job.

"Now Mike, this isn't an April Fool's joke is it?" Yates asked.

"It was a very happy moment," Yates said. "I was going home."

When he was announced as head coach at the Alumni Center, more than 200 friends, former teammates, UC officials and supporters gave him a standing ovation. Yates had to wipe away tears.

Robertson told *The Cincinnati Enquirer*: "Am I happy? You bet. He knows the game. He knows how to recruit. He's just what we need."

BOOT CAMP

It did not necessarily please all the UC players that Yates brought with him a military background of regimen and discipline. The transition from the mostly laid-back Badger to Yates was eye-opening. Some players were certain Yates, a veteran of the U.S. Air Force, was trying to run everyone out of the program.

"It was a miniature boot camp," Yates said. "We wanted the kids who really wanted to be there and who would conform to what we wanted.

"We weeded out the guys who didn't really want to work. They began to leave one by one. A few we asked to leave. The guys who hung in there are the guys who really wanted to be there. Attitudes changed."

Yates set strict in-season and off-season curfews. ("My junior year, you had to be in your room at 10; I can remember me and Joe Niemann sitting across from each other in the doorways talking because we weren't allowed out of our rooms," Doug Kecman said.) Yates required players to sign in at the basketball office by 7:30 a.m. each school day—if not they would have to run five miles at 5 a.m. the next day.

And he was relentless in practice. "We were in a military regime when he came in," Kecman said. "We practiced for four hours every day."

Sometimes longer.

"He had a lot of rules," Derrick McMillan said. "*A lot* of rules."

ICY START

This was Myron Hughes's introduction to Yates.

Hughes had just finished his sophomore season at UC and was rehabilitating an injured knee. Yates called a 3 p.m. meeting, but Hughes had not finished icing his knee. He walked into the meeting a few minutes late and Yates jumped all over him. The two had never met.

"If anybody was always on time, it was me," Hughes said. "My teammates knew I was always on time for everything. At that point, I told myself I was transferring. I didn't want to take the opportunity to get to know him."

Hughes contacted Tennessee and Virginia Tech and was getting ready to leave UC. But he decided that wasn't what he wanted, that he had met so many great people at the university. So he decided to give Yates a chance.

After sitting out the 1983-84 season following knee surgery, Hughes played two seasons for Yates and grew to look at him as a father figure and confidant.

More than 17 years after his UC career ended, Hughes remained close with Yates, phoning him almost monthly.

"If I need advice, he's one of the first people I call," Hughes said.

PRACTICE 'TIL YOU DROP

Yates allowed his players to go home for Christmas in 1983, but they were all to return and get right back to work after the holiday. Back in Cincinnati, it was a cold, cold winter. And when the players returned to town, they found there were no lights and no heat in Dabney Hall, where they lived. There was also no heat in the Armory Fieldhouse, site of the first practice after the break. The players could see steam coming out of their mouths when they breathed.

When it was time for practice to start at 7 p.m., only four players were on hand: Kecman, Niemann, Mike McNally and Marty Campbell. Yates had them play two-on-two full court while they waited for the other players to trickle in. "Practice" continued until after 10 p.m. Derrick McMillan still was not there; he was involved in a car accident in Chicago heading to the airport. Neither was Mark Dorris, who had gotten married during the break. Eventually Yates told the players to head back to the dorm and he'd see them at 7 a.m. the next day.

Yates was obviously not in a good mood. After a four-hour practice in Laurence Hall (which *did* have heat), he had the Bearcats line up for sprints. Lots of them. The players were dropping out one at a time, vomiting on the sideline, unable to continue.

There were six players still running when Luther Tiggs passed out in the middle of the court from dehydration.

"Coach Yates really believed in conditioning," Tiggs said. "It was one of those typical days. As we started our conditioning, one sprint led to another. And that just wasn't enough. He never got satisfied.

"I practiced extremely hard. I didn't believe in saving anything. It just seemed like it was never going to stop. The teammates were encouraging each other. The coaches were really pushing us. I was out of gas. I remember getting extremely light-headed. I looked at the coaches and they indicated we needed to get back on the line. I was totally exhausted. The only thing I remember after that was I was in the student medical center and I had an IV in my arm and a couple of the guys were giving me a hard time because they thought I was bailing out."

After Tiggs went down, Kecman looked at Niemann and said, "We've *got* to be done."

As soon as Tiggs was taken out of the building, Yates said, "Get back on the line."

They ran some more, then had to come back for a 4 p.m. practice.

ONE ON ONE

That wasn't the last time Tiggs got a hard time from his teammates. Or Yates.

He missed two games during the 1983-84 season when he suffered a broken finger playing against … a girl!

OK, to be fair, Tiggs wasn't playing just any female when he got hurt. He was in the Armory Fieldhouse playing one on one against Cheryl Cook, the greatest player in UC women's basketball history whose jersey number is retired and hangs in Shoemaker Center.

"She was the best women's player I ever saw," Tiggs said. "She was extremely competitive. She always wanted to play with the guys. They called her a few names, but nobody gave her an out. That's what she wanted.

"One day, she wanted to play one on one at a side basket. She had the ball and she made a move toward the baseline and my hand went across the body because I wanted to strip her of the ball. I pulled it back. When I looked up, my index finger was completely severed. I ran to the trainer, and my finger was just hanging there. They had to stitch it up. The guys were really on me about that. Coach didn't want to believe it."

As for Cook, Tiggs said she felt badly.

"She was real sweet about it," he said. "She didn't want to make (the men's team) mad."

"It wasn't intentional," Cook said. "Now that you brought it up, I still feel bad about it."

COOKIE MONSTER

Since Tiggs brought up the subject, it's appropriate to take a timeout from the men's program to talk about Cheryl Cook, AKA the Cookie Monster.

In Shoemaker Center hangs the retired jersey numbers of Oscar Robertson, Jack Twyman, Kenyon Martin and ... Cook, No. 24.

A native of Indianapolis, Cook was second in the country in scoring (27.5 ppg) and second-team All-America as a senior in 1984-85, and she remains the women's all-time leading scorer at Cincinnati with 2,367 career points. (That was the seventh best total in NCAA history at the time.)

The five-foot-nine guard was a two-time Metro Conference Player of the Year. She played on the 1983 gold-medal-winning U.S. team in the Pan American Games and on the silver-medal-winning U.S. team in the 1985 World University Games.

Cook was Indiana's Miss Basketball in 1981 as a senior at Indianapolis Washington High School. She said she had 375 scholarship offers from colleges and narrowed her choices to USC, UCLA, Hawaii and Cincinnati.

She wanted to leave the state of Indiana but stay close enough to home so her parents could see her play.

"Plus the (UC) coaching staff was just awesome," Cook said. "They were real people-oriented. It was a close-knit family within the team, and that's what I was looking for.

"I was going there to try to make some noise and get us national recognition."

She would play two years for coach Ceal Barry, then two for coach Sandy Smith.

During her career, the Bearcats went a combined 70-45. Cook's only regret was that UC never went to the NCAA Tournament when she was there.

"But we came a long way as a program," she said. "It opened a lot of doors for other women to come in and try to take it to the next level."

Two memories stand out for Cook.

One was when the Bearcats went to Tennessee in the third game of her senior season and upset the 12th-ranked Volunteers. Cook scored 34 points.

The other is how she sometimes practiced with the UC men's team and competed against guys in pick-up games on campus.

"I grew up with six brothers, so I was accustomed to being the only girl, being knocked down," Cook said. "I played AAU with the boys when I was younger. I wanted to show them at UC that I was capable of playing with them. Some of the guys at the beginning underestimated me—until I got out there and played.

"I grew up with that drive to be better than the next person. I lived in the gym. As far as a personal life and hanging out with friends, I didn't have all that because I was dedicated to the sport."

Cook was one of the top college players in the nation and went on to play four years in Spain and two years in Italy after leaving Cincinnati.

"I feel privileged," she said. "I wish there were more (women's numbers retired), but I'm thankful for every opportunity UC gave me."

SO MUCH FOR THAT IDEA

Seven games into his junior season, Doug Kecman had a great shooting night, scoring 10 points in a 55-50 loss to Miami University at Riverfront Coliseum. He scored the Bearcats' last eight points and hit five jumpers from the corner that would have all been three-pointers if the three-point arc existed then, which it didn't.

The 1-6 Bearcats' next game was against No. 2-ranked Kentucky at Riverfront. At practice the day before meeting the Wildcats, Yates told Kecman that he was going to be in the starting lineup and that with Kentucky playing a 1-3-1 defense, he could get open for that shot in the corner all night. During practice, Kecman said, "I was bangin' them home. I was hitting every corner shot you can imagine."

I'm gonna have a career game against Kentucky, he thought.

Kecman was fired up. He got on the phone that night and called his friends back home in the Pittsburgh area.

"We're playing on ESPN tomorrow night and I'm going to get 20 (points) against Kentucky," he told them. "I've got the green light to shoot everything from the corner."

Well, most UC fans know how this story turns out. Yates told the Bearcat players just before they went out for the tipoff that they were going to hold the ball. All game.

That blows the 20 I'm going to get, Kecman thought, *but I'm still starting on national TV.*

"I played 39 minutes that night and didn't break a sweat," he said. "I did grab a rebound over Sam Bowie—he kind of slipped and fell."

He took one shot all night—and missed. Kecman was scoreless.

The final: Kentucky 24, UC 11.

CINDERELLA STORY

Tony Wilson came to UC from Toledo on a track scholarship (he was one of Ohio's top high school hurdlers), but as a freshman he also was interested in playing basketball. He tried to walk on to UC's team but did not make it.

Derrick McMillan, at Cincinnati on a basketball scholarship, was also on the track team as a freshman and got to know Wilson. The night before walk-on tryouts in the fall of 1982, McMillan said he saw Wilson at a party. Wilson said he wasn't going to try out again. McMillan had seen Wilson play pick-up games, and he liked guys who wanted to play defense and played with a lot of heart. Wilson was also pretty quick, like McMillan.

"It's like 2 a.m.," McMillan said. "I told him, 'You've got to come try out. You're going to practice at 8 o'clock in the morning. I'll be there personally.' I asked (the coaches) to give him a fair shot as a walk-on. The rest is history."

Wilson made the team, impressed coaches with his hustle and determination and was a starter by January of his sophomore year. He is probably best remembered for his 49-foot shot that upset 17th-ranked Alabama-Birmingham at Riverfront Coliseum (69-67) on December 12, 1984.

After UAB tied the score with five seconds left, Wilson got the ball, dribbled once and looked at the clock. "It read :02, and I let it go," he said afterward. "I knew I had the distance."

"I remember the circumstances real well because I wanted the ball so bad," McMillan said. "It was something I practiced every day. Tony reaches out and gets the ball and sends it up, Cinderella style. It was the shot heard 'round the world."

JEKYLL AND HYDE

There were more than 16,000 fans in attendance, but few saw it happen. All of a sudden, Xavier University's Eddie Johnson was on the ground.

It was the January 30, 1985 Crosstown Shootout at Riverfront Coliseum. It was the usual heated battle between the Bearcats and Musketeers.

Myron Hughes and Johnson were battling under the basket.

"We started running down the court and he shot me two elbows," Hughes said. "I just reacted. I turned around and slugged him and knocked him down. I hit him pretty good. He wasn't knocked out, but he was stunned. I didn't think about being kicked out of the game or anything.

"A lot of people say they saw it even though they didn't. The three officials working the game missed it. No one else on the court saw anything. I would venture to say no more than 15 people actually saw it. The referee came up to me and said, 'I don't know what happened but I know something happened. You guys need to clean it up.'"

No foul was called. Hughes was not ejected. Xavier went on to win 55-52. There was no mention of the incident the next day in the morning newspaper.

Hughes is often reminded of the incident before Crosstown Shootouts. But he has no regrets.

"I've been hit in the mouth and upside the head and punched in the side," he said. "When you're playing underneath the basket, there's no telling what will happen.

"There were no hard feelings. He knew what he had done. We've even gone out and had drinks. It is weird. I didn't think too much about it. I would never have thought I'd be talking about it 19 years later and they'd still be showing it on television."

The funny thing is, those who know Hughes off the court would think it was so out of character. But those who played with him, know a different side of Myron Hughes the basketball player.

"He was our protector," Roger McClendon said. "He was the father figure, the big brother. Out of character? Not on the floor. You know how some people could get in the ring, like Muhammad Ali, and punish a guy, but then off the floor he's kissing babies? Myron had that split personality. You knew when you were on the court, if you went through the lane, you'd better be prepared no matter who you were."

ANOTHER "BIG O" ASSIST

Oscar Robertson says University of Cincinnati players have had an "open invitation" to work with him individually for decades. But few over the years have asked for guidance from one of the greatest basketball players of all time.

The summer of 1984, before his senior year, Derrick McMillan was talking to Yates about Robertson.

"Give him a call," Yates said.

"No," McMillan said. "You don't just call Oscar."

"Call him, Derrick," Yates said.

Yates gave Robertson's phone number to McMillan, who soon called.

"He had a shooting problem," Robertson said.

The two met at the Armory Fieldhouse, steaming in the summer heat. McMillan came from a factory job. Robertson came from his office. They got together every day between 4:30 and 5 p.m. for roughly an hour. Robertson showed McMillan a proper shooting technique. He taught him about studying film and watching other players.

"It's amazing, the things he taught me still work today," McMillan said 19 years later. "The things that he taught me in that period of time are things that I share right now with kids.

"There's something about him that really led me toward the things I wanted to do with leadership. I watched the way he carried himself on and off the floor and how he went about approaching things. Even when I'm around him now holding conversations about the way people do business, he just really makes you feel good and makes you look at things that you should be correcting."

It should be noted that as a senior, McMillan averaged a career-high 11.7 points—more than twice his average from his junior year—and was selected second-team all-Metro Conference.

"I tell all the players before the season, if you want to work on some things, here is my number," Robertson said. "Whatever they want to do is fine with me. If they want to work every day, I don't mind. For some reason, most of them never took advantage."

McMillan couldn't be happier that he did.

CLOSE, BUT NO . . .

Going into the final game of his injury-plagued career, Hughes still had a chance to reach the 1,000-point mark. He needed 17 points against Louisville in the 1986 Metro Conference tournament.

"I knew what I needed," Hughes said. "But at that time, I was more worried about how we could win the tournament and get to the NCAA. That was one of my goals, and we never did do it."

Hughes had scored 12 points, and with 12:53 to go in the game he was called for a foul. He thought he only had four, but then he heard the buzzer and saw a person at the scorer's table hold up five fingers. He had fouled out and finished with 995 career points.

"Unfortunately, I did not know how many fouls I had," he said. "It would've been a milestone, but I didn't think about it that much. I knew I missed a lot of games. If I would've played in another couple games, I would've made it to that level with no problem. I was mostly concerned with winning."

Hughes estimates missing roughly 25 games during his career. He had four surgeries on his left knee (including one reconstruction), bursitis in his right knee, a broken finger and nose, a tooth knocked out, 14 stitches above his eye, and torn muscles in his thigh.

Hughes served as executive director of the University of Cincinnati Alumni Association from 2008-14 and is currently UC's senior associate vice president of development for diversity & inclusion.

STUDENT . . . ATHLETE

Roger McClendon was a McDonald's All-American coming out of Centennial High School in Champaign, Illinois, but in choosing a college, he had more on his mind than just basketball.

His father was a professor of African-American History at the University of Illinois. His parents stressed the importance of education. McClendon was interested in majoring in engineering.

When it came time to meet in person with Division I head coaches, the McClendon family prepared just as hard as the coaches. Roger and his parents came up with a list of 25 questions that every coach wanting to sign Roger would have to answer. Among the questions: If Roger got injured his first season and couldn't play anymore, would the school honor his scholarship for as long as it took to get a degree? Or, what if Roger wanted to grow a mustache or beard or wear a goatee? Was facial hair allowed?

It was that one that tripped up Villanova coach Rollie Massimino, who said the rules of his program prohibited facial hair. McClendon's father objected.

"I guess the point was, as you're growing up as a young adult, there are certain decisions you should be able to make, and whether you have a mustache or not doesn't impact the way you play basketball and doesn't define your personality," McClendon said. "You do need some freedom of choice. You're growing as an individual."

So, they all answered the questions. Denny Crum from Louisville. Bobby Cremins from Georgia Tech. Lou Henson from Illinois. C.M. Newton from Vanderbilt. Even Bob Knight, whose Indiana program was not in McClendon's final five.

Of course, there was also Yates, who was in his first year as head coach at the University of Cincinnati. Yates had known McClendon's family for years because he was an assistant at Illinois and had been hoping to lure McClendon to the Fighting Illini.

The more McClendon learned about UC, the more it climbed on his list. He had no idea how successful the program had been in the 1960s. He didn't realize the university boasted a top-flight engineering program and that it had a co-op program that would allow him to gain practical job experience while in school.

"Really what I was looking for was a combination of an academic school that focused on engineering in addition to a high-caliber basketball program," McClendon said.

"The challenge for me would be to carry both of those torches at the same time."

THE PACT

McClendon attended the University of Cincinnati's basketball camp in 1984. Among the other players at camp: Elnardo Givens from Lexington, Kentucky, Levertis Robinson from Chicago and Ricky Calloway from Cincinnati's Withrow High School. Unknown to Yates at the time, the four made a pact to sign letters of intent to attend UC.

All but Calloway—who went to Indiana University—followed through.

"We did talk about it, that it would be a great place to build the program together," McClendon said.

By the way, another player at that camp was Ben Wilson, the top-rated high school player in the country from Chicago who was tragically shot and killed in November 1984.

"Ben Wilson was very interested in coming to Cincinnati," McClendon said.

BALANCING ACT

McClendon was UC's leading scorer for his first three seasons all while holding a double major in chemical and electrical engineering.

How did he pull that off?

"I probably missed out on parties that a lot of people had a chance to make," he said. "I knew where all the action and all the fun was at. You had to make a choice. I didn't regret it. What I had to do was find a balance."

He remembers when a band called Red, White and Blue was performing at Bogart's on Short Vine, and there were rumors Prince was going to show up. A lot of players and people McClendon knew went to the show—and Prince *did* show up.

When his friends returned to Dabney Hall, one had a tambourine from the band and another had a drumstick. They couldn't stop talking about what a great concert they had seen.

"And I'm under a light reading a physics book getting ready for a test," McClendon said.

One of his favorite extracurricular activities was when he was co-campaign manager for Stan Carroll, a candidate for student body president.

McClendon spoke on Carroll's behalf around campus and helped have flyers printed up. "I enjoyed that," McClendon said. "There were things that I wanted to do, and I had to make an extra effort to do them and not be just one-dimensional. I did try to find that balance. But it's always a struggle to try to reach your peak in both academics and athletics."

OLD SCHOOL

McClendon became close friends with teammate Romell Shorter, an exciting player from Chicago Martin Luther King High School. McClendon remembers one game during the 1985-86 season when Shorter, a five-foot-five guard, dribbled four times between his legs, once behind his back, then went around an opposing defender for a layup.

The next day, Yates showed the play on video three or four times in a row and asked the players to analyze whether all those moves were necessary for Shorter to get in position to make the shot.

"Coach Yates was an old-school style of coach," McClendon said. "To him, that was a fancy move. We all laughed. With Romell, that's his game. Without him using that ability, he becomes like everybody else."

WHAT A SHOW

When McClendon was a sophomore, the Bearcats played at Louisville when the Cardinals were ranked 18th in the country (January 20, 1986). Yates calls it "the most fantastic show" McClendon ever put on.

Louisville was ahead 56-43 with 13:20 remaining. From that point on, the UC offensive plays were all called for McClendon. The Bearcats went on a 14-4 run with McClendon scoring 10 of their points.

"We tried eight or nine different players on him and it didn't make a difference," Cardinals coach Denny Crum said afterward.

Always the outstanding student, Roger McClendon (21) passed up a professional basketball career and obtained his UC degree in engineering. Today, he is chief sustainability officer for YUM Brands, Inc., in, of all places, Louisville, against whom he had some of his most spectacular games. (Photo by University of Cincinnati/Sports Information)

"We were all over him and he filled it up anyway," Louisville player Billy Thompson told the media.

McClendon scored 24 of his 35 points in the second half and led Cincinnati to an 84-82 upset victory.

"I just know it was one of those rhythmic type of games where you didn't hear anybody in the stands and things felt like they were in slow motion," McClendon said. "It was easy."

He was 10 of 14 shooting from the field in the second half.

"He hit from all over the place," Yates said. "Louisville played a switching defense. He just beat them all. He penetrated, he pulled up, he shot from the corner, he shot from the wing, and he shot from the top of the key. Everywhere. That was really a special game."

Yates kept a tape of that game and said he plays it every once in a while.

"There was something special about playing Louisville," McClendon said. "I had the opportunity to go there. I knew Milt Wagner. They just had that type of team that would peak at the right time. But there was always something about playing Louisville that brought the level of the game up for me."

UC beat them twice that season. Louisville went on to win the national championship.

SHOULD I STAY OR SHOULD I GO?

UC finished 12-16 in 1985-86, McClendon's sophomore season. Though he had led the Bearcats in scoring two years, McClendon's parents had concerns about Yates's coaching style and philosophy. They attended a lot of games and were not sure their son was reaching his potential as a player.

There were discussions about possibly transferring, though McClendon never contacted another school.

"My dad thought I was probably not reaching my full potential," McClendon said. "I was frustrated but not unhappy. I was frustrated with not winning. The tough challenge with not winning is that nobody's happy. You don't have to be the star of the team. I would've much rather been on those 1960s teams and won a national championship than be the star of the team."

What kept McClendon at Cincinnati was probably this: His priority was not preparing for an NBA career. If it were, he knew there were better places for him to play.

"I was there really to get an education," he said. "That was my focus."

NOT SO EASY GOING

As basketball stars go, McClendon was a pretty levelheaded, calm, easygoing guy. But that demeanor went by the wayside February 16, 1987 when the leading scorer in the Metro Conference (19.7 ppg) learned that he was being benched for the start of a game against Memphis State.

Yates decided to sit McClendon, Joe Stiffend and Calvin Pfiffer and start Marty Dow, Don Ruehl and Romell Shorter.

"It's like being helpless being on the bench," McClendon said. "Not being able to do what you do was a tough thing. For me, it was all about the competition. I'm competitive to this day.

"He probably got the reaction he was looking for. Sometimes as a young player, you can't see what a coach can see with more experience. Coaches have to try different things to motivate players, to motivate the team."

McClendon, Stiffend and Pfiffer entered less than five minutes into the game. The Bearcats went on to win 76-73 at Riverfront Coliseum.

"I'm still angry (17 years later)," McClendon said laughing.

"I CARRIED A LOT OF WEIGHT"

McClendon, who left UC as the school's No. 2 all-time scorer behind Oscar Robertson, is the only Bearcat among the school's 1,000-point scorers to suffer through three losing seasons in his college career.

After UC went 17-14 his freshman year, McClendon's final three teams went 12-16, 12-16 and 11-17.

"I carried a lot of weight on my shoulders," he said. "I felt more responsible for having a losing season. Every game we would lose, I didn't feel like getting up and going to class and showing my face in public. I looked at myself like I should've been able to do more. That was a struggle for me, feeling like I let the team down. I kept that inside, which is not a good thing.

"It's hard to not be in a winning environment. It was very frustrating. Not with the players and not necessarily with the coach, but just going through that experience. I think it made me stronger. I did feel I had the potential and capability to go on to the next level, but I didn't."

McClendon was not picked in the three-round NBA draft. He played for the Miami Tropics of the United States Basketball League in the summer of 1988 and was invited to NBA camps by the Portland Trail Blazers and Chicago Bulls. He pulled a groin muscle while playing for the Tropics and never did attend the camps. He said he also turned down guaranteed money to play in Barcelona.

Instead, McClendon returned to the university for the 1988-89 school year to complete the requirements for his undergraduate degree. Again, he had a chance to begin a basketball career overseas. McClendon decided to accept a full-time engineering job.

He never played organized basketball again.

"I don't know if I really wanted it that bad," he said. "I finally let it go after two years of being in engineering."

XAVIER'S LOSS, UC'S GAIN

Keith Starks grew up in Addyston on the west side of Cincinnati and attended Taylor High School. He was a big Xavier University fan and rooted for the Musketeers each year during the Crosstown Shootout against Cincinnati.

By the end of his sophomore year at Taylor, Xavier was recruiting Starks hard. XU assistant coach Mike Sussli sent letters every day. No school came after Starks more aggressively. "If I would've signed my junior year, I would've gone to X," Starks said.

Gary Vaughn, his high school coach, encouraged Starks to take his time, make some visits to other colleges. Eventually, Starks narrowed his choices to Indiana, Syracuse, UCLA, Xavier, and UC—with UC "a distant, distant fourth or fifth."

Starks visited UCLA and loved it. He was all but ready to commit to the Bruins. Then his grandfather became ill. Starks grew up with his grandparents, and he didn't want to leave Cincinnati at that time.

Two factors ended his desire to go to Xavier. One, coach Bob Staak left and was replaced by Pete Gillen, and Gillen's staff went after another local product, Withrow's Tyrone Hill, and cooled on Starks. Even before that, Starks had decided to play football his senior year at Taylor. Starks said Sussli discouraged it and questioned the decision. UC assistant coach Jim Dudley thought it was a great idea and told Starks it would help his strength and conditioning. Starks—playing organized football for the first time in his life—started at split end and safety in high school.

In the spring of his senior year at Taylor, Starks signed a letter of intent to attend UC, a school that hadn't even been on his so-called radar screen.

"If my grandfather wouldn't have gotten sick, I would've gone to UCLA," Starks said.

LEARNING CURVE

Starks arrived at UC in 1987. He was a big-time scorer at Taylor, and the first day of practice with the Bearcats, he shot the ball almost every time he touched it. Yates stopped practice and tossed Starks the ball. "Here Keith, shoot it," Yates said. He did. Yates gave it back. "Shoot it again." Everyone was looking around, wondering what was going on.

Finally, Yates said, "Have you gotten it out of your system yet? Because you're not going to shoot the basketball. You're just going to go out and play as hard as you can, play defense and rebound. We have plenty of shooters."

The first four games, Starks hardly played. It was a tough transition.

WHAT A FIND

Sometimes, this is how recruiting works.

Yates and assistant coach Ken Turner were traveling through Montgomery, Alabama on the way to try to contact Leon Douglas, a star high school player from Meridian, Mississippi.

Turner was friends with an Alabama high school coach, and he suggested stopping off to see him to inquire about any talented players in the area.

Turns out there was a big kid, a raw talent, at Noxubee County High School in Macon, Mississippi. Yates and Turner dropped by to see him.

The player's uncle was the band director, and the coach had just plucked the kid out of the marching band. He had grown seven inches over the summer and entered his sophomore year six foot six. But he had never played organized basketball.

"He runs the floor like a deer," the coach said. The kid's name was Cedric Glover.

Glover played the drums and trumpet. He had cousins who had received music scholarships to college, and that was the path he was following.

William Triplett was the school's basketball coach, and he also happened to have Glover in his history class. Every day, he talked to Glover about trying out for the team. "I'm coming, I'm coming," Glover would tell him. But he never did show up.

One day, Triplett walked Glover to the gym after class and had him watch practice. Glover expressed interest and said he'd start the next day. He didn't. A few days later, the coach again walked Glover to the gym—and this time he had practice gear waiting for him.

"There was no getting out of it," Glover said. "So I actually got dressed to be a part of a team I had no intention of being a part of. I didn't have a clue about any of the rules. I didn't understand basketball, but I could run a little faster and jump a little higher than other guys."

The UC coaches followed his progress and recruited Glover hard. But so did powerhouses like Houston, Louisville, and Georgetown. All those schools suggested he redshirt as a freshman. Yates told him he'd have the chance to play right away at UC; plus, Glover had relatives in Cincinnati. He signed with the Bearcats.

Yates says Glover was "the worst basketball player in the United States" when he arrived at UC.

"He was big and strong, but he didn't know how to play," Yates said. "He had bad hands. He would travel all the time. He was a very sensitive kid. Not a lot of confidence."

A knee injury forced Glover to sit out his junior season, which gave him time to mature and get stronger. Glover was first-team all-Metro Conference in 1988 and '89.

"He came a long way," Yates said. "He worked very hard and became an excellent player for us."

"Sitting out really, really helped me develop my body physically, helped me get stronger, helped me learn more about basketball," Glover said. "When I look back on it, coming into the university, I should have redshirted. All those other schools that were recruiting me were right. I needed to develop more.

"Everything I earned and gained was due to hard work. I put in a lot of time in the weight room and did what I needed to do to get better. I put on my hardhat every day and I came to work and that was pretty much it for me."

THANKS TO BENCH, ROSE & CO.

Who would have known that the star basketball player from Camden, New Jersey, was such a big Cincinnati Reds fan?

Lou Banks's father loved the "Big Red Machine" and talked about them all the time. He took his son to see the Reds when they were in Philadelphia to play the Phillies.

So when the University of Cincinnati came calling in 1986, Banks felt it was the place to be. He chose UC over Louisville, Temple, and Rutgers and was the fifth-leading scorer in school history when he left.

"When I came on my recruiting visit, I had a great time and already liked the Reds, so it seemed like it was a fit for me," Banks said.

WHERE IS EVERYBODY?

The play was not designed specifically for him. But Vic Carstarphen, a six-foot-one freshman, found himself with the ball as the clock was running out. "I played high school ball with Lou Banks. He said, 'Listen, if it comes to you, take the shot.' That's all I remember," Carstarphen said.

So Carstarphen drove the lane and hit a running 12-foot jumper from just inside the foul line with 10 seconds remaining. That gave UC a one-point lead against Morehead State on December 2, 1988. He would help force a turnover and lay in another basket at the buzzer.

Four points in 10 seconds. The Bearcats won 67-64 at the Cincinnati Gardens.

So how did he get treated afterward? Well, by the time he finished postgame interviews and got dressed, he discovered the team had left the building.

"I really didn't understand the whole leaving on the bus thing," Carstarphen said. "We would have to catch vans back and forth (from campus). I guess everybody left. I remember thinking, 'I hit the game-winning shot and now I'm stuck.' I thought it was a joke actually. I thought it was a freshman joke."

News Record reporter Rodney McKissic ended up driving Carstarphen back to campus.

"I remember Vic walking outside and looking around for the vans, but they were all gone," McKissic said. "I said, 'I think they left you, need a ride?' It was so funny. The guy just won the game for the team and they left him at the arena."

Carstarphen transferred to Temple after the season. He would return to Cincinnati and play at Shoemaker Center as a senior in December 1992. But that didn't turn out to be a pleasant experience. A.D. Jackson fell on Carstarphen while the two went after a loose ball, and Carstarphen broke his left leg in two places.

"I came back in the NCAA Tournament at the end of that year," Carstarphen said. "But I was not 100 percent."

LOU'S GOT A BOARD

UC had just returned from a road trip to Tampa, where the Bearcats lost 82-65 to South Florida, whose six-foot-seven center Hakim Shahid finished with 14 points and 20 rebounds.

The Bearcats were in the locker room before practice December 14, 1988. Miami University was next on the schedule. And Banks and Glover got into an argument.

Glover, the six-foot-eight, 235-pound team captain and the biggest and strongest Bearcat, was telling the UC perimeter players that if they had played better defense, the Bearcats might have fared better against South Florida. USF guards Andre Crenshaw and Radenk Dobras combined for 39 points, 12 rebounds and nine assists.

"What are you talking about?" responded Banks, 6-6, 195 pounds, who had totaled just two points in the game. He pointed out that Glover's man was unstoppable on the boards. South Florida had outrebounded UC, 61-40.

They began to fight. Glover grabbed Banks and dragged his head across the locker-room floor.

"I was the captain of the team," said Glover, who played the South Florida game with the flu and finished with 12 points and five rebounds in 25 minutes. "With every team, there's going to be a guy that for some reason doesn't want to follow the program. He just happened to be that guy. I was the policeman. I was the disciplinarian. I dragged him around. I made him a part of the locker-room decorations. He got a good whipping that day."

Banks was furious.

"He took my face and dragged me on the carpet," Banks said. "I didn't appreciate that. I didn't think because he was bigger he should've been trying to bully me."

Banks left the locker room and went outside. "I didn't collect myself," he said. The first thing he saw was a four-foot-long board with several nails sticking out of it at the Shoemaker Center construction site.

Banks came into the Armory Fieldhouse waving the board in the air and yelling. The players were warming up before practice. Banks headed straight for Glover.

"Lou's got a board!" Yates reportedly yelled.

"Buddy, bring it on," Glover shouted at Banks.

Assistant coach Ken Turner and Yates stopped Banks.

"I was just really hot that day," Banks said. "Yeah, I would've hit him if they wouldn't have grabbed me, because he manhandled me in that locker room. I probably would've hit a couple of those other guys for not helping me."

Banks said he was mad at Glover for "about 10 days." Fifteen years later, the two laugh about the incident.

"I'm not embarrassed about it, because it happened," Banks said. "When I look at now, I'm thinking, yeah, that's crazy, but at that time I was very angry because of the way that he did me. It is funny now. It didn't last very long. I never hold a grudge against a guy."

"It just kind of diffused," Glover said. "It's a big joke now. But at that time, we were in the heat of battle. It just exploded all at once. Once that episode happened, everybody kind of fell in line. And I kind of developed a reputation not only in the locker room, but throughout the football team ... and the entire athletic dorm."

SO LONG, FAREWELL . . .

Glover's senior night was anything but memorable.

Sure, his parents were at the Cincinnati Gardens for his final home game—against South Carolina—and they were on the court before the game with their son, who received a nice ovation.

But Glover was hurt and couldn't play. He had sprained his left ankle at Virginia Tech on February 18 and had not played in three games. Still, Yates wanted him to make an appearance, so he started and played about two minutes. He had no shots, no rebounds, no nothing. He finished 49 points shy of joining the 1,000-point club.

"I'm out there just barely limping around," Glover said. "That's how it ended. It was kind of a downer. But you know what? I developed so many relationships with people associat-

ed with the university, so many relationships with people you
cherish off the court."

HOW IT ENDED

The way the Tony Yates era came to an end somewhat
surprised the coach and some of the players.

"We kind of heard rumors, but we didn't pay attention
to them," Andre Tate said. "We were kind of shocked when it
happened."

UC finished 15-12 in 1988-89 and won four of its last
five games, including a 77-71 upset of No. 14-ranked Louisville
at Freedom Hall. When the season ended, Yates didn't hear a
word from first-year Athletic Director Rick Taylor. Yates had
one year left on his contract.

Around 2 p.m., the day of the team's postseason banquet, Taylor called Yates to his office. Even then, Yates said, he
didn't know what was coming. Taylor told him he was making
a change. "I was caught by surprise," Yates said. "You have a
winning season, you don't expect anything like that to happen.

"I told him, 'This is a helluva time for you to do that.
It's not very fair to me, and it's not very fair for the kids.' We
conducted the banquet as if nothing ever happened."

After the banquet, held in the student union, Yates told
his players in an emotional meeting. Taylor told the media in
his office. Yates did not speak to reporters that night.

He never coached again.

"I was very philosophical about it," he said. "It's just a fact
of life that there are certain times you move on, no matter what
you're doing. It was time to move on. I had my life to live. The
worst thing you can do in life is hang on and brood about those
kinds of things.

"I didn't want to coach anymore. I had my fling. I did
what I wanted to do. I wanted to coach at the University of

Cincinnati. I'm very pleased, very blessed, and very happy about what we had done. There were a lot of very special moments with a lot of special people. There are a lot of great, great memories."

10

BOB HUGGINS ERA (1989-2005)

THERE'S A NEW SHERIFF IN TOWN

The new coach called a 3 p.m. meeting with his players. It was held in Laurence Hall because the new basketball office in Shoemaker Center wasn't ready.

Bob Huggins waited while some guys sauntered in around 3:15. Others strolled in at 3:30.

"Then he just went off," Keith Starks said.

The Bearcats were not just introduced to their new leader, they were treated to a display of, uh, colorful language and verbal assaults the likes of which they were unaccustomed to.

"If this is how you think it's going to be, pack up your stuff and go back to where you came from," Huggins shouted. "I will win with walk-ons."

It was April 1989.

"You can't run a business that way," Huggins recalled, almost 15 years later. "You can't have people sitting around

A 37-year-old Bob Huggins (left) and Dick Vitale take part in the show during UC's Midnight Madness festivities in October 1990. (Photo by David Baxter/University of Cincinnati)

waiting for other people to show up. We start meetings on time. We start practices on time. We leave on time. It could've been the first day, it could've been the 10th day, the message wasn't going to change: Be where you're supposed to be."

He wasn't just talking about basketball; he was talking about life.

Some guys took him seriously, some guys didn't.

Lou Banks and Elnardo Givens didn't. Banks eventually came around; Givens, UC's only point guard and the team MVP the previous season, didn't. He was kicked off the team in September 1989 for missing classes.

"That got everyone's attention," Starks said. He told teammates: "This guy's for real. He's not going to take any crap from anybody."

The players didn't exactly go out of their way to see Huggins that summer. Quite simply, some were a little afraid.

Huggins asked players what were the problems with the program. Of all things, they mentioned the old uniforms and mismatched warmups. "That was easy to fix," Huggins said. He asked them to design new uniforms. He ordered new practice gear. He wanted a fresh start. UC had not been to the NCAA Tournament since 1977—12 long years.

Starks, Banks, Levertis Robinson and Andre Tate were the only returning scholarship players. Michael Joiner and Tarrice Gibson, Huggins's first high school recruits, were freshmen.

"Our first day of practice was hell," Starks said. "We had never practiced that hard, ever. Guys were throwing up, falling down.

"This is what you have to do to win," Huggins told them.

"We had heard certain stories about Coach Huggins," Robinson said. "We had heard he was tough, which is true, but the toughness was not as it was categorized. He was a very level-headed coach and he was passionate about the game. He pretty much let us be young men. The enthusiasm that he had is what really set the tone for me."

"He honestly believed we could win a national championship his first year there," Starks said. "And he made us believe it."

HE SAID IT AND HE MEANT IT

Huggins did believe UC could win a national championship. "If I didn't, I don't know who would," he said.

And he wasn't afraid to let the world know what he expected. In the press conference when he was introduced as UC's new coach, Huggins made it clear that his goals were annual Final Four appearances and an NCAA title.

"We want to win right now," he said the day his hiring was announced. "I don't want to cheat people. If you say you're on a five-year plan, you're basically asking for an excuse to lose."

He never regretted setting the bar so high.

"That's what you play for," Huggins said. "I thought coming in here the Metro (Conference) was a great league. At that time it was. Louisville had won a national championship (in 1986). If you could get to the top of the league and compete with Louisville, you should be able to compete on a national level.

"Some coaching friends said, 'You shouldn't say things like that, people will expect it. Guys get fired for saying things like that.'

"I think the biggest thing we had to change was the work ethic. They didn't really have a strength program, so to speak. They just didn't put the time in for whatever reason. The guys who were here, I thought, were really good. I loved coaching them. There just weren't many of them."

Didn't matter.

UC upset 20th-ranked Minnesota 66-64 in Huggins's first game and went on to a 20-14 season, including a 1990 National Invitation Tournament bid. In Huggins's third season, Cincinnati was back in the Final Four, just as he had predicted.

LAST-SECOND LOU

He had a broken bone in his left hand. He missed practice the day before the game because he went to see a doctor.

Junior Lou Banks's response was to go out and have a career night against Dayton on December 17, 1989. He scored 31 points, added seven rebounds and made the game-winning shot with two seconds remaining in a 90-88 victory.

"I wasn't so much in pain that night," Banks said. "They had it taped up pretty good. I hit it a couple times, but it wasn't throbbing pain.

"That was one of the first times I had a great game in Shoemaker. All my other good games came on other courts."

Banks came to UC's rescue several times during the 1989-90 season. In addition to the Flyers, he had last-second shots to beat Florida State and Creighton, and he made two free throws against DePaul to send that game into overtime.

"I was the captain," he said. "It was my team, so I wanted the ball at the critical times and they wanted to give it to me."

His best game probably came his senior year, when the Bearcats upset No. 11 Southern Mississippi 86-72 at Shoemaker Center. Banks finished with 23 points, nine rebounds and a career-high nine assists. He had averaged just 11.7 points in the previous nine games.

IN FOR THE LONG HAUL

Tarrice Gibson was not the first player to sign with UC after Huggins became coach; that was Michael Joiner (May 1989). But Gibson, who signed a month after Joiner, was Huggins's first four-year player.

Gibson is from Dothan, Alabama, in the southeast corner of the state (population 60,000). Dothan is known as the "Peanut Capital of the World." Gibson really wanted to go to Georgetown—a basketball power in the 1980s under coach John Thompson—but the Hoyas instead signed another guard. Gibson felt that other schools backed off him because they thought he was headed to Georgetown.

Florida State offered him a chance to walk on. But Gibson verbally committed to Howard Community College in Big Spring, Texas.

Cincinnati entered the picture late in Gibson's senior year, 1989. His recruiting trip to Cincinnati was his first airplane ride, and assistant coach John Loyer and Keith Starks met Gibson at the airport.

"As soon as I met Keith, Lou (Banks), and Andre (Tate), I was sold," Gibson said. "The first time I saw Lou, he said,

'We've got to put some muscles on you, little fella.' They called me 'Bama. I went back home, and a week later I signed."

The Howard coaches told him: If you have the chance to play at UC, go for it.

"What Lou, Andre, Keith and Levertis (Robinson) did in 1989 was the best thing that ever could've happened to me," Gibson said. "You've got Lou the hardass, Andre the consummate professional, Levertis the minister of defense, and Keith the workhorse. They taught me everything they knew. Andre's leadership, Lou's tenacity, Keith's will not to give up. Levertis was mild tempered; nothing ever rattled Levertis.

"They laid the foundation for the family."

FAMILY MATTERS

Gibson arrived in Cincinnati with some clothes in a brown paper bag on September 16, 1989. He remembers the date. He owned next to nothing.

Loyer picked him up at the airport and dropped him off on campus. Tate was going to his mailbox in the dorm. "'Dre, I've got your new teammate right here," Loyer said. "Take care of him."

Tate and a female friend took Gibson to K-Mart and bought him sheets, a pillow and blanket. Banks took him to a bank and gave him $10 to open an account. "I didn't have a dime to my name," Gibson said.

All of this is why, 25 years after he came to town, Gibson lives in Cincinnati, keeps in touch with numerous former players from the Huggins era and offers advice to new players who need it.

"That's what we do as a family, we try to go above and beyond the call of duty for each other," Gibson said. "I talk to every teammate that I had at the University of Cincinnati more than I talk to my biological brother and sisters. My four years at UC were the best years of my entire life."

Tarrice Gibson brought tremendous energy and aggressive play off the bench as the Bearcats' top reserve during the team's run to the 1992 NCAA Final Four. Gibson currently ranks eighth at UC with 150 career steals. (Photo by University of Cincinnati/ Sports Information)

WHAT'S IN A NAME?

UC fans probably know Gibson by the name "Tarrance"—which he insists is not his name. He should know, right?

Gibson said a guidance counselor from Northview High School misspelled his name on a form that went to UC. Then UC referred to him as Tarrance in all publications for the next four years.

"It never bothered me," he said. "I thought it was cool that they were renaming me. But it bothered my grandma. I went to (sports information director) Tom Hathaway once and told him, 'That's not the spelling and my grandma doesn't like it.' Tom told me that I needed to bring my birth certificate to show him the spelling of my name. I thought, you think I'm going to lie about my name? I said, 'Forget it.'"

To be fair, Gibson signed his name as "Tarrance," was referred to that way by almost everyone and never complained to UC officials until just before his senior season—too late to make changes in various publications. He finds the confusion somewhat amusing.

Now, he said, he signs all business papers "Tarrice." He is known in Cincinnati by Tarrance, Tarrice and T-Rat, his nickname. "I answer to every one of them," he said.

BREAKTHROUGH RECRUIT

Perhaps the most important recruit in the Huggins's era was Herb Jones, a two-time junior college All-American at Butler County (Kansas) Community College.

"He was a great player," Huggins said. "I thought what we had to do was win, and I thought Herbert was probably the best guy out there that we could get to win."

UC was the first school trying hard to sign him, and that was important to Jones. When Oklahoma coach Billy Tubbs

made a late run for Jones, showing him Final Four and conference championship rings, Jones remained loyal to Cincinnati.

"Huggs came out (to Kansas) and was showing me the
system," Jones said. "I thought I'd fit in. I don't really know
how I was sold. All my friends were saying, 'Why do you want
to go to Cincinnati? You can go anywhere.'"

The six-foot-four Jones was relatively quiet. He stayed
to himself at first more than he hung out with teammates. He
mostly went to class, practice and the cafeteria. But on the
court, it didn't take long for him to make an impression.

"Herb was the real deal," Starks said. "No one could stop
him. Nobody was as strong as him on the block. He was quick
off the floor. We always thought Levertis could jump high.
They had classic battles. If Herb was 6-10, he would've been
(national) player of the year (in 1992)."

"I had never seen anybody that small be able to play down
low the way he did and score in all kinds of ways," Anthony
Buford said. "There's no question he didn't get his due nationally. I think he got his due on our team."

And within the program.

UC coaches would use the fact that they signed the
National Junior College Player of the Year to help land more
top junior college players in the next recruiting class.

"If you would ask Huggs: 'Who's the guy who turned the
program around?' He'd tell you Herb," former assistant coach
Steve Moeller said. "He was the first high-profile guy."

"I didn't really think of it like that at that time," Jones
said, "but that's what people said later, that I broke the recruiting barrier."

Jones was an Associated Press honorable mention All-
American in 1992. UC's previous AP honorable mention All-
American was Robert Miller in 1978.

CHANGE OF ADDRESS

Following Anthony Buford's second season at the University of Akron, his coach, Bob Huggins, accepted the head coaching position at the University of Cincinnati. After Huggins took the job, he returned to Akron to meet with each player. Right away, Buford wanted to know whether there was a spot for him at UC.

"He was who I trusted," Buford said. "The only reason I went to play basketball at Akron was because of Bob Huggins."

Privately, Huggins told people he wanted Buford with him in Cincinnati. But he didn't want it to appear as if he was raiding the Akron program. He encouraged Buford to stay put, saying he didn't know what the situation at UC would be like. Buford was on pace to become Akron's No. 2 all-time scorer; he would have 1,400 points after three seasons.

The players lobbied for assistant coach Steve Moeller, who ended up joining Huggins at UC, to get the Akron job. But instead the school chose Coleman Crawford, who had worked under Huggins, then spent a year as an assistant at Tennessee.

Suffice it to say, Buford did not get along with Crawford for a variety of reasons. Buford would tell Huggins how unhappy he was, but Huggins couldn't say anything in response. When his junior season ended, Buford told Huggins: "I'm not playing my senior year at Akron. I am transferring down there (to UC) whether you like it or not."

Every award Buford earned from his last season at Akron he threw in the trash.

Akron's spring classes ended in May. Buford headed right for Cincinnati. He would have to sit out one year, then would have only one season of eligibility to play for the Bearcats.

That was fine with him.

THE EXAMPLE

Buford had surgery on his right knee in late March 1990, after Akron's season ended. When he arrived in Cincinnati two months later, he could only walk around. No running. No basketball.

His first day on campus, he met some of the players for the first time. Tate, who had just completed his college career, immediately said, "Let's play one on one."

"I can't," Buford said.

But as soon as he did start working out and playing pick-up games, the holdover Bearcats began testing the new guy.

"I finally realized what was going on," Buford said. "When he first came to UC, all Huggs talked about was how tough his former players were. He used me a whole lot as an example. So these guys had heard a lot about me, and now here I am in the flesh and they all wanted to find out firsthand. They were going at me like you can't imagine.

"*I'm* kind of in the mindset that I've played three years of college basketball and I don't have to prove anything to anybody. And I know physically I'm not ready. But they did not like me. You could hear them on the side, saying, 'He ain't all that. Huggs is full of it.'"

Tate, Robinson and Starks—all recruited to UC by Tony Yates—were the main culprits.

"When Buford got there, everybody did want a piece of him," Tate said. "Huggs had built him up to be a tough guy. We had heard so much about him. And we didn't back down from anybody."

"We were a very tight group," Robinson said. "Buford was kind of like an outsider."

Finally, one day, Buford served notice: "Do what you need to do right now because this doesn't mean anything. When the season starts and I'm healthy, I'm going to kill all of you."

The response: Yeah, whatever.

Buford knew Huggins's offense better than anyone on the team. Tate, a graduate assistant that season, also knew the offense well and practiced sometimes with the Bearcats. Together, they posed problems for the starters.

It wasn't until later that Buford would become friendly with some of the players.

He even got into fights with Robinson during practice. One day, while going for a loose ball, Buford caught Robinson with an elbow. Robinson, a second-degree black belt in Tae Kwon Do, responded with a quick punch to Buford's jaw.

"I started to retaliate, then I realized who it was," Buford said. "Being a little bit smart, I decided not to take it any further."

"That's what happens in the heat of battle," Robinson said. "The way our practices went, you couldn't expect anything but that."

THE CALIFORNIA KIDS

Southern California, 1990.

"I didn't know anything about Cincinnati," Corie Blount said. "I didn't even know they had a basketball program."

"All I knew was WKRP," Terry Nelson said. "I didn't even know Oscar Robertson went here."

"I knew about the Big O, but that was a long time ago," Erik Martin said. "I knew Cincinnati didn't do anything in the last decade that would jog my memory."

Such was the mindset of three junior-college recruits being pursued by the University of Cincinnati.

The main targets were Nelson from Long Beach College and Blount from Rancho Santiago. Moeller had recruited the state of California as an assistant at Rice and Texas earlier in his career. In July 1990, he went to the West Coast to see Nelson and Blount.

It was during that trip, at a summer-league game at Cerritos College, that Nelson had what is probably the best game of his life. "I was like 16 of 17 from the field," Nelson said. "I scored 34 points, had a couple dunks. Moe went back and told Huggs: 'This guy's a player. He can score, he's tough, he can rebound and he can defend.'"

It was also during that trip, at an open gym at Rancho Santiago, that coach Dana Pagett told Moeller: "I've got a guy who's better than Corie." The player was Erik Martin, who had left TCU after the 1989-90 season and was to play for Rancho Santiago.

Moeller recruited all three. Junior college players typically didn't sign letters of intent until the spring, but the Cincinnati coaches—in just their second year in Clifton—wanted to secure these three in November.

Nelson and Blount, who knew each other from summertime games, took their recruiting visits together in October. Nelson, who had signed with Cal State-Fullerton out of high school, wanted to leave California. He was the easiest to sell.

"I told Corie the first night in Cincinnati I was coming," Nelson said. "I said I know what I want. If you come, we've got a chance to go to the Final Four. I just liked the chemistry of the guys. We had a good time. I fell in love. I knew this was a place I could settle down and do some fishing. I told Huggs the next day. I don't think he took me seriously."

Blount still wanted to take a trip to Tennessee. He was also considering UNLV and Utah.

After Nelson and Blount returned from UC with good reports, Martin decided he wanted to take a visit to Cincinnati, too. However, he did not want to sign until the spring. His father Edward even told the UC coaches that.

Well, Huggins responded, then Erik has eliminated himself because we need commitments now. Moeller repeated that message to the family.

Eventually, Martin's father called to say his son had changed his mind. Sorry, Huggins said. "The only way I'll bring him in on an official visit is if he comes in here and likes it, he signs without going anywhere else."

Which, of course, is what happened. Then Martin went to work on Blount. "Just imagine, the three of us can go there and turn it around," he'd say.

Blount took a recruiting trip to Utah. Finally, he, too, committed to the Bearcats.

"I told all my friends I was going to Cincinnati with Erik and Terry," Blount said. "My friends didn't even know where Cincinnati was. They were saying, 'That ain't no basketball school.'"

The three California Kids signed in November 1990.

They came to Cincinnati together the following summer, driving in a rented Plymouth Sundance. It took them four days to cross the country.

"We were the California Connection," Blount said. "We felt the hype when we started playing in the summer league (at Purcell Marian High School). Then Nick (Van Exel) came later. … It took off from there."

SETTING A TONE

Early in the summer of '91, some Bearcats played pick-up games at Shoemaker Center—and some did not. Herb Jones played over at Xavier. Some guys rarely played at all.

Huggins returned from a trip out of town and heard all this. He summoned the team to a racquetball court on Shoemaker Center's lower level, then turned out the lights.

He proceeded to blast each and every player, including Buford.

Said Blount: "I'm looking at Erik and he's looking at me, like, man, it's true what they say, this dude is crazy. That did it. We were playing together in the gym all the time after that."

It was during that meeting, Nelson said, that he told everyone he thought his junior college team was successful because the players did everything together.

"If we went to the store, we went together," Nelson said. "Our motto was togetherness. They looked at me like I was crazy and started laughing and making jokes out of it. They thought it was funny, but it soon became our theme. Everything we did from that point, we did together."

"COACH" BUFORD

Herb Jones, Tarrice Gibson, Allen Jackson and Anthony Buford were already in town. Nick Van Exel arrived from Trinity Valley Junior College in Texas. The California Kids— Corie Blount, Terry Nelson and Erik Martin—came from the West Coast.

This collection of players from all over the country started bonding months before the magical 1991-92 season was to start.

Buford watched the talent and felt, if the chemistry was right, if everyone was "on the same page," if the guys could handle Huggins, there was potential for something special.

So he started coaching. He'd warn his teammates old and new about what they would experience with Huggins, how at times he'd be uptight, how there were times the players would not be able to do anything right. "He's going to cuss you out and say crazy things," Buford said. "Don't pay attention to how it's being delivered, just listen to the message."

Buford would gather guys in his apartment and ball up pieces of paper and try to explain the offenses, the defensive presses. Whatever he could show them about Huggins's system, he did.

"Our group trusted each other," Nelson said. "When Anthony said something to me, I didn't get defensive thinking that he was trying to coach me. I just thought he was helping me. I figured whatever he could teach me would get me to play sooner. Everybody wanted to win."

There was tremendous basketball IQ among the group. They really understood the game. By the time preseason practices started, the coaches were able to move through plays quicker and work on more advanced offenses and defenses.

"They were ahead," Huggins said. "I don't know how much ahead. The important thing is we had guys that were leading and guys that were helping. I think their understanding of what was supposed to happen was a lot better."

SHORT RESISTENCE

Blount did not want to lift weights when he got to UC, and he did anything he could to get out of it. "You recruited me to play basketball, you didn't recruit me to be a body builder," he would tell Huggins.

After he missed a few weightlifting sessions, there was a knock on his apartment door at 4:30 a.m. It was Huggins.

"Get your ass up," he said.

He took Blount to the Armory Fieldhouse and had him running. Several miles.

"I did that about three times," Blount recalled, "and then I said, 'All right, I'm going to start lifting.'"

STARTING OFF WITH A THUD

Not many Division I teams lose preseason exhibition games. But that's what happened to kick off the 1991-92 season.

Athletes in Action 82, UC 79.

'Nuf said.

The Bearcats blew a 20-point first-half lead, which prompted Huggins to tell the media afterward: "If I were playing miniature golf with my mother, I'd want to bury her. You can't stop. You've got to keep playing. ... We're not very good right now. But we will be good. This is a great lesson for us."

After listening to a Huggins tirade in the locker room for a half hour after the game, many of the players stayed put for another two or three hours. It was that night the Bearcats put their team goals in writing:

- Work hard every day in practice
- Leave the attitude at the door
- Finish 23-4
- Win the Great Midwest Conference regular-season title
- Win the GMC tournament title
- Go to the Elite Eight of the NCAA Tournament

This was a program that had not gone to the NCAA Tournament in 15 years.

HIT ME WITH YOUR BEST SHOT

Before Martin begins, he cautions: "Huggs is going to try to change the way this story goes."

Now you know it's going to be good.

It was early in the 1991-92 season, and—this is important to know—Martin felt he was in Huggins's doghouse. So naturally, he was mad at Huggins, too.

The first official practice, Martin knew he wasn't in the best shape. Still, he felt everyone was struggling. But when Huggins called the players in for a huddle, he got all over Martin. "He pretty much cursed me out for about five minutes. I had a real bad practice that day. Everything was new as far as drills and all that. I kept thinking, why is he picking on me? Corie and Nick didn't have a great practice, either. It wasn't so much that he was singling me out, but he felt like I had more in me than I was giving that day."

During practice another day, a Bearcat drove for a layup and the defender didn't bother to take a charge. That, of course, enraged Huggins.

"That's it," the coach shouted. "We're going to do the charge drill. I'm going to take the charge. Now who wants to go first?"

Martin was prepared to flatten any teammate who did not let him get to the front of the line. "I was going first," Martin said. "I was going to run over Huggs."

He took one dribble. Two dribbles. Then Martin picked up the ball, put his head down and started running at Huggins "like a football player."

"And Huggs turns," Martin said with a grin. "He takes the charge, but he'll swear to this day he stood in there. He turned his body, man. He knew I was going to plow through him. I knocked him down, ripped his pants a little. Then he got up and said, 'That's the way you take a charge. Now go shoot free throws.' He stopped the drill right there. At first, he was going to take a charge on everyone on the team. After he got up, he went and talked to the trainer."

"He thinks that's really funny," Huggins said. Then turning serious, he added, "But I think that's good. Then they understand that I've never asked them to do anything I would not do."

HIGHS AND LOWS

If Michigan State had recruited Buford out of Flint (Michigan) Central High School, he would've seriously considered joining the Spartans. But Buford heard that then-coach Jud Heathcote told people he was too small.

So when it was time for the Bearcats to play at Michigan State on December 21, 1991, Buford was "all jacked up." Close to 20 friends and family members were in the stands. The Spartans were ranked No. 12 in the nation. Both teams were unbeaten. "Don't hurt us too bad," Heathcote said to Buford before the game.

"He really had no idea what was coming," Buford said. "I was hot when I stepped off the plane, and it never stopped."

It was the eighth game of Buford's UC career, and it was one of his best. He scored 29 points on eight-of-14 shooting. The Bearcats were ahead by 18 with 12:30 remaining.

Everything was going so well. Until the end.

UC led by just two points in the final seconds. Buford ran to double-team one of the Spartans and left his man wide open. The pass went to MSU reserve guard Kris Weshinskey in the corner, and he nailed a three-pointer with 4.6 seconds left. "That mistake probably cost us the game," Buford said.

The Bearcats had one final possession. Buford had the ball, got inside the foul line, a mere 12 feet from the basket, launched the kind of jump shot he had practiced all the time in high school and ... the ball hit the rim and bounced away.

Michigan State 90, UC 89.

"We got exactly the shot we wanted," Huggins said afterward.

"I went through a range of emotions," Buford said. "I felt so good at the beginning of the game and so bad at the end."

It was after that game that Huggins took off his Rolex watch and hurled it at a blackboard in the locker room, breaking the blackboard and watch. Little diamonds fell onto the floor. Nobody moved, then he said: "I hope you all have a miserable Christmas."

WHO'S GOT MY BACK?

After two days off, the team returned for a Christmas Day practice that lasted five hours.

A few days later, during another intense practice, Huggins got upset with Gibson and told him to get off the court.

"No," Gibson said. "This is my team."

He gave the ball to A.D. Jackson and told him to start running a play. "A.D., pick up the ball," Huggins said. "Tarrance, get off the floor."

Gibson wouldn't leave. Huggins was getting angrier. Jackson didn't know what to do. Martin whispered to Blount: "If he gets into it with Tarrance, we're going to jump him."

"We weren't really going to do it, but we were getting our nerve up to say something to him," Blount said.

"C'mon A.D., let's go," Gibson yelled.

"OK, I'm going to say it one more time," Huggins shouted, "If Tarrance doesn't get off the floor, we're going to put the balls away and we're going to run for the next three hours."

Herb Jones looked at Huggins, then at Gibson. "Tarrance, you've got to get off the floor, man! You've got to go."

"We weren't about to run for anybody," Blount said.

Gibson left the court, and the players started laughing.

QUICK EXIT

Nelson felt like he had some good practices leading up to UC's January 8 game at Tennessee, whose star player was Allan Houston. Early in the game, Nelson told some teammates: "I can feel it; I'm going to have a great game today." He was thinking four or five charges, seven or eight rebounds.

Huggins called his name, and Nelson jumped off the bench and pulled off his warmups. He always wore elbow pads, which were pulled down when he was on the bench. Nelson was going to inbound the ball and figured he'd do that, then pull up his elbow pads.

Well, his teammate took the pass and threw the ball right back to him. The Tennessee defender was hand-checking Nelson, pushing at his hip, and Nelson's foot moved. He was called for traveling.

Huggins immediately yanked Nelson after a three-second appearance.

"I didn't even have time to pull my elbow pad up," Nelson said. "Corie was coming to get me and he's cracking up laughing. That's all I played the whole game."

His name didn't even show up in the official box score in the newspaper the next day.

THE GUARANTEE

UC had just beaten Alabama-Birmingham 76-52 on January 25, 1992, at Shoemaker Center, and Nelson was in the hallway outside the media room with former *Cincinnati Post* reporter Bill Koch, who was asking about the Bearcats' next game—against Xavier.

"How do you think you guys are going to do in the Crosstown Shootout?" Koch asked.

"Xavier doesn't have a chance," Nelson said. "We should blow them out."

The next day, Nelson's phone started ringing around 7:30 a.m. A few radio stations wanted him to do live interviews. He was half asleep, answering questions about Xavier and making jokes. He loved the attention.

Of course, he had not seen a newspaper yet.

The phone rang again. Nelson was thinking it was another interview request.

"Get your ass in my office in five minutes." It was Huggins calling from his cell phone.

When Nelson arrived, Huggins was sitting behind his desk with his glasses on. "Any time he has his glasses on, that means he's been up all night watching tape," Nelson said.

"How does a guy, who averages three points and two rebounds, have the nerve to make predictions that we're going to blow somebody out?" Huggins asked.

He held up the newspaper. Nelson's mouth dropped open. He started making excuses, claiming the interview was off the record. It wasn't, of course.

"Why would you even say something so stupid?" Huggins said. "Now you're going to give them bulletin board material. You're going to fire them up. I don't even think we're good enough to beat these guys."

Reporters in town were waiting for the Bearcats before practice. Van Exel started talking about how UC was going to win because Xavier's Aaron Williams and the other post players were soft.

About 30 minutes into practice, Blount twisted his ankle and was carried off the floor.

"There goes our 6-10 post guy getting carted off like a slab of meat and you're saying their post guys are soft!" Huggins yelled.

"You're paranoid," Van Exel shouted back.

Huggins kicked Van Exel out of practice.

Van Exel didn't start the game the next night. Xavier full-court pressed, which worked to UC's advantage. The Bearcats won 93-75.

Afterward, Huggins put him arm around Nelson and said, "Now, why don't you retire undefeated with your predictions?"

IS THE FIX IN?

Huggins rarely got on Herb Jones. Jones was a quiet player who let his game do the talking. He worked on his game constantly and is perhaps one of the most underrated players in school history even though he was an honorable mention All-American in 1992.

UC took a 19-3 record into a February 20, 1992, game against DePaul at The Shoe. The Bearcats had won eight in a row. This night, however, they struggled—and nobody more than Jones, who finished four of 13 from the field with just nine points.

Huggins was ranting and raving in the locker room afterward. Jones sat with his head down.

"I don't know what to think about you," Huggins shouted at Jones. "Are you point shaving, Herb?"

Jones slowly raised his head and looked stunned. "What?" he said.

"It takes a lot to really make me mad," Jones said. "I was fuming mad. I was mad when he said it to me, and I was mad at myself, too. That was probably the worst game of my life. To this day, I don't know why I played so bad. From time to time, I think about that game. That was a real low moment for me."

Several of the players remained in the locker room until 2 a.m. talking. Whatever they said struck a cord. The Bearcats won their next 10 games and didn't lose again until the NCAA Tournament semifinals.

TAKE THAT

Two nights after the DePaul loss, Jones put on a display at South Alabama that even had his teammates shaking their heads.

He scored 17 consecutive points during a four-minute stretch of a 104-78 victory. He finished with 27 points on nine-of-13 shooting to go with eight rebounds.

"I was telling myself I had to play better," Jones said. "I had to do more things to help the team win. I guess I was in a zone. I didn't even know it."

"That was something I couldn't believe," Buford said. "Herb loved playing on the road. He loved those hostile situations. He loved raising up and hitting that three and watching everybody go silent."

YOU'VE GOT TO BE KIDDING?

UC was warming up before its March 7, 1992 game at Memphis when Jones followed a ball that had rolled off the court beyond the baseline. The crowd was close to the court, and when Jones picked up the ball, he came face to face with a rowdy Tigers fan.

"He looked at me, and I said, 'How you doing?'" Jones said.

The man responded by screaming: "F—you. We hate you. You guys are always beating us."

Jones couldn't help it. He started laughing.

As it turns out, the man was right. UC beat Memphis that day 69-59 and would later defeat the Tigers—led by Anfernee Hardaway—in the Great Midwest Tournament and the NCAA Tournament.

A TEXAS (EL PASO) STANDOFF

UC was two victories from the Final Four and meeting Texas-El Paso in the Midwest Regional semifinals in Kansas City. UTEP was unranked; the Bearcats were No. 12 in the country. But the game turned out to be a nail-biter.

Nick Van Exel averaged 12.3 points and 18.3 points during his two seasons at UC. He was third-team Associated Press All-America as a senior in 1993, and was a second-round draft pick of the Los Angeles Lakers. Van Exel played 13 years in the NBA for six teams. He was an All-Star in 1998 and had a career-high 23 assists against Vancouver in January 1997. He finished his NBA career with 12,658 points and 5,777 assists. (Photo by Lisa Ventre/University of Cincinnati)

This didn't help.

Van Exel had picked up a loose ball and fired a pass to a wide-open Jeff Scott, who missed the ball right by the UC basket. It went out of bounds. Huggins started yelling at Van Exel: "Don't pass him the ball anymore. He doesn't want the ball." Van Exel was shouting back: "He was wide open. Shut up." Huggins yanked Van Exel from the game and sat him on the bench.

With two free throws on its next possession, UTEP pulled within 60-57 with 7:44 left.

Blount was getting nervous. "It's getting close again. Let Nick back in the game," he told Huggins.

"(Forget) that!" Van Exel said. "I'm transferring! I'm going to New Mexico State next year."

"That's right," Huggins yelled. "He doesn't want to play. He wants to transfer. He can get out of here right now."

Assistant coach John Loyer kept saying, "I think you need to put Nick back in the game."

"No," Huggins said. "He's not ready."

"I don't care if I go back in the game anyway," Van Exel said.

It was 62-59 with 4:12 remaining. Herb Jones was fouled and went to the line.

Blount, the mediator, was pleading with both parties. "Nick, come on, you've got to get back out there. Will you shut up? ... Huggs, man, talk to him."

"Do you want to play?" Huggins asked Van Exel.

Van Exel didn't say a word. "Let's just go win the game and we'll discuss this afterwards," Huggins said.

Jones missed his first free throw. Van Exel checked back into the game for A.D. Jackson. Jones made his second foul shot to make it 63-59.

UTEP would pull within two points twice in the final minute but couldn't catch the Bearcats.

"We wouldn't have won that game without Nick," Nelson said.

CELEBRITIES UNCENSORED

Gibson wanted a way to remember the experience of going to the NCAA Tournament, so he asked a friend and former roommate from Cleveland whether he could borrow his video camera to record a sendoff at Shoemaker Center.

The friend didn't see the video camera again until that summer.

"It never left my hand," Gibson said. "I had that camera the entire tournament."

In the final minutes of UC's Midwest Regional final victory over Memphis in Kansas City, Gibson asked a student manager to go to the locker room to get the camera.

"I wanted to film the moment," Gibson said. "He brought it back with about 50 seconds left. I went up to Huggs after the game was over and said, 'How do you feel about going to the Final Four?'"

"It's a long way from Dothan, ain't it, Tarrance?" Huggins responded with a smile.

Gibson interviewed media members and teammates and kept that up all the way through the Final Four in Minneapolis.

TRASH TALK 101

As national media members descended upon Cincinnati to learn about the upstart Bearcats, six-foot-five Terry Nelson kept getting questions about how he was going to guard 6-9 Chris Webber, Michigan's star player who was also 20-some pounds heavier.

"My goal is not to let him dunk on me," Nelson said. "I don't know how long it'll last. On the break, that's a different story. But, in the halfcourt, if he gets a rebound, he'll be laying on the floor before he dunks on me."

Nelson and Webber had never met—until right before the NCAA semifinals.

The UC players were shooting free throws and Webber came right up next to Nelson on the foul line. "Aren't you the one who said you're going to take me out? That I'm not dunking on you?"

"That's right," Nelson said.

"Man, don't you know this is your last game?" Webber said.

"No, this is *your* last game," Nelson replied.

The banter continued and included other players.

Webber kind of smirked and went back to the other side of the court.

Once the game started, Webber struck first with a half-hook shot over Nelson for the first points. Buford missed a three-pointer on UC's next possession. Webber rebounded it, then tried to dribble. Nelson stole the ball just above the top of the three-point arc and went in for an uncontested dunk. The game was tied 2-2.

As he ran back down the court, Nelson bumped Webber and said, "Now it's your turn."

"He said, 'Oh, you got me that time,'" Nelson said. "We talked the entire game. Normally, any team that talked trash to us, we got them out of their game. They were the only team that talked trash and won."

Afterward, Webber—who finished with 16 points and 11 rebounds—gave Nelson a hug and said, "You all are fun. Nobody ever talks trash to us. You're a good team. I like you all; let's go hang out."

Michigan won 76-72 before 50,379 at the Hubert H. Humphrey Metrodome in Minneapolis.

Nelson never saw Webber again.

GONE WITH THE WIND

Some of the Bearcats who played on the Final Four team will always feel they were treated as second-class citizens in Minneapolis. By fans. By some national media. By tournament organizers.

"We were treated just like garbage there," Buford said. "We just felt really, really disrespected."

"It's just not right," Huggins said.

The other teams all brought great story lines. There was Indiana and Bob Knight. Duke and Mike Krzyzewski, a former Knight assistant who had perhaps the top program in the country. Michigan and its Fab Five freshmen (Chris Webber, Jalen Rose, Jimmy King, Ray Jackson, Juwan Howard).

UC sports information director Tom Hathaway told Buford about a production meeting with TV representatives who talked about how they were going to present the teams during the telecast. They had met with officials from Duke, Indiana and Michigan—the other teams in the Final Four—to get their OK, but when it came to Cincinnati, Hathaway was told how it was going to be.

"They basically said, 'We're going to show some stuff about Oscar Robertson and we're not going to have much on your team,'" Buford remembers being told. "Hathaway said he was kind of in shock."

All of which is why Buford ending up throwing away the ring he received from the NCAA for being in the Final Four. He said it was silver with a black face that said "NCAA" on it. UC was on the team bus headed back to the airport in Minneapolis. Buford doesn't remember when, but he recalls slipping the ring off his finger and pitching it out of the bus.

"It was a bad vibe," Buford said. "And I felt like my memory of playing in the Final Four is all I need. The ring I got from UC I keep."

STAND BY YOUR MAN

In September 1992, roughly six months after UC's Final Four run, the Bearcats were gearing up for another shot at a national title. Six of the top eight players were returning.

Things were looking good—until the day Huggins called Corie Blount into his office to explain that he was being declared ineligible to play his final year at Cincinnati by the NCAA.

Blount had started his career at Rancho Santiago Junior College in 1988-89. He played four games his first season, then broke a bone in his foot that wouldn't heal. He sat out the rest of that season, then played in 1989-90 and 1990-91. The NCAA considered 1988-89 a full season because it did not recognize medical redshirt years at the junior-college level until January 1992. So when Blount finished one year at UC, he was out of eligibility. UC officials appealed to the NCAA, the governing body of college athletics.

"Huggs said he was behind me 100 percent," Blount said. "Based on the season I already had, of course, I wanted to play, but I wasn't really disappointed. Huggs said I could stay at UC and get my degree. I didn't really have the NBA in my mind back then. I never really could see that I would be a draft pick. I figured I'd have to try out to play somewhere."

In October, the NCAA rejected Blount's appeal and a UC compromise that Blount sit out four games of his senior season. "… We will not stop trying to right this wrong," UC Athletic Director Rick Taylor told *The Cincinnati Enquirer.*

The NCAA did allow Blount to have the opportunity to appeal to an administrative review panel at the NCAA convention in January 1993. While Blount's lawyer hinted at suing the NCAA, he ultimately decided to wait for the review panel to hear the case.

"I really didn't know whether I was going to play again, but I knew I had a good chance," Blount said. "It would've been a shock if they would've said, 'No, you can't play at all this year.'

"Rick (Taylor) was a hard little guy, but he would call me in his office, and I can honestly say he was telling me, 'We're going to do everything we possibly can to help you resolve this problem.' I had a lot of people always telling me, 'Don't worry about it.' That's what made it easier for me."

Meanwhile, the six-foot-10 Blount stayed in school and continued to work out on his own. When the Bearcats were on the road, Chuck Machock would work with Blount on post moves. Blount tried to stay in shape in case a new ruling occurred.

That's what happened.

On January 15, 1993, the day the team was leaving for a game against DePaul in Chicago, Huggins told Blount to come along just in case his eligibility was restored.

In Chicago, the Bearcats had a team meeting to talk about what they wanted their record to be the rest of the way after Blount returned. He was in a hotel room with Van Exel and Martin when Huggins called Blount to his room. "Well, big fella, you're back," Huggins said with a smile, then he gave Blount a hug.

Blount played 28 minutes the next night, coming off the bench for eight points, seven rebounds and five assists. UC won 70-64.

EVERYONE WAS WATCHING

The summer after he left UC, Erik Martin was playing in an NBA summer league game when another player approached him. "Hey man, who's the crazy guy who took his jersey off?" the guy wanted to know.

"That was me, but I ain't crazy," Martin told him. "You just have to know Huggs."

The years may pass, but Martin can't escape the moment on national television when he left the Bearcats' bench in the middle of a game and stripped off his jersey on the way to the locker room. "I try to forget that, but you'd be surprised how many people still say, 'Aren't you the guy who took your jersey off?'"

Be assured, Martin has a sense of humor about it.

So, what did happen?

Cincinnati was playing host to DePaul at Shoemaker Center on January 30, 1993, for a noon game. Martin hated early games. So he was already groggy and in a bad mood when the game started.

But here is what he remembers:

Nick Van Exel threw a pass and a DePaul player tipped it out of bounds. Martin saw the tip and pulled back his hands, letting the ball go. The officials didn't see the deflection and gave DePaul the ball.

"So Huggs took me out," Martin said. "He's screaming, and we're going at each other. Let's just say I said something to him, and he said, 'Go to the locker room!'

"Usually when Huggs said that, you just leave it at that and sit there. That day I got up. I took off my jersey and threw it down. I can remember a fan asking, 'Hey Erik, where ya going?' I just kept walking."

Martin said he went straight into the locker room, got undressed and took a shower. A student manager came in to tell Martin that assistant Steve Moeller said: "Don't go anywhere."

Moeller walked in at the next timeout.

"Where are you going?" he said.

"Back to the dorm," Martin told him.

"No you're not. You're crazy. If you do that, you're off the team," Moeller said.

Soon, another assistant coach, Larry Harrison, came in and echoed that message.

Martin got dressed, sat and waited for halftime. He went into the coaches' locker room and apologized to Huggins. There was a misunderstanding about what Martin had said. Huggins acknowledged that, hugged him and followed him into the locker room. UC was ahead 40-25.

"If coach Mo hadn't come in, in five minutes I probably would've already been at the dorm," Martin said. "When Huggs came in, he said something to me, but to be honest he didn't dwell on that situation at all. He just said, 'You're going to start the second half.'

"My mom and (family) wanted to know what happened. I told people, reporters, fans, that stuff happens in practice all the time. They just happened to have the camera on me as I was walking out of the gym.

"I try not to regret anything I've done in life, but if I had a chance to do that over again, I wouldn't have done it like that. But I'm an emotional person, so if that's what came out that day, that's what was supposed to come out."

YOU OWE ME

UC was in the 1993 East Regional semifinals of the NCAA Tournament against Virginia at the Meadowlands in East Rutherford, N.J. Blount is a California guy who had never been to New York City.

The players were allowed to check out New York during the day, but Blount wanted to see more. Problem was, that night the team had an 11 p.m. curfew because there was a game the next day.

Teammate Mike Harris was from Brooklyn, N.Y., and he took Blount and Darrick Ford home to meet his family. Afterward, the three ran around New York for a while having fun. All of a sudden, they looked at a clock. It was 2 a.m.

The players hurried back to the hotel, walked into the lobby and saw the entire coaching staff sitting there waiting.

Huggins sent Ford and Harris to their rooms. He asked the other coaches to leave.

"Let me tell you something, Corie," Huggins said. "You've got a chance to make more money than anybody on this team.

Coach Huggins was prophetic when he told Corie Blount (44) that he had the potential to earn NBA riches if he was willing to dedicate himself to the game. Blount did, and was taken by the Chicago Bulls in the first round of the 1993 NBA draft. Blount played 11 NBA seasons for the Bulls, Los Angeles Lakers, Cleveland Cavaliers, Phoenix Suns, Golden State Warriors, Philadelphia 76ers, and Toronto Raptors. (Photo by University of Cincinnati/Sports Information)

But you'll be happy going back to Monrovia (California), hanging out with your little gang-banging friends, talking about how I could've done this, I could've done that. You don't understand the opportunity you have right now. We've got an opportunity to do some big things. And instead of you focusing on what we need to do, you're out running around and breaking rules with two young guys.

"Look," Huggins continued, "I'm going to play you tomorrow. But if you don't play your ass off, I'm going to take your ass out as soon as I can."

Blount ended up with 19 points and 11 rebounds in 33 minutes, and the Bearcats won 71-54.

NO PLACE LIKE HOME

Damon Flint remembers the day NCAA officials came to Woodward High School in April 1993 to interview him about his recruitment to Ohio State, the school with which he signed as a high school senior. Flint had hoped to team with Derek Anderson in the Buckeyes' backcourt.

But the NCAA cited the Buckeyes for several violations in recruiting Flint. The most severe: Giving Woodward coach Jimmy Leon $60 for meals and transportation during an October 1991 visit to Columbus. The most petty: Ohio State coach Randy Ayers going to Woodward during a non-contact evaluation period to offer Flint condolences after his mother died in September 1991.

Flint still could have attended Ohio State—if he sat out his freshman year. However, the McDonald's All-American felt he had worked too hard to achieve a high enough standardized test score to be academically eligible.

Flint decided to turn to the hometown school that had been recruiting him as long as he could remember: The

University of Cincinnati. Flint knew Huggins and all the players. He was a frequent visitor to Shoemaker Center.

"I told Huggins I was coming," he said. "I felt welcome."

GETTING THE POINT

Flint was a great scorer in high school, averaging 29.4 points a game as a senior at Woodward. But when he got to UC, Huggins needed him to play point guard as a freshman because there really wasn't a solid playmaker on the roster. Starting point guard Marko Wright broke his foot.

"He's the boss," Flint said. "We didn't have anybody else to do it. But that's the type of player I am. If we win, I'm happy. We won a lot. That was a big sacrifice."

The Bearcats were 99-34 during his four years.

Flint finished his career with 1,316 points and was, at the time, third in career three-point field goals made and third in assists.

He never played point guard in high school but considered himself versatile enough to pull it off in college. "I didn't want to be one dimensional," he said.

Flint played shooting guard most of his last three seasons, but was also a backup point guard.

"I think in the end it was the best thing for Damon," Huggins said. "Because Damon turned out to be a player, not just some guy who stood out there and shot."

With all his offensive talent, Flint said his two most memorable games came on the defensive end.

During his freshman season, he went head to head against California guard Jason Kidd on February 20, 1994, in the 7-Up Shootout in Orlando, Florida The Bearcats lost 89-80, but Flint scored 26 points; Kidd had 22.

In the 1996 NCAA Tournament Southeast Regional semifinals, UC came up against Georgia Tech and its star guard

UC players Damon Flint (3), John Jacobs (55), Curtis Bostic (43), Marko Wright (5) and Mike Harris (32) celebrate after the Bearcats defeated Memphis 68-47 in the championship game of the 1994 Great Midwest Tournament. (Photo by Lisa Ventre/University of Cincinnati)

Stephon Marbury. Flint held Marbury to 15 points on four-of-13 shooting and finished with 18 points, six rebounds and three assists. He was named Player of the Game, and UC won 87-70.

"I was definitely jacked up for that one," Flint said. "That was Marbury's last game. He told me right after the game that he was leaving early for the NBA."

CROSSTOWN LETDOWN

No. 19 UC played rival Xavier, ranked No. 22, at a sold-out Cincinnati Gardens in January 1994.

This would be the only Crosstown Shootout for Cincinnati's Dontonio Wingfield, and it would be a completely forgettable outing for the heralded freshman from Albany, Georgia.

Wingfield sat out the final 7:30 of the first half, and Xavier led 41-31 at intermission. Huggins was yelling at Wingfield in the locker room at halftime.

The Musketeers won 82-76 in overtime that night. Wingfield finished zero of seven from the field in 15 minutes; he barely played in the second half. Jackson Julson started the second half instead of Wingfield, who did not re-enter the game until 7:27 remained. His only two points of the night came on first-half free throws.

"He didn't play well. He hurt us," Huggins said afterward.

THE NON-HANDSHAKE

As it turned out, Wingfield was just a subplot for the evening. The main event was Huggins vs. Xavier coach Pete Gillen.

The context to this is, of course, that Huggins and Gillen were not—how shall we say this?—too fond of each other. The UC-Xavier rivalry may have peaked during this time because of the coaches' dislike for one another.

At some point in the game, Huggins was yelling at one of the officials, when—according to the UC coaches—Gillen looked down the sideline and essentially shouted for Huggins to sit down and shut up.

"I pointed after a few things were said," Huggins said afterward. "They need to coach their team and I'll coach my team."

Gillen said later that Huggins was trying to gain an advantage with the officials and that he was just trying to stick up for his team and "keep the officials from getting intimidated." Huggins said some of the XU assistant coaches started shouting at him during the game.

When the game was over, the Xavier fans rushed the court. As Gillen approached Huggins, the UC coach refused to shake hands. That incensed Gillen.

"If I lost, I would've shaken hands," Gillen said that night.

"I'm not a phony," Huggins countered. "I'm not going to act like everything's all right and shake hands after the game."

The next morning, sitting in his office, Gillen suggested the schools should take a break from playing each other.

"It's just sad, it's a very bitter series," he told *The Cincinnati Enquirer.* "We should definitely play next year, but then we might have to think about a cooling-off period …"

Never happened. Nor did Gillen ever have to coach in another Shootout. He left Xavier after the 1993-94 season to coach at Providence College.

HOW PROPHETIC

Just eight days removed from a devastating loss to Canisius College from Buffalo, N.Y., at Shoemaker Center in the Delta Airlines Classic (the Bearcats blew a 20-point lead), Cincinnati had a game at Wyoming on December 17, 1994.

The team was in a considerably better mood, having won at No. 11 Minnesota (91-88 in overtime) on December 14.

The Bearcats traveled right from Minneapolis to Laramie, Wyoming, to get adjusted to the thin air.

"It was going to be a fight against fatigue," said LaZelle Durden, UC's leading scorer and a team captain. "I pushed myself in practice to prepare for the situation."

Cincinnati had two bad workouts leading up to the game. Huggins told his team: "LaZelle's gonna have to score 50 for us to win because he's the only one who's practiced well."

Well, Huggins was close. Durden ended up with 45 points in a dramatic 81-80 victory.

The Bearcats trailed all game and were behind 80-78 with 15 seconds remaining. Keith LeGree dribbled the ball upcourt for UC and passed to Durden. Durden went to the right side and, with time running out, took a one-handed, off-balance, three-point attempt from roughly 25 feet out. He missed it, but Wyoming's LaDrell Whitehead fouled him in a call disputed afterward by Wyoming coach Joby Wright. "I wasn't sure it would get called," Durden said. "But I know for sure he fouled me."

During a timeout, all the UC players were pumping up Durden. Jim Burbridge, an academic advisor who traveled with the team, pounded his chest and said: "Money. Nerves of steel."

"That gave me confidence," Durden said.

With no time remaining, Durden calmly made all three of his free throws to stun the crowd of 8,688.

"That was a dream come true for me," Durden said. "I would say that was one of my highlights. … And that was the most tired I've ever been in my life."

He finished 16 of 32 from the field, seven of 20 from three-point range and six of seven from the foul line, and totaled the most points for a Bearcat in 45 years.

In the locker room after the game, John Jacobs needled Huggins. "Coach, you lied to us," Jacobs said. "You said LaZelle had to score 50 for us to win."

CAL RIPKEN, WHO?

Around the middle of his senior year, in January 1996, Keith Gregor realized his one chance to land in the UC record books was with his consecutive games played streak.

Make no mistake: It was important to him.

"I'd be forever etched into the history books," he said.

The school record for consecutive games played was held by Dwight "Jelly" Jones, who competed in 112 in a row from 1979-83.

In No. 109, Gregor turned his right ankle against Marquette at Shoemaker Center. He had scored 16 points in the first half and got injured in the first minute of the second half. UC would go on to win 91-70.

It wasn't just his streak that was in jeopardy; the next game four nights later was against rival Xavier. That would be Gregor's last Crosstown Shootout, and the Lakota High School graduate didn't want to miss it.

He temporarily moved into his parents' home in Cincinnati, and for three nights leading up to the Xavier game, Gregor didn't sleep. He spent all night every night icing his ankle for 20 minutes, then taking ice off. Compression. More ice. No ice. Compression. More ice. No ice. Elevated foot. He watched west coast basketball games on ESPN and late-night movies on TBS.

"You can play if you're tired," Huggins reminded him. "But you can't play if you can't walk."

Gregor tested his ankle the night before the XU game, making some cuts on the floor. He was about 90 percent. While loosening it up on game day, he actually weakened his ankle, and by tipoff he was hobbling.

He played a total of 22 minutes off the bench, running out of gas at the end. Gregor finished with four points, four rebounds and three assists. The Bearcats won 99-90. The streak was alive at 110.

The night he would tie "Jelly" Jones, UC was at home against DePaul. Gregor's ankle was in bad shape, and Huggins told him he planned to rest him. Huggins said he'd let Gregor play at the end for a couple minutes to tie the record.

"I thought, that's kind of a cheap way to keep it alive," Gregor said. "But OK, Coach, whatever you say."

UC struggled in the first half. Huggins kept going up to Gregor on the bench, saying, "Can we put you in now?" DePaul led 33-31 at halftime. Gregor felt OK.

"I think I can go, Coach," he told Huggins.

"OK," Huggins responded immediately. "You're starting."

Gregor played the whole second half. UC beat the Blue Demons 71-61.

He wouldn't miss any games the rest of the way and finished with a school-record 131 consecutive games played.

"I always go down there to Shoemaker when Huggins has got a sophomore who's played a lot and tell him 'This kid needs to be benched for a game,'" Gregor said.

"(Steve) Logan broke most games played. That's pretty good company to be in, I guess. I figure as long as Huggins is coaching, my streak is not going to be broken. If there's anybody good enough as a freshman to come in and play there, they'll probably be gone in three years."

Gregor's record was surpassed in 2014 by Sean Kilpatrick, who played in 140 consecutive games. Gregor currently ranks seventh in games played.

THE NICKNAME

During the summer before he entered ninth grade, Melvin Levett was playing in the Ohio Sports Festival. During one game, he went up and tomahawk dunked over an opposing player. "He seemed to hang in the air forever," said Tom Erzen, the assistant coach. "I remembered a professional basketball player who was named the helicopter and I thought it was appropriate to say that about Melvin. I started calling Melvin the helicopter. Soon everyone was calling Melvin the helicopter!"

That didn't stop in Cincinnati, especially after …

… THE DUNK

UC vs. Alcorn State. December 3, 1997.

"I remember it like it was yesterday," Levett said.

The Bearcats were 2-1 and had lost at home to Arizona State in the Preseason NIT Tournament at Shoemaker Center. Levett, a junior and one of the more talented players on the team, had averaged just 12 points in the first three games. He went three of 14 from the field in Game 3 against Morehead State.

"I was in a funk a little bit, because of my performances at the beginning of the season," Levett said. "I was kind of down on myself. Huggs was letting me have it pretty good throughout that week. There was a certain point at halftime (against Alcorn) when we had a little shouting match. I guess it made me just say, 'OK, now it's time.'"

During the second half, Levett dunked twice in a row. But it was the third one that went down in UC folklore.

D'Juan Baker fired up a shot from the left side behind the three-point line.

"I saw it go up, and I just ran and jumped," Levett said. "I never hesitated. I didn't know where I was taking off from. I was going to get that basketball. I took off and I just kept going. I kept rising and rising.

"It hit the rim and bounced off the top of the backboard, and it came right into my hands as I was floating over Bobby Brannen and another guy from Alcorn State. I just slammed it home."

Levett caught himself and ended up swinging on the rim. It would be called the Helicopter Dunk by many.

"There was a lot that went into that," Levett said. "That was pretty much the one to say, 'I've arrived for this season. I'm here. Now is the time to play ball.' The season took off for me from there."

In November 2001, *Slam* magazine included Levett among the 50 greatest dunkers of all time. He came in at No. 32, ahead of folks like Tracy McGrady, Chris Webber, Elgin Baylor, Scottie Pippen and Kevin Garnett. Topping the list (in order): Vince Carter, Michael Jordan, Dominique Wilkins, Julius Erving.

IN A ZONE

Less than three weeks later, Levett scored a career-high 42 points against Eastern Kentucky.

After practice a couple days before the game, Levett stayed in Shoemaker Center and had a shooting contest with guard John Carson. They put up several hundred shots. Some of the players stuck around to watch.

The touch stayed with him. When Levett was warming up before the EKU game, he couldn't miss. Usually, as the adage goes, if a player doesn't miss a shot during warmups, he's in for a bad night.

But Levett's first shot in the game fell, and he thought he had perfect extension on his follow through. Every time he let go, *swish*, the ball went right in. His shot hardly even touched the rim. Levett made 16 of 24 field goal attempts and was 10 of 14 from three-point range.

"It was one of those things that you watch on TV and you wish you were that guy in that moment, like when Mike (Jordan) had 63 in Boston or 69 against Cleveland," Levett said. "You wish you could get in a zone like that. That day, I did. Whenever I am inconsistent with the form on my shot, I go back and watch that film."

LOVE YOU, MOM

Ruben Patterson's teammates learned a lot about him February 19, 1998.

Patterson and Alex Meacham were rooming together on a road trip to UAB. The night before the game, the two were talking when Patterson started opening up.

"He was talking about where he came from in Cleveland and how his goal was to get to the NBA and make lots of money," Meacham said. "His dream was to buy his mother a car and a house and get her out of the 'hood. It was just a typical story of a guy wanting to do better for his family.

"We stayed up until 1:30, 2:00 in the morning. All he talked about was his mom."

Finally, the two fell asleep with the television on. Around 6 a.m., there was a knock on the door. It was Huggins.

Huggins took Patterson back to his room and delivered some horrific news: Patterson's mother, Charlene Patterson, had died of a heart attack in her sleep at age 38.

"Ruben was pretty shaken," Levett said. "Basketball really didn't matter at that point."

At the team's shootaround the day of the game, Huggins tried to convince Patterson to go home to be with his family.

"I'll never forget this," Meacham said. "Ruben said, 'This *is* my family. I'm going to play this game.'"

Ruben Patterson (23), an Associated Press honorable mention All-American in 1998, was selected by the Los Angeles Lakers in the second round of the NBA draft. Patterson played 10 years in the NBA and scored a total of 6,953 points for the Lakers, Seattle SuperSonics, Portland Trail Blazers, Denver Nuggets, Milwaukee Bucks, and Los Angeles Clippers. (Photo by Lisa Ventre/University of Cincinnati)

Back at the hotel, Patterson took his shoes and wrote on them with marker: "Charlene Patterson, #23" and "I am going to miss you."

Then Patterson went out and had one of the best games of his career.

He scored a career-high 32 points and added seven rebounds, three assists and three steals in 37 minutes in a 93-76 victory. "We needed to win this game, and I wanted to play well for my mom," Patterson said that night after the game. "Every time I scored, everybody saw me point up."

"He was playing with an unbelievable amount of concentration defensively and offensively," Meacham said. "And he had a glow to him while he played. After the game in the locker room, everybody was kind of crying. It was a real emotional thing. This is a weird thing to say but it was a good thing for our team in that it brought us a little closer together. And some guys saw a side of Huggins that they had never seen before. There was no doubt that Huggins, his staff and the players truly cared about Ruben and what happened."

"That just shows you the kind of heart he had to overcome something so huge," Levett said of Patterson. "I remember after the game every guy going down to the pay phones in the hotel and waiting to call home to tell their parents they loved them."

THE AGONY OF DEFEAT

There were some tough losses during the Huggins era. The following certainly ranked up there:

UC was the No. 2 seed in the 1998 NCAA Tournament, and the selection committee sure set up an intriguing second-round matchup. After the Bearcats knocked off Northern Arizona in the first round, they earned a meeting with West Virginia.

The subplots? For starters, this was Huggins's alma mater, the school for which he starred as an Academic All-American in the 1970s. He also coached a year for the Mountaineers as a graduate assistant. Coincidentally, West Virginia was coached by Gale Catlett, who left as UC's coach 20 years earlier, took over as the Mountaineers' coach and opted not to retain a young assistant coach named Bob Huggins.

Nice storylines, eh?

Cincinnati uncharacteristically went out and committed 22 turnovers yet remarkably had a chance to win the game. UC led 74-72 with 7.1 seconds remaining.

West Virginia inbounded the ball to Jarrod West, who dribbled to halfcourt and fired up a prayer. UC's Patterson tipped the ball with his middle finger, changing the trajectory. It sailed into the basket for a three-pointer to win the game.

"I think my face was in the floor," Levett said. "I couldn't believe it. I really thought we had a curse on us. If you watch the ball leave his hands, you'll see the rotation on it. It's fast, but as Ruben tips it, it slows down but gains a little bit more flight. If that shot's harder, if Ruben doesn't touch it, we go to the Sweet 16 and possibly the Final Four."

CREATING CAMARADERIE

Teams are allowed to take off-season trips every four years. The advantages: The players get to play games, but more important, they get to bond.

When UC went to Europe after the 1996-97 season, all the players shaved their heads bald. Except, of course, Bobby Brannen, who wasn't going to cut his locks for anyone.

One day after visiting Vatican City in Italy, Darnell Burton, Flint and Levett went to a nightclub. It was a hole-in-the-wall place. Very dark inside.

Once they got seated, servers started bringing drinks, including bottles of champagne. Women were sitting with them. Nobody was speaking English, and the UC players didn't know quite what was going on. After a while, Levett told Burton to find out why drinks were being brought to the table.

An employee told the players they owed $500 in lira, Italy's currency at the time.

"What? We didn't ask for this stuff," the players protested.

"They took us to the back of the club," Levett said. "It reminded you of one of those situations in a movie where you're in a mob joint in some underground place and they want to take you in the back and chop you up. It just happened so quickly. Damon was talking fast. It was so confusing.

"We pull all the money out of our pockets and put it on the table and said, 'This is all we've got.' We didn't get to $500, man. We were well short. We bolted out and walked down the street and we were quiet. Nobody said a word."

Now *that's* bonding.

"That was funny," Burton said. "We were wondering why they were treating us like stars. We didn't know they were keeping a tab on us. ... We were a little scared. It was like one of those scenes from the mafia."

LOOKING INTO THE FUTURE

He was a sophomore who had not yet established himself as a standout player. In fact, Kenyon Martin averaged fewer than 10 points a game and was not the kind of force that caused opposing coaches to alter their game plans.

So there was no way to prepare for what Martin unleashed on DePaul on February 21, 1998. Try this on for size: 24 points, 23 rebounds, 10 blocked shots.

"I was just being more aggressive than everybody," Martin said. "I was grabbing everything and blocking every shot. Guys were scared to come to the hole."

Kenyon Martin (4) gives instructions to teammates Steve Logan (22), Pete Mickeal (32) and Kenny Satterfield (right). (Photo by Lisa Ventre/University of Cincinnati)

It was only the 12th triple-double of any kind in UC history, and Martin was only the third player at the time to have one, joining Oscar Robertson and Rick Roberson. Robertson had 10 triple-doubles during his three seasons, and Roberson's

16 points, 10 rebounds and 10 blocks came 30 years and one month earlier than Martin's.

"Just watching from the sideline, it was unreal," said UC teammate Jermaine Tate, who was sitting out that season after transferring from Ohio State. "I hadn't seen a performance like that by an individual player in a game. It seemed like they were just throwing him the ball. It was unbelievable."

Two years later, Martin would do it again. He finished with 28 points, 13 rebounds and 10 blocks against Memphis during his senior season.

GOOD MOVE

Martin did briefly consider leaving UC a year early for the NBA. Huggins was told by his NBA sources that Martin would be selected between Nos. 19 and 22 in the first round of the 1999 draft.

When he met with Huggins, the coach asked: "What do you want to do?"

Martin replied: "I want to win a national championship."

"That was the only discussion we ever had about leaving early," Huggins said.

CONFIDENCE BOOST

Martin averaged 2.8 points a game as a freshman, 9.9 points as a sophomore and 10.1 points as a junior. He was steadily improving and had a legendary work ethic. But mentally, he did not approach every game as if he were the dominant player on the court until he was a senior.

During the summer 1999, after his junior year, Martin was selected to the U.S. team for the World University Games in Palma del Morca, Spain. He was likely picked for his defense, to provide an intimidating presence near the basket.

Martin brought much more. He would lead the gold-medal-winning team in scoring (13.9 ppg) and rebounding (6.6 rpg). Dayton's Oliver Purnell was the coach.

"A lot of people probably thought I was just going to be another guy on the team," Martin said. "I came back with a different attitude about my game and my ability. That put me over the top. I worked the weight room hard. I worked on my game harder than I ever had. It always takes something for you to realize how good you can be. Those World University Games did it for me."

Walk-on Alex Meacham remembers bumping into Martin when he returned from Spain. They were on their way to play pick-up games in Shoemaker Center. Meacham asked how the Games experience had been.

"I'll never forget this," Meacham said. "Kenyon said, 'I don't mean to brag, but I was probably the best guy on that team.' When he left for those games, he was a little nervous. He knew he was going to be there with some of the best players in the country."

In Shoemaker, team trainer Jayd Grossman told Meacham that he knew the trainer for the World University Games team, and the trainer had said Martin was the best player on the team—by far. That confirmed what Martin had said.

That day, Martin dominated the pick-up games.

"It came down to one thing: Kenyon knew he was a good player, but I don't think Kenyon knew he was *that* good of a player," Meacham said. "He worked out the same, shot the same amount. It was a mental thing."

Huggins said a few other things happened in the summer of 1999: Martin learned to shoot free throws; he built up his leg strength; and he spent a lot of time with former Bearcat Corie Blount, who taught Martin "how to be a professional," Huggins said.

The World University Games also helped Martin get past a game during his junior season that Huggins thinks affected him.

The Bearcats lost 62-60 at Charlotte on January 14, 1999. Trailing by two, UC threw the ball into Martin, who was fouled intentionally with three seconds left. "It was a gamble," 49ers coach Bobby Lutz said afterward. Martin missed the front end of a one-and-one free throw situation, and Cincinnati lost.

"Kenyon's such a good guy, he never wanted to hurt the team," Huggins said. "So I think he didn't want the ball at the end of games after that because he didn't have a lot of confidence in making free throws. I think the World University Games helped him with that because he went to the line and made them."

Martin made 13 of 19 free throws for the U.S. team, which included UC teammate Pete Mickeal.

HAPPY NEW YEAR

UC players may complain privately about Huggins when they're on the team, but after their eligibility expires, most are extremely loyal to Huggins. All he has to do is ask for something, and it's done.

On December 31, 1999, Huggins was at a junior college event in Florida. He called back to assistant coach Dan Peters and wanted the word put out that he needed some former Bearcats to show up for a New Year's Day practice at Shoemaker Center. Huggins gave him phone numbers and said, "Tell those guys I need them at practice."

"Huggs, those guys are not coming in on New Year's Day," Peters said.

"Pete, call them, they'll be there," Huggins said.

They all showed up.

"It really surprised me," Peters said.

UC was 11-3, ranked third in the country and about to play host to UNLV on January 2. But Huggins thought his team needed a test, needed to learn how to compete.

And so they arrived for a little scrimmage: Terry Nelson. Tarrice Gibson. Anthony Buford. Curtis Bostic. A.D. Jackson. Keith Gregor. Donald Little, a freshman center, played with them.

"They just wore them out," Huggins said.

"Could you at least let Satt cross half court so we can start our offense?" Huggins shouted to Gibson, referring to freshman Kenny Satterfield.

"We had a pretty good team, and we couldn't get a shot off against them," Peters said.

"Those guys could play defense at a totally different level," former video coordinator Chris Goggin said. "It was a fiery game. We scrimmaged forever. Those guys came in and absolutely just wiped the floor with them. T-Rat (Gibson) had Kenny Satterfield almost in tears, just locked him up defensively.

"After the whole scrimmage, our guys are exhausted, laying on the ground. Satt's sprawled out on the baseline and T-Rat, just for the hell of it, starts running wind sprints."

Gibson said: "That's just what I usually do. It was out of habit. When we played, we ran after practice. That was fourth quarter and overtime."

The Bearcats blasted UNLV the next day 106-66. They did not lose again until February 20 against Temple.

KENYON HAS TO TOUCH THE BALL

If Martin wasn't already a favorite to be named college basketball's National Player of the Year, he might have clinched the honor March 2, 2000, during a 64-62 victory at DePaul.

The game was on national TV. Huggins benched Pete Mickeal, UC's No. 2 scorer and rebounder. UC's offense was so out of sync that the Blue Demons raced to a 17-point lead.

"Everybody was ready to pack it in," Huggins said. He asked Martin if the game was over with? "Hell no," Martin responded.

With 3:36 remaining and DePaul ahead by 10, Huggins did something unusual for him. In a huddle during a timeout, he told his No. 2-ranked team: "Nobody shoots the ball until Kenyon at least gets a touch. He's the best player in the country. We're shooting quick, taking bad shots. Whoever shoots it before he touches it is never playing again."

Team manager Scott Wilhoit turned to Goggin and said, "We're about to come back." Goggin gave him a look that said, You're crazy!

Martin then got on a roll, scoring the next four baskets. Dick Vitale was raving about him on the ESPN broadcast. The Bearcats were within four points with 2:08 to play. Martin's turnaround jumper with 1:10 remaining tied the game.

Martin finished with 33 points, including his first career three-pointer. He scored 21 in the second half. "He was hitting shots that we had never seen him hit in practice or during the year," freshman DerMarr Johnson said.

"The DePaul players were asking us, 'Does he do this all the time?'" Jermaine Tate said. "We were just as shocked as everyone else."

"I just did not want to lose," Martin said. "I felt I was the leader of the team and I put the team on my back and told them to get on and let's go. A lot of people said that's when I made a true name for myself."

The game was tied with 22 seconds left, and DePaul was in possession. Tate stole a Rashon Burno pass and immediately got it to Martin. Martin then passed to Johnson, who was ahead of the pack racing toward the UC basket.

"All he had to do was drive in for a layup or take an open shot," Goggin said. "He took forever to actually shoot the shot. He said the reason he didn't shoot it right away is because he was looking for Kenyon because that's what Huggs told him to do."

Said Martin: "He was just looking around. I was screaming, 'Shoot it, shoot it!' After the game, Huggs asked him what was he waiting on. He said, 'I wasn't sure if Kenyon touched the ball or not.'"

Johnson said he hesitated because he didn't want to drive to the open lane and somehow end up getting called for a charge. He pulled up for a 15-foot jumper and nailed the game-winning shot with 2.7 seconds remaining.

"I was thinking, 'Should I drive in or sit here and take the shot?'" Johnson said. "I just set my feet and hit the shot."

THE DAY THE MUSIC DIED

UC's overtime loss to Loyola in the 1963 national championship game has to be considered the most heartbreaking day in Bearcat basketball history.

No. 2 may very well be March 9, 2000.

That was the day Kenyon Martin broke his leg in Memphis, Tennessee.

The Bearcats were the nation's No. 1-ranked team, and Martin was the best player in the country. Just three minutes, four seconds into their Conference USA tournament quarterfinal game against Saint Louis, the six-foot-nine Martin went to set a screen on the baseline. He started to fall, and Saint Louis guard Justin Love hit Martin's left knee. Martin fell hard on his own right leg.

"It was a freak accident," he said.

Martin tried to get up but couldn't. He said he knew right away it was broken.

"I felt bad for him," Huggins said. "When I went out there (to the court), all he talked about was how he came back for his senior year to win a national championship. My only thoughts were about him. They weren't about anything else.

Kenyon and I were really, really close. I probably spent as much time with Ken as I did anybody that I've had. The whole half-time, I hardly talked to the team. I was on the phone with the doctors at the hospital. My concern was how bad he felt because of what he wanted to do, but more important my concern was that he was going to be able to play again. It would've been tragic if he wouldn't have been able to play again."

The UC players were stunned. "We didn't know how to respond," DerMarr Johnson said. "That's a game we still should've won even with him out. It affected everybody."

"We all were in shock," Huggins said.

Martin rode in an ambulance to Campbell Clinic in Memphis. His sister, Tamara Ridley, was with him. At the clinic, Martin's leg was X-rayed and put in a cast. He said he rushed staff members because he wanted to return to the arena to cheer on his teammates. "I thought that would mean a lot to them just to see me come back," he said.

"When he walked in and everybody saw him on crutches," Huggins said, "… it was totally the opposite affect.

"Everybody was concerned for him more than anything. Kenyon was and still is the ultimate team guy. He's the greatest team guy you could ever have."

The Billikens, who had lost to UC by 43 points five days earlier, went on to win 68-58.

Huggins was emotional. Not only did Martin's injury likely end UC's bid for a national championship, Martin also is one of Huggins's favorite players.

"He was hurt," Martin said. "He felt the way I did. That was a chance to get to the Final Four and win the national championship. But more than he was hurt about that, he was sad for me because I had worked so hard to get to where I was. He knew all the work I put in."

Martin said he had never suffered a serious injury play-ing sports, and he wasn't sure how to deal with it. He said his family, teammates and coaches and the Cincinnati community helped him through a difficult time with support and kindness.

He did his best to maintain perspective.

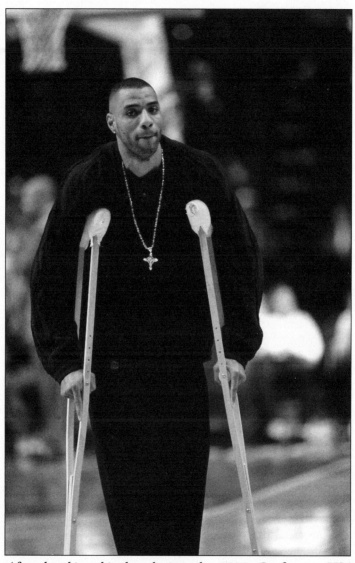

After breaking his leg during the 2000 Conference USA Tournament, UC star Kenyon Martin was on crutches during the Bearcats' NCAA Tournament games. (Photo by Lisa Ventre/ University of Cincinnati)

"I had already made a name for myself and showed how well I could play," he said—and indeed, he would be the No. 1 overall pick in the NBA draft three months later. "It took away a chance to win the national championship, which I thought we would've won. I've had other things in my life that were a little harder than that, but playing sports, yeah, that was the hardest."

After Cincinnati lost to Tulsa in the second round of the 2000 NCAA Tournament, Martin was in tears in the locker room. He had sat on the bench giving Huggins water the whole game. "I'm sorry I wasn't able to help you all," Martin told his teammates. "That kind of touched me," DerMarr Johnson said.

"I was their leader," Martin said. "They looked up to me, not just on the basketball court. It was rough to see those guys struggle and to see us lose like that. It was rough."

SURPRISE, SURPRISE

Martin knew he was going to collect several National Player of the Year and team awards at UC's postseason banquet in 2000. What he didn't know was that his jersey No. 4 was going to be retired, with a banner to hang in Shoemaker Center alongside banners honoring Basketball Hall of Famers Oscar Robertson (12) and Jack Twyman (27).

UC officials decided to surprise Martin. Huggins said some fans called and wrote, suggesting the honor, especially after Martin broke his leg. Athletic director Bob Goin made the decision to retire the number.

"Certainly it wasn't very controversial," Goin said. "It was obvious his performance merited something very special, staying in school and coming back and doing what he did. I did it for Charlie Ward (at Florida State), too."

Goin said maybe a half-dozen people knew of the plan. The "jersey" was hung on the wall and covered up the night before the banquet.

"They didn't tell me," Martin said. "That was exciting. It was touching. You get emotional. I had my jersey retired in high school, too. To have it retired in college, that was even more special."

AUTHOR, AUTHOR

When Alex Meacham, a fan-favorite walk-on (aren't they all?) who totaled 20 points in 21 games in his UC basketball career, told Huggins that he wanted to write a book about his experience as a Bearcat, Huggins said: "You're not going to make a lot of money. All you're going to get is exposure."

That was enough for Meacham, a Roger Bacon High School graduate and a member of UC's team from 1997-99.

"How many people can say they wrote a book?" Meacham said. "My theory is sometimes you do things just for the experience, and sometimes it can lead to bigger opportunities."

Walk of a Lifetime, which was released in August 2000, sold close to 3,000 copies in just over three years. In addition to hoping hardcore UC fans would be interested in the book, Meacham targeted a younger audience, hoping to send a message to junior high and high school players about persevering. Meacham's book is about his overcoming several injuries and his persistence in wanting to achieve his goal of being a Bearcat.

"My senior year, nobody knew my story," Meacham said. "People at the games knew me and would chant my name, but they would think, how the hell did this guy get here?"

Columnist Paul Daugherty of *The Cincinnati Enquirer* wrote about Meacham in February, prompting Simon Anderson, a UC professor of music education who owns Clifton Hills Press, to tell Meacham he should write a book.

"I can barely write these papers for school," Meacham joked.

Meacham would end up working on the project with Anderson, his roommate Sam Dunn, who writes scripts for commercials and writes and edits videos, and *Cincinnati Herald* reporter Marc Brown.

"We were doing something related to the book every day for 14 months," Meacham said. "That's no joke. Every day we did something. If you go to a bookstore and pick up a book, you have no idea what that person went through to do every single piece of that book. Every piece was an adventure."

In the end, Huggins was right on in his advice.

"Everybody who plays for UC should have an opportunity to do something," Meacham said. "Some go play in the NBA. Some guys go play basketball overseas. I've kind of made a career out of playing for UC. My credibility with Shining Star and working with these kids is I wrote a book and I played for UC."

HOTEL, MOTEL, HOLIDAY INN

B.J. Grove was a talented big man from Cincinnati, six foot 11 (the good news) but often weighing upwards of 300 pounds (the bad news). He also didn't always practice to Huggins's standards.

UC had a game February 1, 2001, at Charlotte, and Athletic Director Bob Goin wanted to send Grove a message.

The day before the trip, student manager Corey Brinn was called into a meeting with Goin and told he was going to be put on a special mission in Charlotte: He was in charge of Grove.

The Bearcats were going to be staying at the Embassy Suites in Charlotte, as usual. Grove and Brinn were going to stay in an old hotel with few amenities in the Charlotte area. Grove was not allowed to travel on the team bus, speak to his teammates or be part of the team with the exception of practices and the game.

"From the minute the team left campus, I was with B.J.," Brinn said. "We had to take a cab to the airport. We sat by ourselves at the airport. Once we got into Charlotte, we found our own cab from the airport to the hotel."

Trainer Jayd Grossman, who made the team's travel arrangements, booked Grove and Brinn into another hotel.

"We pulled up not knowing what to expect," Brinn said. "It's 11 or 11:30 at night. When they checked us in, there's a big plate of homemade cookies. Well, B.J.'s in heaven. He starts grabbing cookies and putting them in his pocket.

"We got to our room, and it's one of those old hotels. You've got the two beds, and in between the beds are the sink and a mirror. The bathroom's off in the corner. It doesn't really have a door on it. The shower's right there. The TV had about six or seven stations, and none of them were any good. We were both depressed the minute we walked in."

The next morning, they had to take a $40 cab ride to Halton Arena for shootaround. They had to wait about an hour for a cab to take them back to the hotel. They found their own pregame meal and had to return to Halton.

After the game—Grove had six points in 16 minutes—they met the team at the airport for the flight home.

Finally, Grove and Brinn were allowed on the team bus from the Cincinnati/Northern Kentucky International Airport back to campus.

"It was an experience," Brinn said. "We were laughing. After we first got there and the initial shock, we had a pretty good time together. ... I think he learned his lesson."

THIRTY YEARS LATER...

Oscar Robertson was sitting courtside watching a feat rare to the UC basketball program, though common to Robertson when he played.

Kenny Satterfield, a sophomore point guard from New York City, became only the fourth Bearcat to get a triple-double with 12 points, 11 rebounds, and 10 assists in a 105-57 victory over Tulane at Shoemaker Center. And Satterfield only played 24 minutes. His 10th assist came on a pass to freshman guard Field Williams, who drained a three-pointer with 5:24 remaining.

The only other UC players to have triple-doubles were Kenyon Martin, Rick Roberson, and Robertson. Eric Hicks joined the club in January 2006.

MOTIVATIONAL TACTICS

In five years of playing in the Rock-N-Roll Shootout in Cleveland, the Bearcats had never lost. They beat Temple, Western Kentucky, Massachusetts, Dayton and Gonzaga. But on December 30, 2000, the streak ended with a stunning 69-66 loss to Toledo at Gund Arena.

The new year did nothing to calm Huggins after the defeat. On Thursday, January 4, 2001, he had the doors to the team's plush locker room locked and made the players dress in the smaller, no-frills men's soccer team locker room in the lower level of Shoemaker Center.

"Our locker room is for champions," Huggins told the Bearcats, who dropped to 25th from 19th in the Associated Press poll that week.

For two days, the team was locked out of its customary digs. The third night, Cincinnati pummeled Charlotte 76-66, leading by as many as 20 during the game.

"I think it got the guys' attention," Jamaal Davis said afterward of Huggins's actions.

Not totally.

Two weeks later, UC dropped consecutive games at Saint Louis and at home against a struggling Louisville club. The day after the loss to the Cardinals, Huggins approached student manager Brinn about two hours before practice and told him to find plain gray T-shirts and black shorts for all the players. Much of it ended up being too small. But the guys had to wear it anyway.

"We couldn't find stuff that big quick enough," Brinn said.

The team was also prohibited from entering their locker room again.

"We really don't come out and play like Cincinnati Bearcats, so why should we dress like them?" Davis told *The Cincinnati Enquirer.*

It worked again. In their next game, the Bearcats upset No. 8 Wake Forest 78-72 in a game that would turn around the 2000-01 season.

Two years later, Huggins would dip into the same bag of motivational tactics. In February 2003, after No. 18 Marquette beat UC 82-76 in Shoemaker Center, Huggins again banned the team from its locker room and would not allow the players to wear UC practice clothes. Instead, they were "shirts" and "skins" during practice. This time, they dressed in the women's rowing team locker room in the Armory Fieldhouse.

"It's got nothing to do with motivation," Huggins told *The Enquirer* at the time. "It's loyalty to the people who have played so hard and earned that stuff."

After a 77-71 loss at No. 5 Louisville three days later, the Bearcats upset 11th-ranked Oklahoma State 61-50 at Shoemaker.

MAKING THE CALL

Sometimes it's fate that lands a player in a certain basketball program.

Huggins remembers watching a high school player in Louisiana whom he'd been recruiting. The player was very athletic but—with Huggins in the stands—shot miserably in the first half of the game, going something like three for 20 from the field. Huggins turned to then-assistant coach Mick Cronin and said, "I'm going to call Logan."

That would be Steve Logan, a chunky five-foot-11 guard from St. Edward High School in Lakewood, on the west side of Cleveland, Ohio. Major colleges did not heavily recruit Logan, and he did not sign a national letter of intent in the fall of his senior year because he held out hope Huggins would offer a scholarship.

Which is exactly what happened.

"We had too many guys who couldn't make shots," Huggins once said.

With Logan, Huggins knew, that would not be a problem.

After leading his high school team to a state championship, Logan was named Ohio's Division I Player of the Year. In four years at Cincinnati, he slimmed down, got stronger, worked relentlessly on his game and left as the Bearcats' No. 2 all-time scorer behind only Oscar Robertson.

Just think: What if that Louisiana prep star had a good first half?

LOGAN 41, SOUTHERN MISS 37

Logan accomplished a great many things at UC—including playing in the most victories—and had his name scattered all over the record books by the end of his senior season. But perhaps one of his most memorable nights came when he out-scored an entire team all by himself.

True.

Southern Mississippi came into Shoemaker Center with a 7-15 record just one year after sharing the Conference USA regular-season championship with the Bearcats. Coach James Green's teams had a reputation for playing good defense. But on February 15, 2002, it really didn't matter what they did.

Steve Logan was hot. He drove to the basket. He pulled up for mid-range jumpers. He fired long-range three-pointers. And at the end of the night, Logan had 41 points. Southern Miss had 37.

"Oh man, he put on a show," teammate Donald Little said that night.

"We tried to double him," Green said afterward. "We tried to keep the ball out of his hands."

Nothing worked.

UC won 89-37. Logan left to a standing ovation with 4:25 left, also finishing with nine assists and six rebounds. He made 12 of his 18 field-goal attempts and was eight of 13 from three-point range and nine of 10 from the foul line.

To make the night even more special, Logan's mother and sister were in the stands, and the game was nationally televised on ESPN.

"To do it in a game like there was nobody in the gym with me, it's amazing," Logan said the next day. "I was just in a zone, I guess."

IT'S BETTER TO GIVE

Leonard Stokes didn't think much about it the night it happened. UC had just defeated Southern Mississippi at Shoemaker Center. As usual, Stokes showered, dressed and went to sign autographs outside the Bearcats' locker room.

Jon Johanson, an 18-year-old UC fan with cerebral palsy, was in his red-and-black wheelchair waiting in line. As Stokes approached and signed an autograph for him, Johanson told Stokes: "You're my favorite player." Stokes soon disappeared back into the locker room.

The junior forward grabbed the shoes he wore that night—size 13 Nike Air Jordans—and asked a student manager

Steve Logan left UC in 2002 owning school records for games played (135), career victories (111) and free throw percentage (.861). He was second in scoring (1,985 points), minutes played, three-point field goals attempted and assists. (Photo by Lisa Ventre/University of Cincinnati)

to give them to Johanson. "Leonard Stokes wants you to have these," the manager told Johanson, who was stunned by the gift.

"I remember it was about twelve o'clock at night," Johanson said. "The first thing I wanted to do was wear them."

Nancy Johanson, Jon's mother, wrote a letter to Stokes and sent a copy to Huggins and a reporter with *The Cincinnati Enquirer.* She wanted everyone to know how moved she was by Stokes's gesture

"You really don't know how much you can impact a person's life by some of the things you do," Stokes said. "That day made me realize that.

"I didn't do it and expect anyone to tell the media and make a big deal out of it. I did it out of the kindness of my heart. That kid was sitting there and telling me how I was his favorite player. That touched me. To me, I was just doing something to make him feel happy."

Stokes's mother, Candace Quarles, was awfully proud. She framed the picture of Johanson and the shoes that later ran in *The Enquirer* and hung it in the family's living room in Buffalo, N.Y., alongside Leonard's basketball trophies and awards.

"That's the way she raised me, to be courteous and kind to others," Stokes said.

"I think it was a magical moment that symbolized the goodness in people," Nancy Johanson told *The Enquirer*. "That a perfect stranger would do something that was so generous and meaningful for a fan. I think that's why it lives on. It was a very loving moment. Everyone I have shared this story with has been really touched; it restores people's sense of goodness."

UNCLE CLARENCE

Logan—a first-team All-American and Conference USA Player of the Year as a senior—almost wasn't around to collect all his accolades.

During his sophomore year, Huggins pulled Logan out of the starting lineup late in the season and used him as a sixth man. The Bearcats had one of the best teams in the country, led by National Player of the Year Kenyon Martin. UC was deep, versatile and appeared to be on the way to a Final Four berth—until Martin broke his leg during the Conference USA tournament.

Logan's disappointment after the season was more personal. He didn't think he was being treated fairly. Huggins didn't think Logan was working as hard as he could. Logan went home to Cleveland and was determined to transfer.

Enter Clarence Newby. Or, as Logan calls him, "Uncle Clarence."

Talk to Logan about Newby long enough and Logan will choke up. "I get chill bumps when I hear his name," Logan told *The Cincinnati Enquirer.* "He saved my life."

Newby owned a shoeshine parlor around the corner from where Logan grew up in Cleveland. Logan was 12 years old and the man of the house after his mother asked his father to leave. Newby hired Logan with the intent of keeping him from getting involved in drugs and gangs like other kids in the neighborhood.

When Logan told Newby he planned to leave Cincinnati, Newby set him straight: "No, son, you're going to stick it out. I don't want to hear no more about transferring. It's not even up for discussion."

Logan listened. He mended his strained relationship with Huggins, then went on to be named Conference USA Player of the Year in 2001 and 2002.

"I grew up a little more and understood I wasn't going to win with him," Logan said of Huggins. "In order for me to be successful ... I had to be a little bit more respectful and not talk back."

MEETING OF THE MINDS

UC lost its first regular-season opener of the Huggins era on November 16, 2001, at Oklahoma State, a game set up by the TV network.

The Bearcats looked horrible offensively (they shot 22.7 percent from the field in the first half), and the Cowboys won 69-62. Stokes, expected to be one of the team's leading scorers, went scoreless in the first half and finished with just 12 points.

The next day, senior forward Jamaal Davis (one point and one rebound in 20 minutes) would quit the team—temporarily.

"I'm coming in from the outside, and I'm looking for the big, bad Bearcats that I've always thought about," said assistant coach Andy Kennedy, who was then in his first year at UC. "And when I got here I looked around and said, 'Where are they?'"

That night, after the game, the UC coaching staff sat around in the lobby atrium of the Holiday Inn in Stillwater, Oklahoma. Artificial trees surrounded them. They could smell the chlorine from the nearby indoor swimming pool, and a manure plant next door was sending out an odor.

"The biggest thing I remember about it was, we don't have meetings," former associate head coach Dan Peters said. "But Huggs called one."

Everyone assembled was trying to figure out how Cincinnati could even become a .500 team that season. It did not look good, they all agreed. They sat around for three or four hours, talking about the best style of play for the team, how to maximize Logan, who had scored 31 against the Cowboys.

Some grand conclusion must have been conceived.

The Bearcats won their next 20 games, climbing as high as No. 4 in the Associated Press poll. Logan would be named first-team All-America and lead UC to a 31-4 record, setting a school record for most victories in a season.

"I certainly did not envision going 31-4," Kennedy said. "I don't think anybody did. That was unfathomable at the time."

HELPING HAND

In 1983, Derrick McMillan took advantage of one of the greatest assets the University of Cincinnati basketball program has: Oscar Robertson.

The Hall of Famer has offered his help to Bearcat players for decades. McMillan seized the opportunity and turned into an all-conference player (see Chapter 9).

It was another 18 years before a UC player turned to the Big O.

Robertson sat courtside for many games during the 2001-02 season, saw some flaws in Leonard Stokes's game and thought he could help.

"I think he has talent he hasn't tapped yet," Robertson told *The Cincinnati Enquirer.* "I don't like to interfere. You can only say so much to a guy. They have to learn to play as it comes and learn to grow with it. I just don't think he's aggressive enough yet."

The two talked on the phone regularly, but Robertson came to practice one afternoon and stayed the whole day. He talked at length with Stokes, a six-foot-six junior, and showed him ways to improve some techniques.

"It's a blessing, definitely, when you've got a guy like Oscar noticing you," Stokes told *The Enquirer.* "I just try to take in everything that he says. If he tells me to clap when I'm on the bench, I'm going to listen."

WEST VIRGINIA: A LONG WEEK

The talk started before UC's 2001-02 season even ended. From the moment Gale Catlett resigned as coach at West Virginia on February 14, 2002, reports surfaced that the Mountaineers would target Huggins to replace Catlett.

It made sense for West Virginia. Huggins played there, was a two-time Academic All-American and the team's most valuable player as a senior. He was a graduate assistant there in 1977. He had friends still in Morgantown. And then there was this: Huggins was interested.

Bob Huggins is UC's all-time winningest men's basketball coach with a record of 399-127 (.759) in 16 years. (Photo by Lisa Ventre/University of Cincinnati)

The Bearcats lost a heartbreaking double-overtime game to UCLA in the second round of the NCAA Tournament on a Sunday. Then ...

Monday: West Virginia officials called UC Athletic Director Bob Goin and asked for permission to speak to Huggins. "I told them to get his thing moving as quickly as they could," Goin said. "Bobby and I had dialogue immediately." Goin expected the phone call. "I wasn't nervous," he said. "I thought when he started putting all the pluses together, what he was seeking at West Virginia he already had here."

Tuesday: Huggins met with West Virginia officials in a Pittsburgh hotel. Some people close to Huggins believe that if West Virginia would have made him a good offer this night, he would have accepted. "If they were going to get him, it would've been when he was emotionally removed from the city," Goin said. "Once they let him come back to Cincinnati, then the city started showing its affection. It was openly expressed to him better than I could do it. It reassured him that everything he had done in the past hadn't gone unnoticed."

Wednesday: Huggins could not return to his Shoemaker Center office. Some members of the media were around all day long. The phone wouldn't stop ringing. He spent a lot of time driving around the city and at Goin's home. It was where the two could have the most privacy. The Athletic Director's wife Nancy was out of town for the week. "Most of the time, it was him weighing what he wanted to do, and not me saying, 'Well, you've got to stay here,'" Goin said. "That was not my approach. Ultimately, I felt very confident."

Thursday: The *Pittsburgh Post-Gazette* reported Huggins was staying at UC. Huggins still couldn't go near his office.

Friday: CBS.Sportsline.com was the first to report that Huggins accepted the West Virginia job, but other reports soon followed, including one Cincinnati television station, which also reported Huggins was leaving UC. Huggins called another TV station that night to deny that any deal was done. Steve Farmer, a West Virginia-based lawyer representing Huggins, met with West Virginia officials Friday and Saturday.

Saturday: This was the most frustrating night for Goin. He had a news release written that said Huggins was staying at UC, and Goin was eager to release it. Then Huggins called to say he was indeed meeting with the West Virginia president in Cincinnati on Sunday night. "I owe that to them," he told Goin.

Sunday: West Virginia president David Hardesty and Athletic Director Ed Pastilong flew to Cincinnati to make Huggins an offer. After that meeting, Huggins went to Goin's house. "He was still torn on emotion versus reality," Goin said. Meanwhile in Morgantown, TV trucks showed up over the weekend outside the WVU Coliseum for a potential press conference. The *Charleston Daily Mail* sent a reporter to Morgantown for a possible announcement.

Monday: Huggins drove around Cincinnati and ended up at Goin's house for the sixth straight day. Goin said: "Bobby, this has gone on long enough. I've got two releases here. One says you're leaving and one says you're staying. I want you to pick one of those." The releases were lying on the sofa. Huggins said he had to make another phone call, and he retreated to Goin's game room in the basement. Goin remained upstairs.

Huggins came back up and tapped one of the releases. "Go ahead and send it out," he said.

"But the one he tapped said he was leaving," Goin said. "Then he looked at it and said, 'No, no, no, not that one. This is the one I want to go out.' And it was the one saying he was staying."

During the previous three days, Huggins received phone calls and visits from former players, who told him they just wanted him to be happy. Brian Goldberg, Ken Griffey Jr.'s agent, called Bret Adams, Huggins's Columbus-based agent, to basically say it isn't always so easy "going home again." Junior wanted Huggins to understand that; his return to his hometown to play for the Cincinnati Reds had not worked out so well.

"It was hard," Huggins said. "I really love the people at West Virginia, but I love the people in Cincinnati, too. I love being here. I love being around my former guys. I really love this town. It would've been kind of neat to go back and kind of right the ship there because they had fallen on hard times.

"What caught me by surprise was the number of people who are Bearcat fans here, from elderly people to guys that you would never think follow sports. The people who follow us in TV and newspapers. I had more people say to me, 'I've never been to Shoemaker Center but I love to watch you guys play.' At the gas station, anywhere I was, they would walk up and talk to me."

Make no mistake—without Goin's presence, Huggins would not have stayed. Goin was the assistant Athletic Director at West Virginia when Huggins played there.

"If he's not the AD, I wouldn't be here," Huggins said a few years later. "But I'd have probably left long before that."

This story is even more interesting in hindsight. After parting with UC in August 2005, Huggins sat out a year, then coached Kansas State for one season. On April 5, 2007, he agreed to become the head coach at West Virginia. The Mountaineers got their man after all.

SEPTEMBER 28, 2002:
THE HEART ATTACK

PITTSBURGH

Huggins was in Pittsburgh on Friday, September 27, to watch a few potential recruits play pick-up games at Baldwin High School. He spent time Friday night with longtime friend J.O. Stright, who was legal guardian to former Bearcat Danny Fortson when UC was recruiting him.

Huggins had a late Saturday morning flight out of Pittsburgh. He was scheduled to be at a Nike coaching clinic in Wisconsin that night.

The UC coach returned his National rental car at Pittsburgh International Airport at about 8:30 a.m. Then Huggins started having chest pains. He called Stright on his cell phone and said, "I'm sweating. I feel like I've got an elephant on my chest. I'm having a heart attack." Huggins's cell phone then lost power. Stright left his home immediately and headed for the airport.

Huggins, 49 years old at the time, ended up lying on the sidewalk near the parking garage. A police officer was with him, waiting for paramedics to arrive. An ambulance transported Huggins to Sewickley Valley Hospital, about five miles west of the airport. He was then transferred to the Medical Center, Beaver (Pennsylvania), 19 miles north of the airport and 35 miles north of downtown Pittsburgh.

Doctors found blockage in three main coronary arteries and had to operate immediately. A stent, a tiny metal mesh device designed to keep Huggins's once-clogged artery open, was implanted. Huggins was in serious but stable condition overnight.

"I don't know if he realizes how close he came to not being here," Goin told *The Cincinnati Enquirer* the next day.

At Conference USA Media Day five weeks later, Huggins said: "They tell me 10 or 15 more minutes, I probably would've been dead."

CINCINNATI

June Huggins was preparing to meet her husband at the Cincinnati/Northern Kentucky International Airport where he was catching a connection to Wisconsin. She was going to join him on the trip to the Nike clinic.

Stright called June to tell her what happened. "Bob just had a heart attack," he said.

"Is it very serious?" she asked.

"Yeah, I think it is," Stright said.

June Huggins and her oldest daughter, Jenna, then a sophomore at UC, headed for the airport to catch a flight to Pittsburgh, where Stright picked them up. They arrived at the Medical Center shortly after Huggins's surgery. Jacqueline, the Huggins's younger daughter, remained in Cincinnati with friends.

"It was pretty scary," June said. "I really kept it together, and I think that's because my daughter was with me. She was scared to death."

As soon as she saw her husband, there was some relief.

"Once I got there and saw him, it was better," June said. "You know him. He wasn't going to act like there was anything wrong, like it wasn't a big deal."

Back on campus, the UC players had just finished lifting weights and were getting ready to play pick-up games. Former associate head coach Dan Peters got a phone call from athletic trainer Jayd Grossman telling him Huggins had suffered a massive heart attack.

Peters called the Bearcats into the locker room and delivered the news. The room fell silent. The players prayed together. Some were in tears. They decided not to play that day.

"It was real emotional," Leonard Stokes said. "I started crying. I walked into a bathroom stall and just stood there. Coach Pete gave me his number and said to call him later, he'd keep me up to date."

PHILADELPHIA

The Bearcats football team was playing at Temple University in Philadelphia. The players were just about to come onto the field for pregame warmups. Goin was standing on the sideline at Franklin Field about 20 minutes before kickoff when trainer Bill Walker walked up and handed him his cell phone. It was Grossman, telling Goin that Huggins suffered a massive heart attack. "And he didn't know if he was going to make it," Goin said. "It was not looking good."

Goin hung up the phone, went to the UC locker room and told associate Athletic Director Paul Klazcak that he was leaving for Pittsburgh. Goin's wife, Nancy, was in the stands at the football stadium. By the time Klaczak got to her, Goin was already on his way to the Philadelphia airport, led by a police escort.

He bought a ticket on a U.S. Air flight, got through security and rushed to the gate.

"I was prepared for the worst," Goin said. "I went there with the idea that if anything happened to Bobby, I wanted to be there for June."

Goin arrived in Pittsburgh and went right to the Medical Center, Beaver (Pennsylvania).

"When I got there, he had just been wheeled into his room after they had done the procedure," Goin said. "He was awake when I walked in. I think only June and his brother were in the room."

CINCINNATI

On Wednesday morning, four days after his heart attack, Huggins was taken out a back door of the Medical Center, Beaver (Pennsylvania), and transported by jet ambulance in 37 minutes to Lunken Airport in Cincinnati. He was then taken by ground ambulance to Christ Hospital, where he was in stable condition in the cardiac care unit.

Stokes had not been able to stop thinking about his coach. Finally, he couldn't take it anymore. He just had to see him. Early Thursday morning, Stokes went to the hospital. He said there were so much media and other people around the front desk and occupying security that he just snuck past everyone and onto the elevator.

When he got to Huggins's floor, some of the workers recognized him and said, "You're not supposed to be here." Stokes just kept walking "like I didn't hear them." He rushed to Huggins's room, ran in and shut the door.

"We talked for like 15 minutes," Stokes said. "Just me and him. It made me feel good because he was sitting up. He was acting like his old self, laughing and joking. He was laughing at me. He said, 'Everybody's always got you pictured as a saint and you snuck in!' I felt much better just to be in contact with him."

Several UC players visited Huggins on Friday for about an hour. "He's ready to roll," Peters told *The Enquirer*. "We've just got to see what the doctors say."

Huggins was released from the hospital October 7, nine days after his heart surgery.

SHOEMAKER CENTER

Goin had already decided to do away with Midnight Madness festivities for October 2002 before Huggins had a heart attack. In its place would be "Breakfast with Bob," the morning of UC's first official practice.

On October 12, Bob Huggins, accompanied by June, walked onto Ed Jucker Court in Shoemaker Center to a loud standing ovation from roughly 3,200 fans.

"I just want to thank everybody for everybody's concern," he told the crowd. "It's overwhelming."

"It was amazing how many people were there and the attention they gave it," June Huggins said. "I'm just always surprised at how many people do care. He got so many cards and letters and flowers."

Later, Bob met with the media for the first time since his heart attack.

"If it's your time to go, it's your time to go," Huggins said at his press conference. "God decided it wasn't my time to go."

He coached practice that day and was on the sideline for UC's season opener, his 14th with the Bearcats.

"He wouldn't have been happy if he didn't (coach)," June Huggins said. "I would kind of worry about him when he'd get so fired up. Dr. (Dean) Kereiakes (Huggins's cardiologist) said he thought everything should be OK. I wouldn't say I think about it all the time, just once in a while when he's really red-faced and veins are popping out. But every time he goes to the doctor, they say his heart is great."

SILENT BUT DEADLY

Jason Maxiell showed up from Carrollton, Texas, in the fall 2001 as the pride of UC's incoming class of newcomers. He was a first-team Class 5A all-state high school player in Texas and was a two-time district defensive player of the year. He was only six foot seven, but he had long arms, could block shots and, oh, how he could dunk.

But unlike a lot of highly touted players, Maxiell seldom said a word during practice, pick-up games, drills, wind sprints, before games, after games—you name it. Whether a teammate made a bad or good play, whether Huggins yelled and scolded, Maxiell's facial expression rarely changed and he almost never uttered a peep.

Not that Huggins had to get on Maxiell much during practice or games, but when he did, Maxiell just listened.

"I never was one to say something back," Maxiell said. "I feel like he's always right. My game has advanced because I listened to him. Defense—I didn't know anything about it until I listened to him."

Maxiell won Conference USA's Sixth Man Award as a freshman and was a key player on the Bearcats' 31-4 team in 2001-02. He had plenty of teammates who spoke up on the court—and off. Ironically, it was a player who was not shy about talking back to Huggins who gave Maxiell advice his first year on campus.

"Even though Donald Little wasn't a quiet one, he always told me to shut up and listen," Maxiell said.

Another player who kept silent at all times was 2004 graduate Field Williams, a shooting guard from Houston.

"Field and Max are as quiet as any two guys I've ever been around," former associate head coach Dan Peters said. "Those guys never say a word. It's good to have guys like that. They're leaders by their actions. They just keep working.

"What they do is buy into the program from Day One because they trust and they believe by what's been done in the past. They've seen the success of guys we've had, so they just roll up their sleeves and go to work."

Maxiell finished his career with 1,566 points and ranked 13th on the school's all-time scoring list. Williams left with 1,030 points and as one of the most prolific three-point shooters ever in the program. He still holds the career three-point field goal percentage record (.401), and he is fourth in three-point field goals made (262) behind Deonta Vaughn and Sean Kilpatrick (313) and Darnell Burton (306).

YOU WANT IT, YOU GOT IT

Armein Kirkland felt he needed a demanding collegiate coach to improve as a player. As a senior at Lee High in Tyler, Texas, Kirkland considered playing for Bob Knight, the new coach at Texas A&M. He said he was also recruited by Nolan Richardson at Arkansas. But Cincinnati commanded his attention.

Steve Logan was lighting it up his senior year. Kirkland was attracted to the C-Paw and the fact UC wore Nike gear and was a Michael Jordan-sponsored school. "I liked the uniforms," he said. "As kids, that's what you're attracted to. I really didn't know much about Huggs until he started recruiting me."

Huggins was certainly the challenging coach Kirkland was looking for, but that doesn't mean the two always got along after Kirkland's arrival in 2002.

"I know me and Huggs bumped heads a lot," Kirkland said. "I think he sometimes didn't know how to relate to me. You've got to kind of know how you can talk to people. You can't throw every batter the same pitch. We just bumped heads, but at the same time he saw a lot of potential in me. The approach on both of our ends was not always healthy. Our relationship probably could've been better. But I learned a lot."

GETTING OFF THE BUS

UC's 2002-03 season ended with a 74-60 loss to Gonzaga University in the first round of the NCAA Tournament in Salt Lake City, Utah. It was a game in which Huggins and radio analyst Chuck Machock were thrown out of the game.

You read that right: Machock, a former UC player and assistant coach, was tossed for repeatedly berating official Mike Kitts after he ejected Huggins, who had received two technical fouls. But the evening's events weren't over just yet.

On the quiet ride back to the hotel, a truck carrying Gonzaga fans pulled up next to the Bearcats' bus and started yelling—and gesturing—at the team and Huggins.

When the bus stopped at a red light, Huggins walked off the bus and started to approach the Gonzaga fans. Assistant coach Andy Kennedy followed, as did strength and conditioning coach Scott Greenawalt. Associate head coach Dan Peters tried to keep the players on the bus.

"It was funny," Kirkland said. "Nothing happened. Huggs said something to them. They kind of got scared. They didn't say anything. They probably weren't expecting to get stuck at a light with us. And you could tell by the looks on their faces they were surprised he got off the bus. I was surprised, too. They weren't ready for that."

CHANGE OF HEART

It was just like old times. The Bearcats, who earned a reputation as a full-court pressing defensive team in the early 1990s, were back at it early in the 2003-04 season. Cincinnati started the season 13-0 and climbed to No. 6 in the Associated Press poll.

UC was trapping opponents in the backcourt and converting turnovers into easy lay-ups and dunks. The players were smiling. The fans loved it.

The Bearcats took a 16-3 record into their February 11 home game against South Florida. The Bulls had just six scholarship players, were on an eight-game losing streak and came in with a record of 6-13, 0-8 in Conference USA.

Cincinnati won 80-67, but it was not as easy as it should have been. South Florida had numerous wide-open three-point attempts and lay-ups. It scored 46 second-half points and shot .522 from the field for the night.

Right after that game, Huggins announced: "We've seen the last of the press. You can't press with guys who won't run back on defense."

"We had to readjust what we were doing," Peters said. "We were really depending on getting steals and run outs and some dunks. We turned teams over, but I don't know if we were getting any better.

"When we stopped pressing, we became a better team. We lost some games, but we became a better team. We pulled our defense back. We started guarding the ball a little better. We guarded the paint better. Our defense was better. It just took some time to adjust."

UC lost its next two—at Wake Forest and at UAB—then won eight of its next nine games.

LEAGUE OF THEIR OWN

In 2003, Marquette won Conference USA's regular-season title. It was the first time since the inception of the league in 1995-96 that Cincinnati did not at least share the championship.

It was up to the 2003-04 UC team to reclaim the conference.

That proved no easy task. The league was getting stronger. Rick Pitino was in his third year coaching at Louisville. John Calipari was in his fourth at Memphis. Marquette had advanced to the Final Four in 2003. UAB and DePaul were vastly improved.

No. 13 UC went into its final regular-season game—at home against No. 20 Memphis—needing a victory to share a piece of its eighth league title in nine years and clinch a first-round bye for the conference tournament.

The Tigers had won 12 of their previous 13 games.

"I can't guarantee a victory, but we can guarantee that guys will come out and give it their best," Tony Bobbitt told *The Cincinnati Enquirer* the day before the game.

It was another classic battle between the two programs.

Memphis was ahead 79-78 when senior guard Bobbitt came to the rescue—after he almost blew it. Bobbitt drove into the lane and sent a high pass out to senior guard Field Williams, who saved it from going out of bounds. Williams threw the ball inside, and another pass went out to Bobbitt in the right corner. He nailed a three-pointer to give UC a two-point lead with 36 seconds remaining.

After the Tigers missed a shot, Bobbitt got the rebound and was fouled. He made both free throws with 19.7 seconds left.

Final score: Cincinnati 83, Memphis 79.

"I just knew I wanted the ball," Bobbitt said. "I told Coach Huggs in the huddle I wanted the ball. I wanted to show I could step up and make a big basket.

"When the shot went up, it felt good. I knew right then not only did I help myself, I helped my team and I helped the program."

BIG-TIME TURNAROUND

On one wall in Shoemaker Center is a list of players who have been named All-America. One day before practice in the fall 2002, Bobbitt looked up and told a newspaper reporter that he wanted his name on the wall, too.

"I wanted to make an impact," he says now.

Bobbitt, a native of Daytona Beach, Florida, came from the College of Southern Idaho as a highly touted junior college transfer who was expected to help UC right away offensively.

But Bobbitt's Division I career did not get going the way he envisioned. In his first 17 games, he averaged just 12.3

minutes and never started. He scored in double digits only three times. His defense wasn't up to Huggins's standards. After missing a game with a sprained ankle, Bobbitt averaged 8.7 minutes over the next six games. He was frustrated with the limited playing time.

The day before UC played at No. 5 Louisville on February 5, Bobbitt left the team.

"Stupid move," he said, "but that was my decision. I don't even like to talk about it anymore. It happened. There's nothing I can do about it."

Bobbitt wasn't the first player to leave the Bearcats in midseason (he wasn't even the first that season), and he won't be the last. After a meeting with Huggins, he was reinstated to the team. He apologized to his teammates and told *The Cincinnati Post*, "It will never happen again. I'm better than that. I just tried to copout the easy way."

UC lost at Louisville 77-71. Bobbitt returned for the next game and played six minutes against Oklahoma State.

In the final seven games of the season, he averaged 11.1 points and 18.7 minutes.

During the summer of 2003, a former Bearcat stepped in and became kind of an unofficial mentor to Bobbitt. Corie Blount, who played on UC's Final Four team in 1992, was in the weight room with Bobbitt one day and the two decided to have lunch. Blount talked to Bobbitt "about being a man and responsibilities," Huggins said. "Corie's been unbelievable for Tony. Tony's been a different kid."

"We just went to lunch and discussed some basketball things, as well as personal things," Bobbitt said. "He was talking to me about who to be around, who not to be around, watching game film, preparing better for practice. More than basketball. He knew what I could do on the court, he just wanted to make sure I was doing the right things off the court.

"He told me the real things that I needed to hear. Corie said, 'Don't fight with Huggs. Act like a professional.' Why not listen to a guy who's been in the (NBA) making millions of dollars? It helped me a lot. I knew if I didn't listen, it would shoot me in the butt later."

Blount helped. The year of maturity and a year of experience with Huggins helped. Bobbitt's approach to his life off the court helped.

"I let a lot of the friends I used to hang with go—friends in Cincinnati and Florida," Bobbitt said. "I cut ties. I had to. It was hard.

"And my approach with Huggs was excellent. I think that's one of the reasons I had a better season. He didn't yell and I didn't have to yell. Though he still got on me a little bit."

Bobbitt turned things around all right.

He continued to come off the bench but was UC's second-leading scorer at 13.4 ppg. He was third-team all-league and Conference USA's Sixth Man Award winner. He tied a school record with eight steals against Coppin State (November 29, 2003), was most valuable player of the C-USA tournament and hit the game-winning shot with 16.1 seconds left in Cincinnati's first-round NCAA Tournament victory over East Tennessee State.

"I think he dealt with Huggs better," Peters said. "He just bought in to the whole thing, and you saw the results."

END OF A SPECIAL ERA

It was no secret that University of Cincinnati President Nancy Zimpher was not a fan of Bob Huggins. Mike DeCourcy of the *Sporting News* reported in a 2010 article that among Zimpher's charges by the board of trustees when she was hired in 2003 was to "do something about Huggins." DeCourcy attributed that to former Athletic Director Bob Goin.

Zimpher's contempt for Huggins only escalated after Huggins was arrested for driving under the influence of alcohol in June 2004, an episode captured on video and aired repeatedly on national television.

Coach Bob Huggins and 2000 National Player of the Year Kenyon Martin embrace during Martin's final home game—an 84-41 victory over St. Louis on March 4, 2000. (Photo by Lisa Ventre/University of Cincinnati)

While Huggins was not dismissed after that, Zimpher refused to renew Huggins' contract. Late in the summer of 2005, the impasse came to a head.

Huggins was on his way back to Cincinnati on August 24, 2005, after attending the Michael Jordan Fantasy Camp in Las Vegas.

Kennedy and assistant coach Frank Martin were sitting in the basketball office when they saw a fax had arrived.

"It was basically the terms of the end," Kennedy said. "It said, 'You resign by this time and here are the terms; if not here's the other option.' I just remember Huggs wasn't in the office. We didn't know if he was even aware of it. I'm sitting there holding this fax thinking, *OK, what does this mean? Does Huggs know this?* That was three or four hours of uneasiness.

"I just kind of sat tight. I didn't feel it was my place to call Mr. G [Goin]. I just waited until Huggs was back."

The day is well documented. After 16 years as head basketball coach at the University of Cincinnati, Huggins was given the choice to resign or be fired.

Kirkland said he found out from reporters. Eric Hicks said he saw the news on TV while in an airport returning from playing with the U.S. team at the World University Games in Turkey.

This can't be true, Hicks thought. He called Kennedy, who confirmed what was happening. "I was angry as hell," Hicks said. "I had bought into the program completely. I had given myself to the team. It felt like I was betrayed. If Andy Kennedy didn't get the job as interim, I was transferring to North Carolina."

Kennedy didn't know what was going to happen. He tried to reach out to players, most of whom hadn't yet arrived on campus for the school year. He didn't know if he should start looking for a job. The next day, UC asked whether he would take over as interim coach with a contract through the following March.

Kennedy first wanted to speak with Huggins face-to-face and drove to his Loveland home.

"I don't really know how to feel about this," he told Huggins. "I don't really know what to do. I'm certainly not going to do it without your blessing. I need to know you're OK with it."

"He obviously was in an emotional state based on all he had poured into the program and now within a few short days he was no longer captain of that ship," Kennedy said. "But he said without hesitation, 'Hey, if you think you can do it, do it.' He understood it would be a challenge based on the roster. ... His concern was not about UC and how he had been treated; his concern was more about wanting me to have a chance to be successful. He felt responsible for bringing those kids into the program, especially the seniors, and said, 'We have a responsibility to see this through. It's a no-brainer if you're up to the task.'"

Kennedy accepted the challenge.

11

ANDY KENNEDY ERA (2005-2006)

IRONY

The first victory of the Andy Kennedy era came in the first game of the 2005-06 season ... at home.

... in overtime.

... against Murray State.

... coached by—wait for it, wait for it—*Mick Cronin.*

Not once during that night did Cronin envision becoming UC's head coach, he said. In fact, on the bus ride home to Murray State, he told his assistant coaches he felt the Cincinnati program would be decimated after that season, as it was losing five seniors and rumors were already circulating that freshman guard Devan Downey would transfer.

"Whoever takes that job next is screwed," Cronin says he told his assistants.

Little did he know.

WHO NEEDS SLEEP?

After an encouraging 3-0 start, UC lost back-to-back games at home to the University of Dayton and the University of Memphis. The loss to the Flyers was the first ever against UD in Shoemaker Center. And it was the first time *ever* that UC lost consecutive games at The Shoe.

"My popularity was soaring," Kennedy recalled, laughing.

The next game was December 10, 2005, in Nashville against Vanderbilt University, which had a 28-game home winning streak versus non-conference opponents.

The Bearcats were fitting in one more practice in Cincinnati before flying to Nashville. As practice began, light snow flurries fell from the sky; by the time they left, heavy snow covered everything.

It wasn't until they were on the bus to catch their flight that Kennedy and the team learned the airport was closed.

What the heck? Let's drive, Kennedy thought. It's typically about a four-hour drive to Nashville.

"They had given us a bus that was only supposed to take us to the airport; it wasn't a real nice bus," Kennedy said. "We simply had no choice. We couldn't risk it and try to fly on game day. So we had to go. We drove to Nashville, and it took us like 11-12 hours. We got into Nashville in the wee hours of the morning."

The Cincinnati players showed no ill effects from the journey. All five starters scored in double figures, led by Downey and James White with 18 points each, and the Bearcats won 92-83.

That kicked off a 10-game UC winning streak. "From that point on we soared," Kennedy said.

UNTIL ...

Armein Kirkland suffered a heartbreaking season- and college-career-ending knee injury—at a time when he was playing his best basketball.

"He had this talent, this Scottie Pippen-like point-forward game," Kennedy said. "Everybody was waiting for this kid to show what he could do consistently. He really started playing well."

In Milwaukee on January 7, 2006, Kirkland helped hold Marquette star Steve Novak—coming off 41 points against the University of Connecticut—to 17 points in a 70-66 Bearcats victory. Also in that game, Eric Hicks collected a triple-double with 22 points, 12 rebounds, and a career-high 10 blocked shots.

"That was a special game because I almost broke my ankle," Hicks said. "I think I got a rebound and landed on somebody's foot and rolled it. ... I didn't even know I had a triple-double until the end, when [then-associate Athletic Director Brian] Teter told me. I knew the rebounds were there. I didn't know how many blocks I had. I was just playing to get a win."

Anticipation was building for the next game on January 9 against the No. 4 UConn Huskies. The Bearcats finally entered that season's Associated Press rankings at No. 25. It was ESPN's Big Monday game. ESPN's Andy Katz was working on a story about UC's turnaround. And, a number of NBA scouts were on hand.

"There was all this hype," Kennedy said. "People were starting to get excited about the team."

"I remember telling James [White], 'We're gonna get paid tonight,'" Kirkland said. He thought if he could impress the scouts, his NBA stock would rise. "I was getting my confidence back. I felt good about the game."

Kirkland started out impressive, all right. He scored 14 of UC's first 18 points, including three 3-pointers, and helped the Bearcats stay within 21-18.

And then it happened.

"I just went up for a normal layup and my left knee gave out," Kirkland said. "It was a split-second thing. It was a freak accident. I felt the pop. I kind of hopped to the sidelines. I was just holding my knee. [Athletic trainer David] Fluker was looking at me as they were trying to examine it."

He left with 7:49 remaining in the first half. After his knee was wrapped, he limped to the locker room with 4:55 to play.

"I went back to the visitor's training table inside the locker room," Kirkland said. "Their team doctor came in there. He checked my knee, and I just remember him saying, 'Armein, I'm not going to sugarcoat anything. I've been doing this a long time. I'm pretty sure you tore your ACL.' I was hurt. My season was over with. I was hoping to go to the NBA and have a career and now I couldn't even finish my senior year.

"I was crying. My teammates came in and tried to console me after Coach Kennedy's halftime speech. They put a brace on me. I was on crutches. I kind of just chilled on the bench the rest of the game.

"It was tough to deal with for a while. That's not how I wanted to spend my senior year. I guess it was definitely in God's plan. At least I went out playing the start of the best game I had."

UC lost the game, 70-59.

Said Kennedy: "I was depressed for the kid, for our program, for everything that transpired."

HELP WANTED

Monday was Kirkland's last game.

Kennedy's team was already low on numbers, and he was even more concerned about merely having enough players to practice.

Tuesday, Kennedy visited Bearcats football coach Mark Dantonio to inquire if he had a player with high school basketball experience good enough to help with practices.

Dantonio suggested true freshman Connor Barwin, a 6-foot-4, 230-pound tight end who played football *and* basketball at the University of Detroit Jesuit High School and Academy.

Wednesday, Kennedy met with Barwin.

Thursday, Barwin practiced with the basketball team.

Saturday, against perennial power Syracuse, Barwin suited up in jersey No. 51 without a name on the back.

"I'm sure he's thinking, *I'm here to put on a uniform and just go through layup lines,*" Kennedy said.

Instead, Barwin played eight minutes and finished with two points (on free throws) and one rebound. He played in 18 games that season, averaging 9.9 minutes and scoring a total of 18 points.

Barwin played one more season of basketball for incoming coach Mick Cronin, scoring 27 points in 23 games. On the football field, Barwin moved from tight end to defensive end and helped lead UC to its first Big East football championship while leading the league in sacks.

He was selected by the Houston Texans in the second round of the 2009 NFL draft and made his first NFL sack against Cincinnati's Carson Palmer. In March 2013, he signed a six-year, $36-million contract with the Philadelphia Eagles.

SENIOR NIGHT SPECIAL GUEST

In the time leading up to his final game in Shoemaker Center on March 4, 2006, Hicks called Bob Huggins, the coach who recruited him to UC, and said, "If you're not there for my Senior Night, I'm not playing. It's as simple as that."

Hicks echoed that to Kennedy and anyone else who would listen. Hicks wanted Huggins to walk out with him on the court before the game. "I know they wanted him to be there," Kennedy said of the seniors.

"It's going to cause too much controversy," Huggins told Hicks. "I don't want to cause any more controversy. I'll just be in the building. You'll see me."

"I don't recall having any issues with that," then-UC Athletic Director Mike Thomas said. "As a matter of fact, I probably thought it was the right thing to do. Certainly you always want to look at what's in the best interest of your team. Bob Huggins was part of the fabric of the basketball program, and he still is."

In pre-game ceremonies, Hicks received a loud ovation from the sellout crowd of 13,176. Carrying a framed photo of himself—a gift from the school traditionally given to seniors—he hugged Kennedy and a few teammates, and then walked to the far corner of the court where Huggins stood. It was the first time Huggins was at a home game since leaving the university.

The two embraced and Hicks started crying. An emotional Huggins hugged all five seniors, including James White, Chadd Moore, Armein Kirkland, and Jihad Muhammad. Hicks walked back toward the bench, using his warm-up shirt to wipe away tears.

"You never saw me cry like that," Hicks said. "I just broke down. Those were tears of joy. Huggs was a father figure to a lot of us. He's the man who got me there. He needed to be there for my last [home] game. It just felt right."

"I wanted to be here," Huggins said that night, "but I didn't want to do anything they didn't want me to do."

UC's opponent West Virginia was ranked 16th in the country. Led by Kevin Pittsnogle and Mike Gansy, the Mountaineers had beaten UC a month earlier.

It didn't matter, though. The Bearcats won 78-75. Hicks scored 18 and went into the student section to celebrate when the game ended. He said it was the most special game of his college career.

"I thought it took a lot of courage for Coach [Huggins] to come," Kennedy said afterward. "It shows you what kind of man he is. It's a tribute to these seniors. They wanted him to come. I thought it was fitting going against his alma mater in a game that decided our season."

Not only was West Virginia Huggins' alma mater—it's the team he would take over as head coach in 2007.

AWKWARD TRANSITION

Kennedy thought the West Virginia victory would be enough to boost UC into the 2006 NCAA Tournament. UC went 6-9 to finish the regular season, then lost in its first Big East Tournament game to Syracuse 74-73 on a Gerry McNamara runner at the buzzer.

At 19-12, the Bearcats were still predicted by bracketology expert Joe Lunardi to make the field of 64 as a 10th seed. The team watched the NCAA Tournament Selection Show in its locker room. "I thought we were in," Kennedy said. "Lunardi doesn't miss. I was relieved because we had been to like a thousand straight tournaments and I didn't want it to end on my watch. Well, we didn't get in. I kept thinking, *there's got to be another bracket.* Our locker room was in stunned silence."

Cincinnati settled for a bid to the National Invitation Tournament. It won home games against Charlotte and Minnesota. After those games, Kennedy asked Athletic Director Mike Thomas for permission to speak with other schools about jobs, and Thomas agreed.

That's when Kennedy had his first conversation with University of Mississippi Athletic Director Pete Boone. Boone flew to Cincinnati to meet with Kennedy on March 23, 2006, the morning of UC's NIT quarterfinal game at home against South Carolina.

Kennedy woke up and went to meet with Ole Miss officials, including chancellor Robert Khayat and senior associate Athletic Director for finance John Hartwell, at the downtown Omni Hotel.

Upon his return to campus, he retrieved a voicemail summoning him to a meeting, where he was informed James White and Jihad Muhammad were academically ineligible. Their seasons were over. Kennedy then went to UC's shootaround to tell the players and the team.

"Again, we have to regroup," he said. Kennedy told Boone he would keep his cell phone turned on until an hour before the game. It turns out that while Kennedy was in the coaches' locker room in Shoemaker Center, Boone called to offer him Mississippi's head coach position. Kennedy accepted.

As he walked on to the court before the game, Kennedy approached his wife, Kimber, in the corner stands and told her, "We're going to Ole Miss."

"She had no idea," he said. "She didn't know the job had been offered."

The Bearcats played a gutsy game but lost 65-62 to South Carolina before 7,775 fans, many of whom gave Kennedy multiple standing ovations and shouted their support for him to remain as head coach.

Kennedy said he knew long before that night it wasn't going to happen. He said he and Thomas had candid conversations during which Kennedy expressed he wasn't interested in the job.

"I just didn't think it was the right fit," Kennedy said. "I will always be a Huggs guy. I am not going to divorce myself from Bob Huggins. I am not going to act is if I was there for any reason but because of him. It wasn't in anyone's best interest."

Thomas said that when he arrived as UC's Athletic Director in December 2005, he was open-minded and considered Kennedy a candidate for the job. "There was no foregone conclusion that I was going down a certain path," Thomas said. He felt that early on, Kennedy was interested in the job. But as the season went on, the two agreed it was indeed not the right fit.

The aftermath of UC's final game was, well, active. Longtime UC reporter Bill Koch of *The Cincinnati Enquirer* wrote

In his one year as UC's interim head coach, Andy Kennedy's team went 21-13. The Bearcats started the season 13-2, and Kennedy was selected as CBS Sportsline's Mid-Season National Coach of the Year. (AP Photo/Al Behrman)

that the day "will be remembered as one of the most bizarre in the history of the UC basketball program."

Kennedy held his standard postgame interview with radio announcers Dan Hoard and Chuck Machock, but instead of his comments being broadcast in the arena for the fans, as they usually were, the sound was turned off. The crowd, which had waited around to hear Kennedy, was angry.

Soon after, Kennedy and Thomas met in Thomas' office.

"I think by that point in time we both knew where it was going," Thomas said. "I wish I could tell you how the conversation went. I am sure my mouth opened first, but what came out I don't really remember."

Within an hour of the final buzzer, UC issued a press release announcing Mick Cronin had been hired as its new basketball coach. Cronin was unavailable to the media. Thomas left the building without talking.

Mississippi announced Kennedy as its new basketball coach.

Oh, and earlier that same day, Huggins had been hired as head coach at Kansas State University.

"I think this is the end of the chapter for Bob Huggins basketball," Kennedy said that night.

Later, Kennedy said, he, assistant coach Frank Martin, and Huggins all met at the Holy Grail in Clifton and talked about the strange previous seven months.

"It was really a crazy year," Kennedy said. "But I have a lot of good memories."

12

MICK CRONIN ERA (2006-PRESENT)

HOME-GROWN HEAD COACH

Leading up to Murray State University's first-round 2006 NCAA Tournament game against No. 3 seed University of North Carolina, Mick Cronin heard Cincinnati might be interested in interviewing him for its head coaching position. But he was concentrating on his team and had no direct contact with UC at that point.

The Friday night game on March 17 didn't begin until after 9:30 p.m. The 14th-seeded Racers lost to the Tar Heels 69-65 at University of Dayton Arena. After the loss, which left some Murray State players in tears in the locker room, it was after 1 a.m. before the team returned to its hotel. It was then that Cronin learned from Murray State Athletic Director Allen

Ward that Cincinnati had asked permission to speak with him about its vacancy.

"My phone had been off," Cronin said. "When I turned it on, I had all kinds of messages—from my agent and from people in Cincinnati. They wanted to meet with me *immediately*—the next day."

Cronin sent his team back to Murray State the next morning and drove to a Five Seasons Sports Club between Cincinnati and Dayton, where he met with UC Athletic Director Mike Thomas and Deputy Director of Athletics Bob Arkeilpane.

"I didn't know either one of them," Cronin said. "I had no time to prepare. To be honest, I figured it was a token interview so they could say they did interview me. I told Mike Thomas that. I figured anybody tied to Bob Huggins had no chance. He said, 'That has no bearing on anything.'"

Cronin was a Cincinnati native and graduated from La Salle High School and UC. He worked for Huggins for five years—one as video coordinator and four as an assistant coach.

The talk started with Xs and Os, academics, and how Cronin would run his program. Thomas and Arkeilpane then shifted to sales mode. They wanted Cronin to know Cincinnati did indeed care about its basketball program. Cronin left that interview wondering if anyone else was interested in the job. As he drove back to Murray, Kentucky, he pondered the conversation with his assistants four months earlier on the bus after the Bearcats loss:

"Whoever takes that job next is screwed."

Thomas said other coaches were considered.

"We did have interest in the position," Thomas said. "We had vetted other candidates and talked to other candidates. I think Mick was a good fit in a lot of ways. He was obviously born and raised in Cincinnati. He went to school there. He had a long history there with Huggs and understood the university and the community. He knew Cincinnati and the region. And he had been in some battles himself as a head coach."

A WILD WEEK

After returning to Kentucky, Cronin then left to recruit at the National Junior College Men's Basketball Championship in Hutchinson, Kansas. Other schools showed interest in Cronin. On one hand, he was receiving calls from Cincinnati boosters and Big East Conference officials urging him *not* to take another job because UC was going to make him an offer; others, however, were concerned going back to UC was a bad move.

"Everybody professionally was telling me not to take it, saying whoever got the job was going to get fired and that I should be the *next* guy after that if I wanted to go back home," Cronin said. "They said it could be career suicide."

Louisville coach Rick Pitino, another Cronin mentor and one-time boss, advised that Cronin stipulate in his contract a certain amount of time to rebuild Cincinnati's program. "It's going to take you five years," Pitino told Cronin. "There's no other way to fix it."

"He was right on the money," Cronin said. "Once I felt confident I was going to be given time to do it the right way, I thought I couldn't turn down the job I really wanted; I thought I may never get the chance again. I figured I was going to get beat up for three or four years, but I could take that if it meant I was going to be able to be the coach at my alma mater and go home."

"It wasn't as joyous as you would think," Cronin added, "because I knew how brutal it was going to be. I knew I wasn't riding in on a white horse with the band playing. It wasn't like Coach Huggins retired and everybody was happy. It wasn't how you would want it to be."

On March 24, 2006, one week after Murray State was eliminated from the NCAA Tournament, Cronin was introduced as the head coach of UC's men's basketball team.

RUDE AWAKENING

A few weeks after accepting the job, Cronin walked through campus near UC's baseball stadium with recruit Mike Williams when a man wearing an Elder High School shirt turned to Cronin and said, "Hey Mick, welcome home."

Cronin was feeling good, but the man continued: "You've got absolutely no chance. They don't care about sports here. They're tearing this place apart. They won't support you. I don't know why you came back."

Williams' jaw dropped. But he still signed with UC.

HOOSIERS LOSS, BEARCATS GAIN

Indianapolis native Deonta Vaughn initially committed to Indiana University while he was attending Arlington High School in his hometown. But, he said, he backed out when rumors started circulating that Indiana coach Mike Davis was not going to stay in Bloomington. (Davis did resign as the Hoosiers' coach in February 2006.)

Vaughn also was not yet academically eligible for college, so he transferred to Harmony Community School in Cincinnati for the 2005-06 school year, when he became better acquainted with the Bearcats.

Vaughn got the test scores he needed but was not heavily recruited after suffering a high ankle sprain at Harmony, even though he averaged 17.4 points and 6.6 assists while playing for former Bearcat Rodney Crawford.

"When I got the job, I had a list of every unsigned player in the country," Cronin said. "I knew what [Vaughn] was capable of. I saw him play in the Nike camp before he committed to Indiana a year and a half prior. I went to Harmony to see him right away. His ankle was still swollen.

"My goal was not to sign a high school player just to make it look good in the media. I was only going to sign a high school player I knew was good enough—and I knew he was good enough. Extenuating circumstances made him available."

Vaughn would become instrumental in UC's rebuilding process.

IT HAS TO START SOMEWHERE

UC started the 2006-07 season 3-0, with victories all coming at home against Howard University, the University of Tennessee-Martin, and High Point University out of North Carolina. In the morning shoot-around before the Bearcats' fourth game, against Wofford College from South Carolina, Cronin gave Vaughn the news he would get his first college start.

"I didn't tell anybody, though," Vaughn said. "I didn't tell my parents, who were coming to the game. I was surprised. We had a point guard named [Timmy] Crowell with us. I thought he was going to start because he was more experienced at the college level."

There were two surprises in the game:

1. UC lost 91-90, only Wofford's second victory over a Big East team in its history.
2. Vaughn delivered an eye-opening performance. He scored 33 points (22 in the first half) and finished 9-of-17 from 3-point range. He also had six assists.

"It was a super exciting game for me," Vaughn said. "Everything just worked. I was running the team. I was coming off screens and popping open, shooting 3s. I felt like I couldn't miss. That game made me realize I belonged here.

"The first couple of games I was nervous. You don't know if you're going to be able to play at a big-time school like

Cincinnati. Once I got the opportunity to prove I could be here, I never looked back."

NOT A PRANK CALL

Around 9:30 p.m. on Selection Sunday 2008, Mike Waddell, then associate Athletic Director at UC, received a call on his cell phone that sounded like it was from the inaugural College Basketball Invitational, a new postseason tournament that would choose teams left after the NCAA and National Invitation Tournaments announced their fields.

The battery in Waddell's cell phone was all but dead; he had to go to his car and plug his phone into a charger in order to return the phone call.

"I thought it was a prank," he said.

It wasn't. The CBI was inviting the 13-18 Bearcats to its tournament.

Waddell collected the information and called Thomas. Thomas told Waddell to call Cronin, who was in the middle of putting his daughter to bed.

"I thought you had to have a winning record to get invited," Cronin said. "I told Mike Waddell that if Mike Thomas is OK with this—we'll never do this again—but for what these guys have done for us, if they want to play, we owe it to them. I called the guys and asked if they wanted to play. I remember how excited they were. They started running back and forth to each other's rooms saying, 'Hey, we can still play!'"

Waddell called the CBI officials and said the Bearcats would play. However, UC could *not* host a game and insisted on playing on Wednesday instead of Tuesday.

UC was first going to play at Penn State, but CBI officials called Waddell and said Penn State had backed out and asked again if UC would host a game. The answer was still no.

Waddell was then given four opponents from which to choose, including two that were far away. It came down to Bradley University or Wichita State University. Waddell said Cronin had him pull up statistics of both and compare 3-point percentages.

Ultimately, UC chose to play Bradley in Peoria, Illinois. Bradley won 70-67 and UC finished 13-19. It has not had a losing season since.

"We were a mess—all beat up and injured," Waddell said. "We ended up losing late. We bussed there and back, and when we returned that night, Fifth Third Arena was on lockdown for a Barack Obama rally."

Waddell continued. "A CBI banner never quite made it up to the rafters. Mick joked that we should put a Post-It note with CBI 2008 on it next to the two national championship banners. We all laughed and agreed to never be in that position again to have to go to that event."

"It certainly was not where we wanted to be," Thomas said. "Let's face it: That's not the standard that Cincinnati basketball was used to."

IMMEDIATE ADVERSITY

In February 2007, Cashmere Wright verbally committed to attend Clemson University, during his junior year at Urban Christian Academy in Savannah, Georgia. But he decided to open up his recruiting process and six months later committed to the University of Cincinnati. Larry Davis, named a UC assistant coach in 2006, was previously the head coach at Furman University, where he had recruited Wright.

"He was the first coach to recruit me from any school," Wright said. "I had a relationship with him. He just seemed like a straight-shooter. He said, 'We want you to play [at UC], but we're not saying you're going to come in here and start.'"

Wright came from a graduating class of eight. The idea of being on television and playing in the Big East Conference was intriguing.

His freshman year at UC was the first time Wright was away from home. Everything was going well until the first official day of practice in the fall 2008. The Bearcats had two workouts. In the final drill of the second practice, he was getting back on defense in a 3-on-2 drill when he tore the anterior cruciate ligament in his left knee.

"It was just a simple drill, the same thing I had been doing my whole life," Wright said. "Before that, I never even turned my ankle."

Within the week, he underwent surgery and would be sidelined his first collegiate season.

"Mentally it kind of tore me down," Wright said. "I was ready to go home."

He said that for two or three weeks he isolated himself and did not talk to anyone. He did not want to attend practice. He didn't want to do anything associated with basketball. "There were days I just locked my room and sat there," Wright said. "No class. No nothing. Just sitting around."

Cronin sent a student manager to Wright's room to force him to attend practice.

Ultimately, Gene and Patricia Wright each took a leave of absence from work to visit Cashmere in Cincinnati; they weren't about to let him give up on his dream of college *or* basketball. His father told him: "You can't come home. This is what you chose to do, so you're going to finish it."

"It helped me grow up," Wright said.

"The first two months were horrible for me—once my parents left I was all by myself. After surgery it's more painful because you have to go through training your muscles again. At first I couldn't even lift my leg up. The first time I walked again I felt better. That was maybe two months later. I started to see the light ahead."

SHOULD I STAY OR SHOULD I GO?

After the 2008-09 season ended, Vaughn said he was "about 80 percent" certain he would declare himself eligible for the NBA draft. He asked Cronin to get him the paperwork he needed to sign. Cronin said he turned in the forms to an advisory council which contacts NBA general managers and in turn reports back to the players.

Deonta Vaughn, left, and Lance Stephenson celebrate the University of Cincinnati's 69-66 victory over Louisville in the second round of the 2010 Big East Tournament. Stephenson (12.3 ppg) and Vaughn (11.7 ppg) were the Bearcats' top scorers during the 2009-10 season. (AP Photo/Henny Ray Abrams)

"They came back, told him late second round at best, probably undrafted," Cronin said. "I told him if you're going to go, go. I'll support you. Back then you could test the waters. You could put your name in and pull it out."

Cronin told Vaughn: "You need to come back for yourself if you think you need it and want to be part of our team."

Which is exactly what Vaughn did.

BORN READY

Lance Stephenson arrived at UC with more hype than any player in the Cronin era.

The six-foot-six McDonald's All-America player from Abraham Lincoln High School in Brooklyn, N.Y., was rated among the Top 15 high school players in the country. He averaged 28.9 points, 10.2 rebounds, and 3.9 assists as a senior and left high school as the top scorer in the history of New York State, with 2,946 points. Also, he had already been featured in an online documentary series called *BornReadyTV*.

He became part of Cronin's fourth UC team.

"Knowing you were ranked high and you're coming into a situation where you're just learning how to play college basketball and everyone is expecting you to do great, it was tough," Stephenson said. "That's when I got with the coaches to try and learn the game and help me be more comfortable on the floor."

Cronin tried to alleviate pressure on Stephenson. He did not allow the media to talk to Stephenson until the second half of the season. He also had him room with Sean Kilpatrick, another New Yorker from White Plains Senior High School who was redshirting that season.

"Sean was extremely mature for his age, but his game needed development," Cronin said. "Lance was the dead opposite. He was a typical 18-year-old immature kid, but his game and his body were extremely developed."

"Whenever you'd see Lance, you'd see me a couple of steps away," Kilpatrick said. "Coach would call us Frick and Frack. We were good for each other on and off the court."

Kilpatrick said he wanted to be a teammate, friend, and brother to Stephenson.

"There were times I would be at his door saying, 'Come on, we've got class.' That's what best friends do," Kilpatrick said. "They make sure their friends don't slack off when it comes to taking care of their business."

Said Stephenson: "Sean came from the same environment I came from. We bonded as soon as I came to the team. He was one of the reasons I came to Cincinnati. At an all-star game back home, he was like, 'Man, you should come to school with me.' We were laughing and joking about it. I am so happy I decided to go there.

"Sean definitely helped me adjust. He was always doing the right things, making sure he did his work, making sure he went to class. He helped me focus. When you have somebody around you doing everything right, it helps. He definitely was a role model for me."

MODEL WORK ETHIC

Turns out, Stephenson's work ethic served as a model for his teammates.

"Energy level off the charts," Cronin said.

"Out of all the people I have played with in my life, he may have been the hardest worker I have seen on a daily basis," Wright said. "When you hear about Lance, you're thinking he's going to come in here big-headed not thinking he has to do the work. When he got here and you started to see him practice and work out and how he was always in the gym, then you see why he gets what he gets.

"Right now he's doing well [in the NBA] and I'm not surprised. You could see that happening when he was here. He may be the only person I've seen who works hard at everything he does. No matter what drill it is, you're going to get 100 percent out of him."

Said Stephenson: "I just tried to be the first one in and the last one out. I had a goal. I wanted to become the best player and be in the best shape I could be."

That's what makes this story so interesting:

Stephenson recalls his first day of conditioning when he had to run "ladders"—a series of sprints. On this particular day, the Bearcats had to run 13 ladders.

"You get timed," Stephenson said. "You get almost no rest. We went to 13. I couldn't finish. I just broke down. It was my first college practice. Ever since that day, I knew I had to work harder and be in better shape. That was one of the toughest practices I ever had. I just gave up on the practice. I couldn't even go anymore."

REDSHIRT YEAR

In the fall prior to the 2009-10 season, Cronin looked at his roster and saw a glut of shooting guards. Vaughn and Stephenson were locks to start. Dion Dixon and Larry Davis were veteran reserves. Cronin just didn't see an opportunity for Kilpatrick to get a lot of minutes.

So he called Kilpatrick into his office and recommended that he redshirt his freshman year.

"I was hoping he wasn't going to say what I thought he was going to say," Kilpatrick said. "I was really eager to play. He brought up the redshirt process. I told him no. That was my first instinct. That was one of the hardest moments of my college career."

"I told him, 'Look, I don't want you to transfer. You're not ready to play,'" Cronin said. "These other guys are older. They were ahead of him, and he was struggling a little in practice early on. I told him, 'I believe you're going to be a great player, and I don't want you to be a great player for somebody else. I'm worried if you don't redshirt, everybody back home is going to tell you to transfer. You're going to be the captain of my team and you're going to be my best player. But I think this is the right move for you.'"

Cronin gave Kilpatrick the choice, but reiterated he needed to trust him. Kilpatrick left the office and Cronin called Kilpatrick's mother to break down the scenario.

Kilpatrick's mother told her son: "This might be a good thing for you. At the end of the day you don't want to waste a year of basically not playing. Next thing you know your time is up."

After a few days of reflection, Kilpatrick ultimately decided to redshirt and put his trust in his coach.

IN THE CLUTCH

In the first Big East Conference game of his career, Stephenson and the squad faced No. 10 Connecticut and star Kemba Walker, who would lead the Huskies to the 2011 NCAA title.

Cincinnati watched a 12-point second-half lead disappear and faced a tie game after Walker made a 3-pointer with 9.4 seconds remaining. Cronin did not call a timeout. Stephenson got the inbounds pass and dribbled up the floor. He made a few moves to try to get open and ended up forcing up a shot in a crowd in the lane. It missed. The buzzer sounded. And Stephenson lay on his stomach on the floor.

But a foul was called on Gavin Edwards. After officials reviewed the game footage, they put .7 seconds on the clock.

Stephenson went to the foul line and made both free throws to complete UC's 71-69 victory.

"I remember how close and how physical the game was," Stephenson said. "The whole crowd was into it. It was like a championship-game experience. I got excited about games like that. I like physical games.

"I felt real comfortable [shooting the free throws]. I felt like I could be one of the clutch players on the team."

Stephenson finished with 21 points and sensed a change in how people felt about him.

"I thought Coach trusted me after that game," Stephenson said. "It was a turning point of my season. When you hit clutch shots like that with the game on the line, a lot of people have a lot of faith in you."

ONE AND DONE

By the time UC was playing in the Big East Tournament, Stephenson said he knew he was going to declare for the NBA draft.

Stephenson averaged 12.3 points and 5.4 rebounds in his one year of college basketball with high games of 23 points against Georgetown University and 22 against Xavier University. He had a double-double with 18 points and 10 rebounds against DePaul. He grabbed 11 rebounds against Texas Southern.

He was named Big East Rookie of the Year and, at times, showed glimpses of why there was so much hype surrounding him coming out of high school. He also shot just 21.9 percent from 3-point range.

"I felt like I was physically ready," he said of the decision to turn pro. "It was a family decision. I wanted to get to the NBA and learn as much as possible."

The Indiana Pacers selected Stephenson with the 40th overall pick in the second round of the 2010 draft. In 2013-14, his fourth NBA season, Stephenson led the Pacers in rebounding and assists and was their No. 3 scorer; he was second in voting for the NBA's Most Improved Player award.

"Cincinnati definitely helped me on the court and helped me become a man," he said.

Cronin said the decision to leave was harder for Stephenson than people think.

"Lance is a pretty bright guy," Cronin said. "He knew that he didn't dominate college basketball. He knew he needed to improve. He liked Cincinnati. His first year with the Pacers, he was in Cincinnati almost every off day."

HELPING HAND

Despite the fact that the team went 24-38 in Vaughn's first two seasons, Vaughn said he never considered transferring to another school.

Six games into his senior year, the Bearcats were ranked for the first time under Cronin, coming in at No. 22. Unfortunately, Vaughn never got a chance to play in the NCAA Tournament.

"I don't know how we would've scored for a few years without him," Cronin said. "He was the first rock the program was rebuilt on; no question about it."

Vaughn's role changed somewhat as a senior. He shot fewer times. And at the end of games, it was Stephenson who often had the ball in his hands.

"It was different because we had somebody else who could create just as good as me," Vaughn said. "At the same time, it was something that I never focused on. We were a team; it's not like I had to shoot every shot now for us to win."

Vaughn averaged 11.7 points as a senior, shooting 37.8 percent from the field and 33.8 percent from 3-point range. He took and made fewer shots than he had in his previous three seasons.

"I did everything that I could with the help of my teammates," Vaughn said. "I liked the way they rebuilt the program. It was a great opportunity for anybody because of the family atmosphere and how everybody treats you there. And we took Cincinnati from nothing back to something."

By the time Vaughn was done, he had set school records for career assists (511), minutes played (4,310), games started (123), 3-point field goals (313), and 3-point field goals attempted (913). He left as UC's No. 3 all-time scorer (he was later passed by Kilpatrick) and was the first Bearcat ever to total 1,800 career points and 500 assists.

"It sounds like somebody who worked hard to get to somewhere that no one thought that he could get to," Vaughn said. "It boggles my mind. I can tell my kids, 'Your daddy went to college and he became a player people will know later.'"

LEADING BY EXAMPLE

Early in the 2010-11 season, Cronin was unhappy with this players because he didn't think anyone was diving on the floor for loose balls. He called for a drill to help solve that.

"He rolled the ball down the court," Wright said. "You had to chase it, and instead of picking it up you had to dive on it."

After less than a handful of players did not perform the drill to Cronin's satisfaction, he stepped to the front of the line. He threw the ball down the court and went and dove on it himself.

"Once Cronin gets upset, you have no choice but to get into it, or you're going to do it all day," Wright said. "It got to the point where the trainer was looking at him and saying, 'Hey, that's enough.' He was like, 'It's not enough until I say so.'

"We thought it was funny, but he was serious. He was full-out Mick Cronin-style-serious and yelling. You can't laugh then. We waited until we got into the locker room, and then everybody started laughing.

"It definitely set the tone for the season. I think it more so changed how we looked at him. We realized he may yell a lot, but you have to figure out the difference in what he really means and what he's trying to say. Once he dove on that ground to show us 'I'm with you all, and this is how we're going to play,' the team kind of bought into the whole system."

REVENGE PLUS

The 2009-10 season ended with a disappointing 81-66 loss to the Dayton Flyers in the National Invitation Tournament at Fifth Third Arena. That UC team had Vaughn, Yancy Gates, and Stephenson.

No question that game was on the Bearcats' minds when they faced an undefeated Flyers team on November 27, 2010, at U.S. Bank Arena.

"Everybody was talking about how they were better than us," Wright said.

"I have never seen a team more focused on winning. Details. Knowing everything about the scouting report and everything we had to do. The whole team wanted to win to prove everybody wrong. That showed me what a focused team could do."

Before the game, Wright, said, there was complete silence in the locker room. Players were reviewing scouting reports. "A memorable moment," Wright called it.

"We really wanted to make sure everything was perfect," he said. "Not good, but perfect. We didn't want them to even think they could score."

Well, UC won 68-34, leading by as many as 36 at one point. It was ahead 42-19 at halftime. Dayton shot just 20 percent from the field.

"It was real satisfying," Wright said. "It shut up all the Dayton fans."

The Bearcats started the season 15-0 on the way to their first NCAA Tournament under Cronin.

YANCY 'JUST LIKE MICK CRONIN'

Bob Huggins often said that Herb Jones was the most important recruit he signed.

Cronin said Yancy Gates, a six-foot-nine power player from Cincinnati's Withrow High School, was his most important recruit.

"Yancy was a recruit that I *had* to sign," Cronin said. "I don't think I make it here if he doesn't come to Cincinnati. I don't know if we would've been able to get things turned around.

"The program was a mess. When Yancy signed on, he knew all the things that I knew. He knew the fans were upset. He had read in the paper that Nancy Zimpher didn't care about basketball. But, like me, he said, 'I love the Bearcats and I love Cincinnati. This isn't how I wanted to go to Cincinnati, but I'm coming.' He was just like Mick Cronin."

Gates became the only player in UC history to lead the team in rebounding four consecutive seasons. He finished his career with 1,485 points and 916 rebounds.

"The program has been rebuilt the right way," Cronin said. "Our academics are in order. Guys graduate. I don't believe we get the corner turned if he doesn't come."

All of which made the December 2011 Crosstown Shootout even more upsetting to Cronin.

CROSSTOWN PUNCH-OUT

The Cincinnati-Xavier rivalry has included many memorable episodes. Punches thrown. Crutches thrown. Handshakes ignored. Pushing. Jawing. Lots of rhetoric from both sides.

Xavier's 76-53 victory on December 10, 2011, at Cintas Center involved perhaps the ugliest moments in Crosstown Shootout history. But there were so many variables that led up to the fight at the end of that game:

- **December 13, 2008:** XU won by 10. Six technical fouls were called—two on UC and four on Xavier. XU freshman center Kenny Frease and Gates each received a technical foul. Xavier's Derrick Brown was ejected after his second technical for trash talking after being fouled with 1:20 left. Xavier's C.J. Anderson received a technical foul for taunting UC's Rashad Bishop. *Cincinnati Enquirer* columnist Paul Daugherty wrote that night: "It was a sloppy, chippy, ill-mannered game. The better team won, without distinguishing itself. Recent wisdom has had it that the Shootout has lost some luster, some interest. The players didn't get that memo."

- **December 13, 2009:** The Musketeers won in double overtime. Xavier guard Jordan Crawford and Bishop were each called for technical fouls after jabbering at each other. Bishop even went after Crawford and had to be restrained. During a TV timeout, players from both teams confronted each other. There was pushing, shoving, and lots of talking. The officials brought Cronin and Xavier coach Chris Mack together to try and calm things down. "My guys lost their cool, no doubt about it," Cronin said that night. "The intensity of this game is unique," Mack said.

- **January 6, 2011:** The Bearcats won by 20. Xavier's Tu
  Holloway, held to a season-low five points, received a
  technical foul with 13:11 remaining for throwing an
  elbow at Cincinnati's Ibrahima Thomas.
- **December 10, 2011:** In the days leading up to the
  game, this was the exchange in a radio interview
  between UC guard Sean Kilpatrick and host Andy
  Furman on WQRT-AM 1160:
  Furman: "Are you better than Tu Holloway?"
  Kilpatrick: "I'll let the fans decide."
  *Furman: "I need to know. No one's listening. Just
  between you and me."*
  Kilpatrick: "Yes, I am."
  Furman: "Would Tu Holloway start for UC?"
  *Kilpatrick: "Would he, with the players we have now? I
  would say no."*

Cronin said Furman "stirred the pot" and instigated the
exchange, which became a focal point of the pre-game buildup.
Cronin did not talk to Furman for more than two years after
that.

"The questions I asked were inbounds and fair questions,"
Furman said. "I think the general public probably loved to hear
the answers."

Any way you look at it, a solid foundation was in place for
an intense showdown.

"We had a meeting the night before the game," Cronin
said. "I told my guys that we are walking into the fire. We
won easy last year; they're going to play the best game of their
lives tomorrow. I said that no matter what happens, we are *not*
getting in a fight. If they beat us, then we're going to go to the
locker room, get our stuff, and get back to Clifton."

If only ...

The Musketeers led by 23 points in the final seconds.
Then Holloway got in the face of UC freshman guard Ge'Lawn
Guyn and was yelling at him not far from the Bearcats bench.

Holloway slapped Guyn. Xavier's Dez Wells shoved Guyn to the floor. Gates threw the ball at Holloway.

Both teams' benches emptied. There was plenty of pushing and several punches thrown. Gates threw a punch at Frease that connected, knocking Frease to the ground. Frease was bleeding from under his left eye. As he tried to get up, he was kicked by UC's Cheikh Mbodj. More pushing. More punches. More trash talk.

The officials ended the chaos *and* the game with 9.4 seconds still on the clock. It took several minutes before the teams left the court and headed back to their locker rooms.

"It was a national humiliation for the Queen City, and a blow for two great schools and fine basketball programs," *The Cincinnati Enquirer* later wrote in an editorial. "Their programs' reputations have been tarnished."

CRONIN'S FINEST HOUR

For the first five minutes of his postgame press conference, Cronin answered questions about the game itself. But as the topic turned to the fight at the end, Cronin started to get worked up. He was upset with the Xavier players, his own players, as well as the officials. He instructed his players to take off their jerseys in the locker room immediately after the game and said that he physically removed jerseys from some players.

Excerpts from his press conference:

"... there is no excuse for any of it. On our side. On their side. Guys need to grow up."

"I'm not blaming anybody from our standpoint. We accept full responsibility, and it will be handled. There is zero excuse for that in basketball. You've got to learn how to win on one side, and you've got to learn how to lose on the other side."

"The fact is guys are here to get an education. They represent institutions of higher learning. Xavier's been a great school for years. We're trying to cure cancer at Cincinnati. I [work at a] place where they discovered the vaccine for polio and created Benadryl. I think that's more important than who wins a basketball game. And our guys need to have appreciation for the fact that they're there on a full scholarship, and they better represent institutions with class and integrity."

"... If my players don't act the right way, they will never play another game at Cincinnati. Right now I just told my guys I will meet with my AD and my president and I'm going to decide who's on the team going forward; that's what the University of Cincinnati is about. Period. I've never been this embarrassed. I'm hoping President [Gregory] Williams doesn't ask me to resign after that."

" ... I made everybody take their jersey off—and they will not put it on again until they have a full understanding of where they go to school and what the university stands for and how lucky they are to even be there—let alone have a scholarship, 'cause there's a whole lot of kids that can't pay for college and don't get to go."

There was more. Plenty more.

Cronin said he has been told by "a thousand people," including Xavier fans, that he was viewed differently after that press conference.

"I have never listened to it," he said. "What I don't understand is, I didn't become a different person all of a sudden. It wasn't hard for me; I was pissed off. I guess people got to see who I am and how I view the whole situation. I didn't just develop those opinions walking down the hall."

AFTERMATH

Over the next few days after the game, UC suspended Gates, Mbodj, and Octavius Ellis for six games each and Guyn

In June 2014, Bearcats coach Mick Cronin signed a seven-year contract extension that extended through the 2020-21 season. In his first eight seasons, Cronin's team went 162-107, making him the second-winningest men's basketball coach in school history behind only Bob Huggins (399-127). (AP Photo/Al Behrman)

for one game. Xavier suspended Wells and Landen Amos for four games, Mark Lyons for two, and Holloway for one.

There were lots of apologies from both sides—from the presidents, Athletic Directors, coaches, and players. Frease texted Gates; Gates texted back and apologized. All involved agreed it was one of the most embarrassing episodes in the storied history of the rivalry and for college athletics as a whole.

At a UC press conference, all the suspended players apologized. Gates said that as a senior he should have been the one holding back the freshmen—not throwing punches. He said his parents didn't raise him like that and he has to show he's a better person than he did at the game. He said he thought his college career might be over.

Then he said: "I'm not that type of person. A lot of people have been calling me a thug, a gangster …"

And with that, tears started flowing. Gates stopped talking, lowered his head, and cried, rubbing his eyes.

"I want to apologize really to the whole city of Cincinnati for my actions because I'm homegrown. I'm from here," Gates said that day. "A lot of people expect me to represent not just the University of Cincinnati but everybody—my family, kids back in Madisonville running around, from downtown. Everywhere I go a lot of kids look at me and say, 'There goes Yancy Gates.' The actions that I displayed are not what I'm about. This is not what the University of Cincinnati is about. It's not what my family's about."

What saddens Cronin—to this day—is the way Gates was perceived after that game.

"It was the end of him," he said of Gates. "I care about Yancy. It's just sad for me ... I know he's a great guy. Obviously he'd love to have it back. We all would; not just him. He didn't start it, and he's not the only guy who threw a punch. Yancy's a great guy, and I'm not talking about Yancy as a player."

After that game, Cronin said, Gates received some of the cruelest hate mail the coach had ever seen.

"Racist beyond belief," Cronin said. "He showed me some stuff that was just unbelievable. I told him, 'You go to college to learn to get ready for the real world. Let's look at this as a positive. What did you just learn? Everybody's not forgiving. Everybody's not a good person. Everybody doesn't love all humanity.' Young kids don't understand all that. They're innocent. He learned a lot about the real world through that incident."

On the court, the Bearcats moved to a smaller lineup and ran off seven consecutive victories, six without Gates. When he returned, Gates told his teammates: "This is your team. You did well without me. My job right now is to try and fit in with you all."

"That told me a lot," Wright said. "We all had our moments when we had to grow up as people. For him, to come in there and say that, it meant so much to the team. It showed so much character. It got everyone's respect quickly.

"Plus, it was nice to have him back."

FIRST OF MANY

Kilpatrick had many memorable showdowns with Connecticut guard Shabazz Napier. This was one of the classics.

Connecticut was ranked 13th in the country when it played host to the 14-4 Bearcats on January 18, 2012.

Napier scored a then-career-high 27 points, including a long-range 3-pointer that tied the game with 9.5 seconds left. But it was Kilpatrick who pulled up from the top of the 3-point line and hit the game-winning shot with 2.5 seconds to play.

"All I remember is [Napier] hitting the 3 and I'm thinking to myself when the ball is rolling that Coach is going to call a timeout," Kilpatrick said. "Then they threw the ball to me. I was a sophomore. I thought they were going to go to Cashmere.

"I didn't want to go into overtime. I really wanted to get this thing over with once they threw the ball to me. I was running down the court thinking that if Coach doesn't call a time-out, I have to figure something out. Once I got past half court and he didn't call a timeout, I saw them come down to try and strip the ball from me. I just pulled up at the 3 and hit the shot."

UC won 70-67. Kilpatrick said it was the first game-winner of his career.

"That's when everything started," he said. "Honestly, I think it opened up a lot of eyes. People didn't know who I was. I was just somebody playing the role that coach asked me to play. But that shot really started everything. It was definitely a confidence booster. That helped me get to where I am now.

"If you look at when I was a senior, I knew what to do in that position. I wasn't nervous. I wasn't scared. With 10 seconds left, I was really comfortable having the ball in my hands."

'A MOMENT THAT WILL FOREVER STICK WITH ME'

Wright remembers that he was having a horrible game. He was 3-of-8 shooting from the field and had missed both his 3-point attempts. He had four turnovers and only one assist.

UC, ranked No. 17, was playing Alabama at home on national television (ESPN) on December 1, 2012.

With the game tied and just six seconds remaining, the Bearcats called a timeout. The play called for Wright to look for Kilpatrick and if he wasn't open to make a play.

Titus Rubles inbounded the ball to Wright, who dribbled straight up the middle of the court. As he neared the 3-point arc, he went left and shot a step-back fade-away jumper over Alabama's 7-foot center Moussa Gueye. Wright fell on his back just about off the court and never saw the ball go in the basket at the buzzer. But he knew from the reaction of the crowd and his teammates what happened. "I'm looking at Sean's man, who is face-guarding him," Wright said. "By the time I pass half court, I realize that I've got to take the shot. All I thought was: *How am I going to get separation from [Gueye] to get this shot off?* My preference was going left. As long as I could get to my left hand, I felt comfortable with whatever shot I was going to take.

"I could hear in my mind my father telling me, 'Shoot the ball with arc. Shoot the ball with arc.' It was like a rainbow shot to get over his hand. Before I could hit the ground, SK was jumping on me so I realized I hit the shot. I never saw it go in. All I heard was the crowd and then SK jumped on me. That was a moment that will forever stick with me. To this day I even watch it on YouTube and try to figure out how it happened."

SK CARRIES THE LOAD

UC started the 2012-13 season 12-0, then went 3-3 over its next six games. Next up was 25th-ranked Marquette, riding a six-game winning streak, at Fifth Third Arena.

Wright, the point guard and the team's second-leading scorer behind Kilpatrick, had sprained his knee in the previous game, a victory at DePaul four days earlier. Now Kilpatrick was going to be called upon to play some point guard, as well as shooting guard.

"I knew it was going to be tough," Kilpatrick said. "I was going to have to carry the load."

Kilpatrick came in having made only 12 of his previous 40 attempts from 3-point range. And two of his first four shots against Marquette missed badly.

But then he got hot, scoring 25 of UC's first 50 points. However, it was most important how he finished. With 4.3 seconds left in overtime, Kilpatrick made a driving layup from the left side over 6-foot-11 Chris Otule to give UC a 71-69 victory.

Marquette's Junior Cadougan missed a runner off the glass at the buzzer.

Kilpatrick's shot capped a career-high 36-point outing.

"I remember that Coach didn't call timeout again," Kilpatrick said. "I was just dribbling up the court. I saw the clock winding down. I made a left-hand layup to make us win the game. That was really special to me. I remember Fifth Third Arena was so loud; it felt like the whole floor was shaking after I made that bucket."

PLAYING WITH PAIN

Wright was pretty much used to dealing with injuries throughout his UC career, especially his knees. He missed his freshman season with a torn ACL in his left knee. He severely sprained his right knee midway through his senior season. And then there was his shoulder.

Wright injured his left shoulder during practice in his junior season in a collision with JaQuon Parker. After that, the shoulder kind of popped in and out of place maybe seven or eight times. "I kind of knew how to put it back in and keep going," Wright said.

On February 2, 2013, during his senior season, No. 24 UC played at Seton Hall, which was pressing the Bearcats late in the game. Wright kind of got pushed into the scorer's table and his shoulder came out of place.

Cronin looked at him and saw it.

"He knew I was tough and I could take pain, but I don't think he realized how much," Wright said. "Before he turned around and looked at the ball, I pushed it back in place and ran back on the floor. He was just looking at me like, 'Wow, OK.' Nobody knows that but me, him and the team. I think I shocked him.

"One thing I told my team: No matter what happens, how hurt I am, we're going to make the NCAA Tournament, even if I am out there in a wheelchair. That was my mind-set."

Wright finished his career having played the most games in UC history (139). He also was the team's career leader in steals with 198. To that point, no Bearcat ever had tallied more than 1,300 points, 475 assists, and 175 steals.

Oh, and he ended up having surgery on his shoulder after his final season.

"Considering that I was never actually fully healthy, it was a marvelous career," Wright said. "I don't think the Cincinnati fans were ever able to see me play 100 percent unless you saw the summer league when I first got there.

"That's what makes everything feel good to me. I was basically playing with one arm my senior year. Even Cronin said it's kind of odd to see you playing with one arm and get the steals record."

RIVALS TO THE SOUTH

Over the years, many Cincinnati-Louisville games have been special. For starters, the schools have been rivals through a series of leagues: Metro, Great Midwest, Conference USA, Big East, and the American Athletic Conference.

It was especially intense when Bob Huggins coached against Denny Crum and then Rick Pitino. And then came Pitino versus Cronin, who was Pitino's associate head coach from 2001-03.

When the teams played in Louisville on January 30, 2014, Louisville was ranked No. 12 and the Bearcats No. 13. Louisville had one of the top players in the country in Russ Smith. UC had one of the top players in the country in Kilpatrick.

This was another classic. Cincinnati surrendered a 17-point lead, only to come back from a three-point deficit in the final two minutes to beat the Cardinals 69-66. Kilpatrick made 6 of 6 free throws at the end and finished with 28 points. He went 11-of-11 from the foul line.

Cronin said the arena was "louder than a NASCAR event" in the second half.

"SK just said, 'You're not winning,' and he just went and got baskets," Cronin said.

"They didn't leave him open and he still shot it in. He went from a guy who couldn't handle the ball as a young player to someone who had the ball at half court against the best, quickest, defensive guy in the country in Russ Smith and he's making dribble crossover moves and slicing by Smith and through two other guys for a layup. I'm standing over there thinking, *you've got to be kidding me. This guy couldn't dribble through cones without losing the ball four years ago.*"

Former UC assistant coach Tony Stubblefield, who had helped recruit Kilpatrick, called Cronin that night from Oregon, where he was an assistant coach. "I was watching the game," he told Cronin. "It's unbelievable how good he is."

WHATEVER IT TAKES

Kilpatrick's development is not so unbelievable, as Stubblefield put it, when you consider his work ethic.

Cronin tells the story of Kilpatrick going through individual workouts during the summer of 2013 with UC assistant coaches Larry Davis and Darren Savino. They were having him dribble through cones, and Kilpatrick was struggling and kept losing the ball. "You can't dribble with your left hand," the coaches were yelling at him. "You're not working hard enough."

The coaching staff flew out that night to go recruiting. The next morning, they were all getting coffee when they received a text message from Kilpatrick.

"It's a YouTube video clip, and he is in the practice gym at 2 in the morning," Cronin said. "He's got the cones out, he's doing the drill and he's yelling at us the whole time he's doing it: 'You said I couldn't do it!' Then he'd go through the cones with his left hand.

"Coaches like to tell stories about guys working hard. They're not 'stories' with this guy. They're true. There are many of those stories."

Cronin continues:

"Last summer [2013], I'm on the road. It's Friday night. I'm eating with a friend of mine. It's 11:45 p.m. and I get a text message. It's SK. He sends me a picture. It's the whole team and they're in the gym. You can tell they've all been playing because they're all sweating. And the caption is: *Nobody else is playing like the Bearcats tonight.* That's a Friday night in July. That's when you know as a coach you're going to have a good year."

AND IT WAS

Cronin's 2013-14 team went 27-7 and shared the American Athletic Conference championship with a 15-3 record.

Without question, the season belonged to Kilpatrick. He was the team's leader, top scorer, big-shot maker, clutch performer. You name it, Kilpatrick did it.

The night before UC's final home game of the season, March 6, 2014, against Memphis, Kilpatrick and Justin Jackson—long-time roommates on the road—stayed up talking until about 2 a.m. in their hotel room. They reminisced about games past and wondered how the program would look after they left.

Mostly, though, they talked about how hard they planned to play against Memphis and how they wanted the home fans to remember them.

"We're going to go out the way we want to go out," they told each other. "We've got to leave everything on that court. We've got to get to the point where you can't breathe; where you'll crawl on the floor to get to where you want to go."

"I really wanted to make that night special, not only for me, but for the fans as well," Kilpatrick said.

As soon as Jackson was announced to the crowd before the game, he started crying. Then tears started rolling down Kilpatrick's face. Once he was announced, the ovation was so loud and long that it "sent chills" through Kilpatrick.

Kilpatrick said that Cronin hugged him and said, "I love you, man, and I appreciate everything you've done for me and this program. If you need anything, and I mean anything, I'm always here for you."

"That made me cry," Kilpatrick said. "He gave me the chance to come to the University of Cincinnati and make things work. Once I got here, when I told him what my dream was, he said it's going to be a lot of work but it's not impossible. That's something I really thought about on Senior Night. I remembered everything he said to me. That caused me to cry the most."

Then, it was show time. No. 20 Memphis never stood a chance.

The Bearcats raced to an 18-4 lead and went on to a 97-84 victory. Kilpatrick scored 34. Jackson finished with 13 points, nine rebounds, three steals, and three assists. Classmate Titus Rubles had a career night with 24 points and five rebounds.

"Once that ball was thrown up in the air, it was all over," Kilpatrick said. "We just saw blood. If you were standing in the lane, Justin was dunking on you. If you were trying to guard me, I was crossing you over. Titus had the biggest game of his life. We really put everything we had onto the court.

"It's a night I will never forget. Honestly, that was the best game of my life. It was the result, how things went, the atmosphere. It was so loud in there. You couldn't even hear Coach call any plays because it was so loud."

SPECIAL POSTGAME

When Kilpatrick emerged from the locker room after UC's victory, his friend Ricardo Grant told him that a fan was waiting to meet him and wanted his shoes. "You know these are my favorite sneakers," Kilpatrick said. "SK, you've got to do it," Grant said.

Kilpatrick met the fan. It was a boy in a wheelchair.

"I ran back in the locker room, signed those sneakers, and gave them to him," Kilpatrick said. "I took a picture with him. It made my day.

"I always said to myself that I would never, ever make a kid feel that I was too stuck up or too good to sit down and try to talk for 10 or 15 minutes. I always wanted to leave a mark on younger kids. I want to be somebody who is recognized for his off-the-court ability, as well as on the court."

CONSIDER IT DONE

As good of a player as Kilpatrick was at UC, he was equally—if not more so—appreciated because of the way he handled himself publicly, in the media, in games, and the way he represented the program and the university.

For five years he stayed out of trouble. He said he chose the gym over parties. He mostly hung out with teammates. "I understood really early in my life what my mom and dad expected from me," he said. "If I did get in trouble, that would be very disappointing to them."

Kilpatrick earned his degree and was selected to join Sigma Sigma, a UC men's honorary fraternity founded in 1898 that emphasizes leadership and loyalty to the University of Cincinnati.

"It's the top honorary on campus," Kilpatrick said. "Do you know how hard it is to get in Sigma Sigma? There are not a lot of people who get in.

"I never had heard about it until Leonard Stokes told me about it. Then I did my homework on it. I took it with open arms. I am able to be a part of this university forever now and really lay my mark down knowing that my name will forever be paved on this campus."

When Cronin talks about Kilpatrick, it's clear he meant more to the program than all the points he scored and victories he participated in.

"This is what I'm most proud of: Not the wins, but when you think of a Cincinnati basketball player right now, what comes to your mind?" Cronin said. "You think of Sean Kilpatrick. He's a good guy. That benefits all our former players. It helps them all get better jobs, whether regular jobs or in basketball. And it's great for our university."

ICING ON THE CAKE

On March 31, 2014, Kilpatrick was named first-team All-America by the Associated Press. It was the culmination of a memorable senior season and five years at the University of Cincinnati.

Kilpatrick left as the school's No. 2 all-time scorer with 2,145 points and is the only player other than Oscar Robertson to amass 2,000 points. He tied Vaughn for most 3-pointers made in school history (313) and set school records for games played (140) and career minutes (4,315).

He played in four NCAA Tournaments. He led the American Athletic Conference in scoring with a 20.6 ppg scoring average. And he graduated with a degree in criminal justice.

"It went so fast," Kilpatrick said. "I had a helluva life here. If the NBA wasn't in existence, I would never want to leave college. When I write things on Twitter and Instagram and I hashtag #thehottestcollegeinamerica, that's something that I really mean.

"This college took me to a whole 'nother level. It made me a man. It made me who I am today. There are a lot of guys in the NBA who went to Cincinnati who never come back. I will try to come back every year for a game. I know that may be impossible, but you better believe I will try. This is who I am. I bleed Cincinnati red."